GLEIM®

2016
EDITION

CIA Review

Part 2

Internal Audit Practice

by

Irvin N. Gleim, Ph.D., CPA, CIA, CMA, CFM

Gleim Publications, Inc.
P.O. Box 12848
University Station
Gainesville, Florida 32604
(800) 874-5346
(352) 375-0772
Fax: (352) 375-6940
Internet: www.gleim.com
Email: admin@gleim.com

For updates to the first printing of the 2016 edition of *CIA Review: Part 2*

Go To: www.gleim.com/updates

Or: Email update@gleim.com with **CIA 2 2016** in the subject line. You will receive our current update as a reply.

Updates are available until the next edition is published.

ISSN: 2332-0540

ISBN: 978-1-58194-608-6   *CIA Review: Part 1*
ISBN: 978-1-58194-609-3   *CIA Review: Part 2*
ISBN: 978-1-58194-610-9   *CIA Review: Part 3*
ISBN: 978-1-58194-626-0   *How to Pass the CIA Exam: A System for Success*

First Printing: May 2015

ACKNOWLEDGMENTS FOR PART 2

The author is grateful for permission to reproduce the following materials copyrighted by The Institute of Internal Auditors: Certified Internal Auditor Examination Questions and Suggested Solutions (copyright © 1980-2015), excerpts from *Sawyer's Internal Auditing* (5th and 6th editions), parts of the 2013 *Certification Candidate Handbook*, The IIA Code of Ethics, *International Standards for the Professional Practice of Internal Auditing*, Practice Advisories, and parts of Practice Guides.

CIA® is a Registered Trademark of The Institute of Internal Auditors, Inc. All rights reserved.

Environmental Statement -- This book is printed on recyclable, environmentally friendly groundwood paper, sourced from certified sustainable forests and produced either TCF (totally chlorine-free) or ECF (elementally chlorine-free).

ABOUT THE AUTHOR

Irvin N. Gleim is Professor Emeritus in the Fisher School of Accounting at the University of Florida and is a member of the American Accounting Association, Academy of Legal Studies in Business, American Institute of Certified Public Accountants, Association of Government Accountants, Florida Institute of Certified Public Accountants, The Institute of Internal Auditors, and the Institute of Management Accountants. He has had articles published in the *Journal of Accountancy*, *The Accounting Review*, and *The American Business Law Journal* and is author/ coauthor of numerous accounting books, aviation books, and CPE courses.

REVIEWERS AND CONTRIBUTORS

Garrett W. Gleim, B.S., CPA (not in public practice), received a Bachelor of Science degree from The Wharton School at the University of Pennsylvania. Mr. Gleim coordinated the production staff, reviewed the manuscript, and provided production assistance throughout the project.

Grady M. Irwin, J.D., is a graduate of the University of Florida College of Law, and he has taught in the University of Florida College of Business. Mr. Irwin provided substantial editorial assistance throughout the project.

Lawrence Lipp, J.D., CPA (Registered), is a graduate from the Levin College of Law and the Fisher School of Accounting at the University of Florida. Mr. Lipp provided substantial editorial assistance throughout the project.

Dr. Steven A. Solieri, CPA, CMA, CIA, CISA, CITP, CFF, CRISC, is an Assistant Professor at Queens College in Flushing, New York, and is a Founding Member in the Firm of Solieri & Solieri, CPAs, PLLC, New Hyde Park, NY, where he currently practices. Dr. Solieri earned his Ph.D. from Binghamton University and holds four Masters from the University of Michigan, Pace University, Kettering University, and Binghamton University. Dr. Solieri helped develop the instructor materials to be used in conjunction with this text.

A PERSONAL THANKS

This manual would not have been possible without the extraordinary effort and dedication of Jacob Brunny, Julie Cutlip, Kelsey Olson, Jake Pettifor, Teresa Soard, Justin Stephenson, Joanne Strong, and Elmer Tucker, who typed the entire manuscript and all revisions and drafted and laid out the diagrams and illustrations in this book.

The authors also appreciate the production and editorial assistance of Jessica Felkins, James Harvin, Kristen Hennen, Jeanette Kerstein, Katie Larson, Diana León, Cary Marcous, Shane Rapp, Drew Sheppard, and Martha Willis.

The authors also appreciate the critical reading assistance of Brett Babir, Ellen Buhl, Paul Davis, Jack Hahne, Nathan Kaplan, Melissa Leonard, Yating Li, Monica Metz, Tyler Rankin, Sunny Shang, Justin Shifrin, Daniel Sinclair, Tingwei Su, Nanan Toure, and Diana Weng.

Finally, we appreciate the encouragement, support, and tolerance of our families throughout this project.

TABLE OF CONTENTS

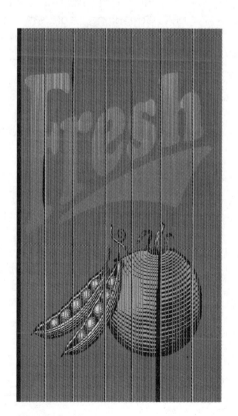

GLEIM® Updates

Keeping your CIA Review materials FRESH

gleim.com/CIAUpdates

Updates are available until the next edition is published

DETAILED TABLE OF CONTENTS

PREFACE

The purpose of this book is to help **you** prepare to pass Part 2 of the CIA exam. Our overriding consideration is to provide an inexpensive, effective, and easy-to-use study program. This book

1. Explains how to optimize your grade by focusing on Part 2 of the CIA exam.

2. Defines the subject matter tested on Part 2 of the CIA exam.

3. Outlines all of the subject matter tested on Part 2 in 7 easy-to-use-and-complete study units, including all relevant authoritative pronouncements.

4. Presents multiple-choice questions from past CIA examinations to prepare you for questions in future CIA exams. Our answer explanations are presented to the immediate right of each question for your convenience. Use a piece of paper to cover our explanations as you study the questions.

5. Suggests exam-taking and question-answering techniques to help you maximize your exam score.

The outline format, the spacing, and the question-and-answer formats in this book are designed to facilitate readability, learning, understanding, and success on the CIA exam. Our most successful candidates use the Gleim CIA Review System*, which includes books, Test Prep, Audio Review, Gleim Online, Exam Rehearsals, and access to a Personal Counselor. Students who prefer to study in a group setting may attend Gleim Professor-Led Reviews, which combine the Gleim Review System with the coordination and feedback of a professor. (Check our website for live courses we recommend.)

To maximize the efficiency and effectiveness of your CIA review program, augment your studying with *How to Pass the CIA Exam: A System for Success*. This booklet has been carefully written and organized to provide important information to assist you in passing the CIA examination.

Thank you for your interest in our materials. We deeply appreciate the thousands of letters and suggestions we have received from CIA, CMA, CPA, and EA candidates and accounting students and faculty during the past 5 decades.

If you use Gleim materials, we want YOUR feedback immediately after the exam and as soon as you have received your grades. The CIA exam is NONDISCLOSED, and you must maintain the confidentiality and agree not to divulge the nature or content of any CIA question or answer under any circumstances. We ask only for information about our materials, i.e., the topics that need to be added, expanded, etc.

Please go to www.gleim.com/feedbackCIA2 to share your suggestions on how we can improve this edition.

Good Luck on the Exam,

Irvin N. Gleim

May 2015

PREPARING FOR AND TAKING THE CIA EXAM

READ *HOW TO PASS THE CIA EXAM: A SYSTEM FOR SUCCESS*

1. Scan the Gleim *How to Pass the CIA Exam: A System for Success* booklet and note where to revisit later in your studying process to obtain a deeper understanding of the CIA exam.

    a. *How to Pass the CIA Exam: A System for Success* has six study units:

    Study Unit 1: The CIA Examination: An Overview and Preparation Introduction
    Study Unit 2: CIA Exam Syllabus
    Study Unit 3: Content Preparation, Test Administration, and Performance Grading
    Study Unit 4: Multiple-Choice Questions
    Study Unit 5: Preparing to Pass the CIA Exam
    Study Unit 6: How to Take the CIA Exam

2. *How to Pass the CIA Exam: A System for Success* is available as an e-book at www.gleim.com/PassCIA.

OVERVIEW OF THE CIA EXAMINATION

The total exam is 6.5 hours of testing (including 5 minutes per part for a survey). It is divided into three parts, as follows:

CIA Exam (3-Part)			
Part	Title	Exam Length	Number of Questions
1	Internal Audit Basics	2.5 hrs	125 multiple-choice
2	Internal Audit Practice	2 hrs	100 multiple-choice
3	Internal Audit Knowledge Elements	2 hrs	100 multiple-choice

All CIA questions are multiple-choice. The exam is offered continually throughout the year. The CIA exam is computerized to facilitate easier testing. Pearson VUE, the testing company that The IIA contracts to proctor the exams, has hundreds of testing centers worldwide. The Gleim CIA Test Prep, Gleim Online, and Gleim CIA Exam Rehearsals provide exact exam emulations of the Pearson VUE computer screens and procedures to prepare you to PASS.

SUBJECT MATTER FOR PART 2

Below, we have provided The IIA's abbreviated CIA Exam Syllabus for Part 2. The percentage coverage of each topic is indicated to its right. The IIA provides a range of % coverage, but for simplicity Gleim provides the average of that range. We adjust the content of our materials to any changes in The IIA's CIA Exam Syllabus.

Part 2: Internal Audit Practice

I.	Managing the Internal Audit Function	45%
II.	Managing Individual Engagements	45%
III.	Fraud Risks and Controls	10%

Appendix B contains the CIA Exam Syllabus in its entirety as well as cross-references to the subunits in our text where topics are covered. Remember that we have studied and restudied the syllabus in developing our *CIA Review* materials. Accordingly, you do not need to spend time with Appendix B. Rather, it should give you confidence that Gleim *CIA Review* is the best review source available to help you PASS the CIA exam.

NONDISCLOSED EXAM

As part of The IIA's nondisclosure policy and to prove each candidate's willingness to adhere to this policy, a confidentiality and nondisclosure statement must be accepted by each candidate before each part is taken. This statement is reproduced here to remind all CIA candidates about The IIA's strict policy of nondisclosure, which Gleim consistently supports and upholds.

> *This exam is confidential and is protected by law. It is made available to you, the examinee, solely for the purpose of becoming certified. You are expressly prohibited from disclosing, publishing, reproducing, or transmitting this exam, in whole or in part, in any form or by any means, verbal or written, electronic or mechanical, for any purpose, without the prior written permission of The Institute of Internal Auditors (IIA).*

> *In the event of any actual or anticipated breach by you of the above, you acknowledge that The IIA will incur significant and irreparable damage for each such breach that The IIA has no adequate remedy at law for such breach. You further acknowledge that such breach may result in your certification being revoked, disqualification as a candidate for future certification, and suspension or revocation of membership privileges at The IIA's discretion.*

> *If you do not accept the exam non-disclosure agreement, your exam will be terminated. If this occurs, your registration will be voided, you will forfeit your exam registration fee, and you will be required to register and pay for that exam again in order to sit for it in the future.*

THE IIA'S REQUIREMENTS FOR CIA DESIGNATIONS

The CIA designation is granted only by The IIA. Candidates must complete the following steps to become a CIA®:

1. Complete the appropriate certification application form online and register for the part(s) you are going to take. The *How to Pass the CIA Exam: A System for Success* booklet contains concise instructions on the application and registration process and a useful worksheet to help you keep track of your process and organize what you need for exam day. Detailed instructions and screenshots for every step of the application and registration program can also be found at www.gleim.com/accounting/cia/steps.

2. Pass all three parts of the CIA exam within 4 years of application approval.

3. Fulfill or expect to fulfill the education and experience requirements (see *How to Pass the CIA Exam: A System for Success*).

4. Provide a character reference proving you are of good moral character.

5. Comply with The IIA's Code of Ethics.

ELIGIBILITY PERIOD

Credits for parts passed can be retained as long as the requirements are fulfilled. However, candidates must complete the program certification process within 4 years of application approval. If a candidate has not completed the certification process within 4 years, all fees and exam parts will be forfeited.

Candidates who have not successfully completed their exam(s), or who have been accepted into the program but have not taken their exam(s), have the opportunity to extend their program eligibility by 12 months. To take advantage of The IIA's one-time Certification Candidate Program Extension, candidates must pay a set fee per applicant.

MAINTAINING YOUR CIA DESIGNATION

After certification, CIAs are required to maintain and update their knowledge and skills. Practicing CIAs must complete and report 40 hours of Continuing Professional Education (CPE) every year. The reporting deadline is December 31. Complete your CPE Reporting Form through the online Certification Candidate Management System. Nonmembers must submit a US $100 processing fee with their report. Contact Gleim for all of your CPE needs at www.gleim.com/cpe.

HOW TO USE THE GLEIM REVIEW SYSTEM

To ensure that you are using your time effectively, we have formulated a three-step process that includes all components (book, CIA Test Prep, Audio Reviews, and Gleim Online) together and should be applied to each study unit.

Step 1: Diagnostic

    a.   Multiple-Choice Quiz #1 (20 minutes, plus 10 minutes for review) – In Gleim Online, complete Multiple-Choice Quiz #1 in 20 minutes. This is a diagnostic quiz, so it is expected that your scores will be lower.

        1)   Immediately following the quiz, review the questions you flagged and/or answered incorrectly. For each question, analyze and understand why you flagged it or answered it incorrectly. This step is essential to identifying your weak areas. "Learning from Your Mistakes" on page 7 has tips on how to determine why you missed the questions you missed.

Step 2: Comprehension

    a.   Audiovisual Presentation (30 minutes) – This Gleim Online presentation provides an overview of the study unit. The Gleim CIA Audio Review can be substituted for audiovisual presentations.

    b.   True/False Quiz (45 minutes) – Complete the True/False quiz in Gleim Online and receive immediate feedback.

    c.   Knowledge Transfer Outline (60-80 minutes) – Study the Knowledge Transfer Outline, particularly the troublesome areas identified from your Multiple-Choice Quiz #1 in Step 1. The Knowledge Transfer Outlines can be studied either online or in the book.

    d.   Multiple-Choice Quiz #2 (20 minutes, plus 10 minutes for review) – Complete Multiple-Choice Quiz #2 in Gleim Online.

        1)   Immediately following the quiz, review the questions you flagged and/or answered incorrectly. This step is an essential learning activity. "Learning from Your Mistakes" on page 7 has tips on how to determine why you missed the questions you missed.

Step 3: Application

    a.   CIA Test Prep (40 minutes, plus 20 minutes for review) – Complete two 20-question quizzes using the Practice Exam feature. Spend 20 minutes taking each quiz and then spend about 10 minutes reviewing each quiz as needed.

Final Review

1.   CIA Exam Rehearsal (2 hours/120 minutes) – Take the Exam Rehearsal at the beginning of your final review stage. It contains 100 multiple-choice questions, just like the CIA exam. This will help you identify where you should focus during the remainder of your final review.

2.   CIA Test Prep (10-20 hours) – Use Test Prep to focus on your weak areas identified from your Exam Rehearsal. Also, be sure to do a cumulative review to refresh yourself with topics you learned at the beginning of your studies. View your performance chart to make sure you are scoring 75% or higher.

The times mentioned above are recommendations based on prior candidate feedback and how long you will have to answer questions on the actual exam. Each candidate's time spent in any area will vary depending on proficiency and familiarity with the subject matter.

GLEIM KNOWLEDGE TRANSFER OUTLINES

This edition of the Gleim *CIA Review* books has the following features to make studying easier:

1.   **Guidance Designations:** In an effort to help CIA candidates better grasp The IIA authoritative literature, we have come up with visual indicators to help candidates easily identify each type of guidance.

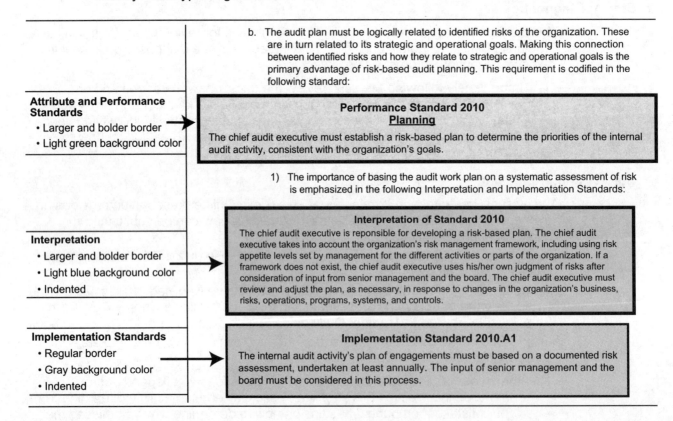

Attribute and Performance Standards
- Larger and bolder border
- Light green background color

b.   The audit plan must be logically related to identified risks of the organization. These are in turn related to its strategic and operational goals. Making this connection between identified risks and how they relate to strategic and operational goals is the primary advantage of risk-based audit planning. This requirement is codified in the following standard:

> **Performance Standard 2010**
> **Planning**
> The chief audit executive must establish a risk-based plan to determine the priorities of the internal audit activity, consistent with the organization's goals.

1)   The importance of basing the audit work plan on a systematic assessment of risk is emphasized in the following Interpretation and Implementation Standards:

Interpretation
- Larger and bolder border
- Light blue background color
- Indented

> **Interpretation of Standard 2010**
> The chief audit executive is reponsible for developing a risk-based plan. The chief audit executive takes into account the organization's risk management framework, including using risk appetite levels set by management for the different activities or parts of the organization. If a framework does not exist, the chief audit executive uses his/her own judgment of risks after consideration of input from senior management and the board. The chief audit executive must review and adjust the plan, as necessary, in response to changes in the organization's business, risks, operations, programs, systems, and controls.

Implementation Standards
- Regular border
- Gray background color
- Indented

> **Implementation Standard 2010.A1**
> The internal audit activity's plan of engagements must be based on a documented risk assessment, undertaken at least annually. The input of senior management and the board must be considered in this process.

2. **Examples:** We use illustrative examples, set off in shaded, bordered boxes, to make the concepts more relatable.

EXAMPLE

An internal auditor discovered fraud committed by members of management and is unsure of whom to disclose this information.

In most cases of whistleblowing, whistleblowers will disclose sensitive information internally, even if not within the normal chain of command. If they trust the policies and mechanisms of the organization to investigate the problem, information can be shared with the appropriate internal parties. However, if the whistleblower doubts the problem will be properly investigated by the corporation, (s)he may consider disclosing the problem to an outside party.

---

3. **Gleim Success Tips:** These tips supplement the core exam material by suggesting how certain topics might be presented on the exam or how you should prepare for an issue.

 An internal audit activity can add value to its organization by performing many types of engagements. CIA candidates must know not only the requirements of these engagements but also when and where to perform each kind of engagement.

---

4. **Memory Aids:** We offer mnemonic devices to help you remember important concepts.

The Seven Seas (7 Cs) is a useful memory aid. Good writing is

1) Clear.
2) Correct (accurate and objective).
3) Concise.
4) Consistent.
5) Constructive.
6) Coherent.
7) Complete and timely.

TIME-BUDGETING AND QUESTION-ANSWERING TECHNIQUES FOR THE EXAM

The following suggestions are to assist you in maximizing your score on Part 2 of the CIA exam. Remember, knowing how to take the exam and how to answer individual questions is as important as studying/reviewing the subject matter tested on the exam.

1. **Budget your time.**

   a. We make this point with emphasis. Just as you would fill up your gas tank prior to reaching empty, so too should you finish your exam before time expires.

   b. You have 120 minutes to answer 100 questions. We suggest you attempt to answer one question per minute, which would result in completing 100 questions in 100 minutes to give you 20 minutes to review questions that you have flagged.

   c. Use the wipeboard provided by Pearson VUE for your Gleim Time Management System at the exam. List the question numbers for every 20 questions (i.e., 1, 21, 41, etc.) in a column on the left side of the wipeboard. The right side of the wipeboard will have your start time at the top and allows you to fill in the time you have remaining at each question checkpoint. Stay consistent with 1 minute per question.

2. **Answer the items in consecutive order.**

   a. Do **not** agonize over any one item. Stay within your time budget.

   b. Note any items you are unsure of by clicking the "Flag for Review" button in the upper-right corner of your screen, and return to them later if time allows. Plan on going back to all the questions you flagged.

   c. Never leave a question unanswered. Make your best guess in the time allowed. Your score is based on the number of correct responses out of the total scored questions, and you will not be penalized for guessing incorrectly.

3. **For each multiple-choice question,**

   a. **Try to ignore the answer choices.** Do not allow the answer choices to affect your reading of the question.

      1) If four answer choices are presented, three of them are incorrect. These incorrect answers are called **distractors** for good reason. Often, distractors are written to appear correct at first glance until further analysis.

      2) In computational items, distractors are carefully calculated such that they are the result of making common mistakes. Be careful and double-check your computations if time permits.

   b. **Read the question carefully** to determine the precise requirement.

      1) Focusing on what is required enables you to ignore extraneous information and to proceed directly to determining the correct answer.

         a) Be especially careful to note when the requirement is an **exception**; e.g., "Which of the following is **not** an indication of fraud?"

   c. **Determine the correct answer** before looking at the answer choices.

      1) However, some multiple-choice questions are structured so that the answer cannot be determined from the stem alone. See the stem in b.1)a) above.

   d. **Then, read the answer choices carefully.**

      1) Even if the first answer appears to be the correct choice, do not skip the remaining answer choices. Questions often ask for the "best" of the choices provided. Thus, each choice requires your consideration.

      2) Treat each answer choice as a true/false question as you analyze it.

   e. **Click on the best answer.**

      1) If you are uncertain, you have a 25% chance of answering the question correctly by blindly guessing. Improve your odds with educated guessing.

      2) For many of the multiple-choice questions, two answer choices can be eliminated with minimal effort, thereby increasing your educated guess to a 50-50 proposition.

4. After you have answered all 100 questions, return to the questions that you flagged. Also, verify that all questions have been answered.

5. **If you don't know the answer:**

   a. Again, guess but make it an educated guess, which means select the best possible answer. First, rule out answers that you think are incorrect. Second, speculate on what The IIA is looking for and/or the rationale behind the question. Third, select the best answer, or guess between equally appealing answers. Your first guess is usually the most intuitive. If you cannot make an educated guess, read the stem and each answer and pick the most intuitive answer. It's just a guess!

   b. Make sure you accomplish this step within your predetermined time budget per checkpoint.

LEARNING FROM YOUR MISTAKES

Learning from questions you answer incorrectly is very important. Each question you answer incorrectly is an **opportunity** to avoid missing actual test questions on your CIA exam. Thus, you should carefully study the answer explanations provided until you understand why the original answer you chose is wrong, as well as why the correct answer indicated is correct. This study technique is clearly the difference between passing and failing for many CIA candidates.

Also, you **must** determine why you answered questions incorrectly and learn how to avoid the same error in the future. Reasons for missing questions include

1. Misreading the requirement (stem)
2. Not understanding what is required
3. Making a math error
4. Applying the wrong rule or concept
5. Being distracted by one or more of the answers
6. Incorrectly eliminating answers from consideration
7. Not having any knowledge of the topic tested
8. Employing bad intuition when guessing

It is also important to verify that you answered correctly for the right reasons. Otherwise, if the material is tested on the CIA exam in a different manner, you may not answer it correctly.

HOW TO BE IN CONTROL WHILE TAKING THE EXAM

You have to be in control to be successful during exam preparation and execution. Control can also contribute greatly to your personal and other professional goals. Control is a process whereby you

1. Develop expectations, standards, budgets, and plans
2. Undertake activity, production, study, and learning
3. Measure the activity, production, output, and knowledge
4. Compare actual activity with expected and budgeted activity
5. Modify the activity, behavior, or study to better achieve the desired outcome
6. Revise expectations and standards in light of actual experience
7. Continue the process or restart the process in the future

Exercising control will ultimately develop the confidence you need to outperform most other CIA candidates and PASS the CIA exam! Obtain our *How to Pass the CIA Exam: A System for Success* booklet for a more detailed discussion of control and other exam tactics.

IF YOU HAVE QUESTIONS ABOUT GLEIM MATERIALS

Content-specific questions about our materials will be answered most rapidly if they are sent to us via the methods described below. Our team of accounting experts will give your correspondence thorough consideration and a prompt response.

There are two methods for submitting an inquiry to our accounting experts:

1. The preferred method is to utilize the "Submit Question Feedback" link that appears beneath the answer explanations of all questions in a Review Session. Use this method if you have an inquiry about a question in Gleim Online, CIA Test Prep, Exam Rehearsals, or Diagnostic Quizzes.

2. For inquiries regarding your Gleim Review book or Test Prep Software Download, please visit www.gleim.com/questions and submit your inquiry using the on-screen form.

In order for us to deliver your response directly to your Personal Classroom, you will need to log in to your Gleim account to submit your inquiry.

Questions regarding the information in this introduction (study suggestions, studying plans, exam specifics) should be emailed to personalcounselor@gleim.com.

Questions concerning orders, prices, shipments, or payments should be sent via email to customerservice@gleim.com and will be promptly handled by our competent and courteous customer service staff.

For technical support, you may use our automated technical support service at www.gleim.com/support, email us at support@gleim.com, or call us at (800) 874-5346.

FEEDBACK

Please fill out our online feedback form (www.gleim.com/feedbackCIA2) IMMEDIATELY after you take the CIA exam so we can adapt to changes in the exam. Our approach has been approved by The IIA.

STUDY UNIT ONE
STRATEGIC AND OPERATIONAL
ROLES OF INTERNAL AUDIT

(22 pages of outline)

This study unit is the first of four covering **Section I: Managing the Internal Audit Function** from The IIA's CIA Exam Syllabus. This section makes up 40% to 50% of Part 2 of the CIA exam and is tested at the **proficiency level** (unless otherwise indicated below). The relevant portion of the syllabus is highlighted below. (The complete syllabus is in Appendix B.)

I. MANAGING THE INTERNAL AUDIT FUNCTION (40–50%)

A. Strategic Role of Internal Audit

1. Initiate, manage, be a change catalyst, and cope with change
2. Build and maintain networking with other organization executives and the audit committee
3. Organize and lead a team in mapping, analysis, and business process improvement
4. Assess and foster the ethical climate of the board and management
   a. Investigate and recommend resolution for ethics/compliance complaints, and determine disposition of ethics violations
   b. Maintain and administer business conduct policy (e.g., conflict of interest), and report on compliance
5. Educate senior management and the board on best practices in governance, risk management, control, and compliance
6. Communicate internal audit key performance indicators to senior management and the board on a regular basis
7. Coordinate IA efforts with external auditor, regulatory oversight bodies and other internal assurance functions
8. Assess the adequacy of the performance measurement system, achievement of corporate objective -- *Awareness Level (A)*

B. Operational Role of IA

1. Formulate policies and procedures for the planning, organizing, directing, and monitoring of internal audit operations
2. Review the role of the internal audit function within the risk management framework
3. Direct administrative activities (e.g., budgeting, human resources) of the internal audit department
4. Interview candidates for internal audit positions
5. Report on the effectiveness of corporate risk management processes to senior management and the board
6. Report on the effectiveness of the internal control and risk management frameworks
7. Maintain effective Quality Assurance Improvement Program

C. Establish Risk-Based IA Plan

1.1 INTRODUCTION TO INTERNAL AUDITING

Performance Standard 2100
Nature of Work

The internal audit activity must evaluate and contribute to the improvement of governance, risk management, and control processes using a systematic and disciplined approach.

---

1. **Nature of Work**

    a. According to The IIA's Definition of Internal Auditing, the internal audit activity "helps an organization accomplish its objectives by bringing a systematic, disciplined approach to evaluate and improve the effectiveness of risk management, control, and governance processes."

        1) These processes are closely related. The IIA Glossary (see Appendix A) defines them as follows:

            a) **Governance** – "The combination of processes and structures implemented by the board to inform, direct, manage, and monitor the activities of the organization toward the achievement of its objectives."

            b) **Risk management** – "A process to identify, assess, manage, and control potential events or situations to provide reasonable assurance regarding the achievement of the organization's objectives."

            c) **Control** – "Any action taken by management, the board, and other parties to manage risk and increase the likelihood that established objectives and goals will be achieved. Management plans, organizes, and directs the performance of sufficient actions to provide reasonable assurance that objectives and goals will be achieved."

                i)   **Control processes** – "The policies, procedures (both manual and automated), and activities that are part of a control framework, designed and operated to ensure that risks are contained within the level that an organization is willing to accept."

    b. Internal auditors should educate senior management and the board about best practices in governance, risk management, control, and compliance.

        1) **Compliance** is defined in The IIA Glossary as "adherence to policies, plans, procedures, laws, regulations, contracts, or other requirements."

            a) The internal audit activity must evaluate the risks involved in governance, operations, and information systems that relate to compliance with laws, regulations, policies, procedures, and contracts. The internal audit activity also must evaluate the controls regarding compliance.

2. **Reasonable Assurance**

    a. Governance, risk management, and control processes are **adequate** if management has planned and designed them to provide reasonable assurance of achieving the organization's objectives efficiently and economically.

        1) **Efficient** performance accomplishes objectives in an accurate, timely, and economical fashion. **Economical** performance accomplishes objectives with minimal use of resources (i.e., cost) proportionate to the risk exposure.

        2) **Reasonable assurance** is provided if the most cost-effective measures are taken in the design and implementation stages to reduce risks and restrict expected deviations to a tolerable level.

3. **Basic Types of Internal Audit Engagements**

    a.   The essential strategic function of the internal audit activity is to provide assurance services and consulting services. Thus, the Definition of Internal Auditing describes internal auditing as "an independent, objective assurance and consulting activity."

    b.   Separate groups of Implementation Standards have been issued for assurance services and consulting services. These services are defined in The IIA Glossary as follows:

        1)   **Assurance services** – "An objective examination of evidence for the purpose of providing an independent assessment on governance, risk management, and control processes for the organization. Examples may include financial, performance, compliance, system security, and due diligence engagements."

        2)   **Consulting services** – "Advisory and related client service activities, the nature and scope of which are agreed with the client, are intended to add value and improve an organization's governance, risk management, and control processes without the internal auditor assuming management responsibility. Examples include counsel, advice, facilitation, and training."

4. **Reporting**

    a.   Reporting to senior management and the board provides assurance about

        1)   Governance,
        2)   Risk management, and
        3)   Control.

    b.   Periodic reports also are made on internal audit's purpose, authority, responsibility, and performance.

    c.   Reporting to senior management and the board is covered in more detail in Study Unit 6.

Stop and review! You have completed the outline for this subunit. Study multiple-choice questions 1 and 2 on page 31.

1.2 INTERNAL AUDIT ADMINISTRATIVE ACTIVITIES

1. **Overview**

    a.   The chief audit executive (CAE) is responsible for management of internal audit activity resources in a manner that ensures fulfillment of its responsibilities. Like any well-managed department, the internal audit activity should operate effectively and efficiently. This can be accomplished through proper planning, which includes budgeting and human resources management.

    b.   Management oversees the day-to-day operations of the internal audit activity, including the following administrative activities:

        1)   Budgeting and management accounting
        2)   Human resource administration, including personnel evaluations and compensation
        3)   Internal communications and information flows
        4)   Administration of the internal audit activity's policies and procedures

---

Performance Standard 2040
Policies and Procedures

The chief audit executive must establish policies and procedures to guide the internal audit activity.

2. **Degree of Formalization**

    a. According to Practice Advisory 2040-1, *Policies and Procedures*, policies and procedures developed by the CAE do not necessarily need to be contained in formal administrative and technical manuals.

        1) A small internal audit activity may be managed informally through daily, close supervision and memoranda.

        2) In a large internal audit activity, more formal and comprehensive policies and procedures are essential to guide the execution of the internal audit plan.

    b. The importance of the relationship of the particular internal audit activity to the extent of its formal policies and procedures is made clear in this Interpretation:

Interpretation of Standard 2040

The form and content of policies and procedures are dependent upon the size and structure of the internal audit activity and the complexity of its work.

---

3. **Budgeting**

    a. The CAE is responsible for creating the operating and financial budget. Generally, the CAE, audit managers, and the internal audit activity work together to develop the budget annually. The budget is then submitted to management and the board for their review and approval.

4. **Human Resources**

    a. The skill set and knowledge of the internal audit activity are essential to its ability to help the organization achieve its objectives. According to *Internal Auditing: Assurance & Consulting Services* (Redding, et al), "The CAE is responsible for hiring associates to fill the organizational structure of the internal audit function in a way that maximizes efficiency, effectively provides the necessary skill base, and makes good use of the financial budget."

    b. Internal auditors should be qualified and competent. Because the selection of a superior staff is dependent on the ability to evaluate applicants, selection criteria must be well-developed.

        1) Appropriate questions and forms should be prepared in advance to evaluate, among other things, the applicant's (a) technical qualifications, (b) educational background, (c) personal appearance, (d) ability to communicate, (e) maturity, (f) persuasiveness, (g) self-confidence, (h) intelligence, (i) motivation, and (j) potential to contribute to the organization.

    c. Internal auditors need a diverse set of skills to perform their jobs effectively. These skills are not always apparent in a standard resumé. Developing effective interviewing techniques will ensure that the internal audit function acquires the proper set of skills, capabilities, and technical knowledge needed to accomplish its goals.

    d. Effective interviewing techniques involve structured interviews and behavioral interviewing.

        1) Structured interviews are designed to eliminate individual bias. These interviews use a set of job-related questions with standardized answers, which then are scored by a committee of three to six members. According to *Management* (Kreitner & Cassidy, 12th edition), interviewers can use four general types of questions:

            a) Situational – "What would you do if you saw two people arguing loudly in the work area?"

            b) Job knowledge – "Do you know how to do an Internet search?"

        c)   Job sample simulation – "Can you show us how to compose and send an e-mail message?"

        d)   Worker requirements – "Are you able to spend 25 percent of your time on the road?"

    2)   Behavioral interviews determine how candidates handled past situations. Past performance is generally indicative of future performance.

Stop and review! You have completed the outline for this subunit. Study multiple-choice questions 3 through 8 beginning on page 31.

1.3 STAKEHOLDER RELATIONSHIPS

1.   **Stakeholder Relationships**

   a.   For internal auditors to be effective, *Sawyer's Guide for Internal Auditors*, 6th edition, states that they must build and maintain strong constructive relationships with managers and other stakeholders within the organization.

   b.   These relationships require conscious ongoing focus to ensure that risks are appropriately identified and evaluated to best meet the needs of the organization.

   c.   Internal auditors have a responsibility to work together with external auditors and other stakeholders to facilitate work efforts and compliance with regulators.

   d.   Key stakeholders include the board of directors, audit committees, management, external auditors, and regulators.

2.   **The Board and the Audit Committee**

   a.   For the internal audit activity to achieve organizational independence, the chief audit executive (CAE) must have direct and unrestricted access to senior management and the board.

      1)   The IIA Glossary defines a **board** as an organization's governing body, such as a board of directors or other designated body of the organization, including the **audit committee**, to whom the CAE may functionally report.

   b.   The audit committee is a subunit of the board of directors. However, not every member of the board is necessarily qualified to serve on the audit committee.

      1)   Some statutes have imposed the following significant restrictions on the membership of the audit committee:

          a)   No member may be an employee of the organization except in his or her capacity as a board member.

          b)   At least one member must be a financial expert.

      2)   Many stock exchanges require that all listed organizations have an audit committee.

3.   **Role of the Audit Committee**

   a.   The most important function of the audit committee is to promote the independence of the internal and external auditors by protecting them from management's influence.

   b.   The following are other functions of the audit committee regarding the internal audit activity:

      1)   Selecting or removing the CAE and setting his or her compensation

      2)   Approving the internal audit charter

      3)   Reviewing and approving the internal audit activity's work plan

      4)   Ensuring that the internal audit activity is allocated sufficient resources

      5)   Resolving disputes between the internal audit activity and management

      6)   Communicating with the CAE, who attends all audit committee meetings

7) Reviewing the internal audit activity's work product (e.g., interim and final engagement communications)

8) Ensuring that engagement results are given due consideration

9) Overseeing appropriate corrective action for deficiencies noted by the internal audit activity

10) Making appropriate inquiries of management and the CAE to determine whether audit scope or budgetary limitations impede the ability of the internal audit activity to meet its responsibilities

c. The following are other functions of the audit committee regarding the external auditor:

1) Selecting the external auditing firm and negotiating its fee
2) Overseeing and reviewing the work of the external auditor
3) Resolving disputes between the external auditor and management
4) Reviewing the external auditor's internal control and audit reports

4. **Relationships with Management**

a. According to *Sawyer's Guide for Internal Auditors*, 6th edition, internal auditors are responsible for performing their mission, maintaining their objectivity, and ensuring the internal audit activity's independence. They also should develop and maintain good working relationships with management.

b. Good relationships are developed by communicating effectively, resolving conflicts constructively, and using participative auditing methods.

1) Participative auditing is a collaboration between the internal auditor and management during the auditing process. The objective is to minimize conflict and build a shared interest in the engagement. People are more likely to accept changes if they have participated in the decisions and in the methods used to implement changes.

2) However, internal auditors are ultimately responsible for guiding and directing the audit because the responsibility for the final audit opinion is theirs.

Stop and review! You have completed the outline for this subunit. Study multiple-choice questions 9 and 10 on page 33.

1.4 ETHICAL CLIMATE

CIA candidates should understand the governance process, governance principles, and ethical culture. The IIA may ask questions that require candidates to apply knowledge to a set of facts.

1. **Definitions**

a. Business ethics are an organization's policies and standards established to ensure certain kinds of behavior by its members.

b. Individual ethics are the principles of conduct expected to be followed by individuals.

2. **Issues in Business Ethics**

a. The following are the major issues:

1) General business understanding of ethical issues
2) Compliance with laws (e.g., tax, securities, antitrust, environmental, privacy, and labor)
3) External financial reporting

        4) Conflicts of interest

        5) Entertainment and gift expenses

        6) Relations with customers and suppliers (Should gifts or kickbacks be given or accepted?)

        7) Social responsibility

3. **Factors That May Lead to Unethical Behavior**

    a. In any normal population, some people behave unethically. If these people hold leadership positions, they may have a bad influence on subordinates.

        1) **Organizational Factors**

            a) Pressure to improve short-run performance is an incentive for wrongdoing.

            b) Emphasis on strict chain-of-command authority may excuse unethical behavior when following orders.

            c) Informal work-group loyalties may result in tolerance of others' unethical behavior.

            d) Committee decision processes reduce individual responsibility.

        2) **External Factors**

            a) Competitive pressures may result in unethical compromises in the interest of survival.

            b) The advantage obtained by a competitor's wrongdoing is an excuse for imitation of that behavior.

            c) Definitions of ethical behavior may vary from one culture to another. For example, bribes to officials or buyers may be consistent with customary business practices in some countries.

4. **Criteria for Evaluating Ethical Behavior**

    a. The following questions aid in defining an ethical issue:

        1) "Would my behavior be acceptable if people I respect were aware of it?"

        2) "What are the consequences of this behavior for myself, other employees, customers, and society?"

    b. Ethics are individual and personal. They are influenced by the following:

        1) Life experiences (rewards for doing right, punishment for doing wrong)

        2) Friendship groups (professional associations, informal groups)

        3) Organizational pressures (responsibilities to superiors and the organization)

5. **Codes of Ethics**

    a. An organization's code of ethics is the established general value system the organization wishes to apply to its members' activities by

        1) Communicating organizational purposes and beliefs and

        2) Establishing uniform ethical guidelines for members.

            a) This guidance extends to decision making.

    b. Laws and specific rules cannot cover all situations. Thus, organizations benefit from establishing a code of ethics that effectively **communicates acceptable values** to all interested internal and external parties. For example, a code may do the following:

        1) Require compliance with the law

        2) Prohibit conflicts of interest

        3) Provide a method of policing and disciplining members for violations through

            a) Formal review panels and

            b) Group pressure (informal).

4) Set high standards against which individuals can measure their own performance

5) Communicate to those outside the organization the value system from which its members must not be asked to deviate

c. A typical code for auditors or accountants in an organization requires the following:

1) Independence from conflicts of economic or professional interest

a) They are responsible for presenting information fairly to stakeholders rather than protecting management.

b) They are responsible for presenting appropriate information to all managers. They should not favor certain managers or conceal unfavorable information.

c) They are responsible for maintaining an ethical presence in the conduct of professional activities.

   i) They should do what they can to ensure organizational compliance with the spirit as well as the letter of pertinent laws and regulations.

   ii) They should conduct themselves according to the highest ethical and legal standards.

   iii) They should report to appropriate internal or external authority any fraudulent or other illegal organizational act.

2) Integrity and a refusal to compromise professional values for personal gain

3) Objectivity in presenting information, preparing reports, and making analyses

6. **Role of the Internal Audit Activity**

a. This topic is covered by the following Implementation Standard:

> ### Implementation Standard 2110.A1
> The internal audit activity must evaluate the design, implementation, and effectiveness of the organization's ethics-related objectives, programs, and activities.

b. The internal audit activity's role in this process includes monitoring compliance with the corporate code of conduct and assessing the ethical climate of the board and the organization. The ethical culture of an organization has a significant effect on the success of the overall governance process. The following outline, based on a publication of The IIA, describes that role:

1) The governance process meets four responsibilities:

a) <u>C</u>ompliance with legal and regulatory rules
b) <u>S</u>atisfaction of generally accepted norms and social expectations
c) Providing <u>b</u>enefits to society and specific stakeholders
d) <u>R</u>eporting fully and truthfully to ensure accountability

**Governance Process
Responsibilities**

<u>C</u>ompliance	<u>C</u>reditors
<u>S</u>atisfaction	<u>S</u>end
<u>B</u>enefits	<u>B</u>illing
<u>R</u>eporting	<u>R</u>eminders

2) Governance practices reflect the organization's culture and largely depend on it for effectiveness. The culture

  a) Sets values, objectives, and strategies;
  b) Defines roles and behaviors;
  c) Measures performance;
  d) Specifies accountability; and
  e) Determines the degree of sensitivity to social responsibility.

3) Because of their skills and position in the organization, auditors should actively support the ethical culture. Auditor roles may include

  a) Chief ethics officer,
  b) Member of an ethics council, or
  c) Assessor of the ethical climate.

4) The minimum internal audit activity role is assessor of (a) the ethical climate and (b) the effectiveness of processes to achieve legal and ethical compliance. Internal auditors should evaluate the effectiveness of the following features of an enhanced, highly effective ethical culture:

  a) A formal code of conduct and related statements and policies (including procedures covering fraud and corruption)
  b) Frequent demonstrations of ethical attitudes and behavior by influential leaders
  c) Explicit strategies to enhance the ethical culture with regular programs
  d) Easily accessible means of confidentially reporting alleged violations
  e) Regular declarations by employees, suppliers, and customers about the requirements for ethical behavior
  f) Clear delegation of responsibilities for (1) providing counsel, (2) investigation, and (3) reporting
  g) Easy access to learning opportunities
  h) Positive personnel practices that encourage every employee to contribute
  i) Regular surveys of employees, suppliers, and customers to determine the state of the ethical climate
  j) Regular reviews of the processes that undermine the ethical culture
  k) Regular reference and background checks

c. Other internal audit activity roles include (1) recommending resolution of ethics complaints, (2) determining the disposition of ethics violations, (3) fostering a healthy ethics climate, (4) administering the business conduct policy, and (5) reporting on compliance.

1) A conflict of interest policy should

  a) Prohibit the transfer of benefits between an employee and those with whom the organization deals.
  b) Prohibit the use of organizational information for private gain.

Stop and review! You have completed the outline for this subunit. Study multiple-choice questions 11 through 13 on page 34.

1.5 COORDINATION

Performance Standard 2050
Coordination

The chief audit executive should share information and coordinate activities with other internal and external providers of assurance and consulting services to ensure proper coverage and minimize duplication of efforts.

---

1. **Coordinating the Work of the Internal Audit Activity with Other Auditors**

   a. Detailed guidance is provided in Practice Advisory 2050-1, *Coordination*:

      1) "Oversight of the work of external auditors, including coordination with the internal audit activity, is the responsibility of the board. Coordination of internal and external audit work is the responsibility of the chief audit executive (CAE). The CAE obtains the support of the board to coordinate audit work effectively" (para. 1).

      2) "Organizations may use the work of external auditors to provide assurance related to activities within the scope of internal auditing. In these cases, the CAE takes the steps necessary to understand the work performed by the external auditors, including:

         a) The nature, extent, and timing of work planned by external auditors, to be satisfied that the external auditors' planned work, in conjunction with the internal auditors' planned work, satisfies the requirements of Standard 2100.

         b) The external auditor's assessment of risk and materiality.

         c) The external auditors' techniques, methods, and terminology to enable the CAE to (1) coordinate internal and external auditing work; (2) evaluate, for purposes of reliance, the external auditors' work; and (3) communicate effectively with external auditors.

         d) Access to the external auditors' programs and working papers, to be satisfied that the external auditors' work can be relied upon for internal audit purposes. Internal auditors are responsible for respecting the confidentiality of those programs and working papers" (para. 2).

      3) "The external auditor may rely on the work of the internal audit activity in performing their work. In this case, the CAE needs to provide sufficient information to enable external auditors to understand the internal auditors' techniques, methods, and terminology to facilitate reliance by external auditors on work performed. Access to the internal auditors' programs and working papers is provided to external auditors in order for external auditors to be satisfied as to the acceptability for external audit purposes of relying on the internal auditors' work" (para. 3).

      NOTE: Professional standards place sole responsibility for the attest function on the external auditors. Only the external auditors have the necessary independence to permit the provision of assurance to external parties. Unlike circumstances in which the external auditors use the work of other independent auditors, the responsibility cannot be shared with the internal auditors.

      4) "Planned audit activities of internal and external auditors need to be discussed to ensure that audit coverage is coordinated and duplicate efforts are minimized where possible. Sufficient meetings are to be scheduled during the audit process to ensure coordination of audit work and efficient and timely completion of audit activities, and to determine whether observations and recommendations from work performed to date require that the scope of planned work be adjusted" (para. 5).

5) "The internal audit activity's final communications, management's responses to those communications, and subsequent follow-up reviews are to be made available to external auditors. These communications assist external auditors in determining and adjusting the scope and timing of their work. In addition, internal auditors need access to the external auditors' presentation materials and management letters. Matters discussed in presentation materials and included in management letters need to be understood by the CAE and used as input to internal auditors in planning the areas to emphasize in future internal audit work. After review of management letters and initiation of any needed corrective action by appropriate members of senior management and the board, the CAE ensures that appropriate follow-up and corrective actions have been taken" (para. 6).

6) "The CAE is responsible for regular evaluations of the coordination between internal and external auditors. Such evaluations may also include assessments of the overall efficiency and effectiveness of internal and external audit activities, including aggregate audit cost. The CAE communicates the results of these evaluations to senior management and the board, including relevant comments about the performance of external auditors" (para. 7).

2. **Coordinating with Regulatory Oversight Bodies**

   a. Businesses and not-for-profit organizations are subject to governmental regulation in many countries.

      1) Below is a sample of typical subjects of regulation:

         a) Labor relations
         b) Occupational safety and health
         c) Environmental protection
         d) Consumer product safety
         e) Business mergers and acquisitions
         f) Securities issuance and trading
         g) Trading of commodities

      2) Local and regional governments may have their own regulatory bodies.

   b. Particularly in larger organizations, entire departments or functions are established to monitor compliance with the regulations issued by these governmental bodies.

      1) For example, broker-dealers in securities establish compliance departments to ensure that trades are executed according to the requirements of securities laws. Moreover, manufacturers have departments to monitor wage-and-hour compliance, workplace safety issues, and discharge of toxic wastes.

   c. Among the responsibilities of the internal audit activity is the evaluation of the organization's compliance with applicable laws and regulations.

      1) The internal audit activity coordinates its work with that of inspectors and other personnel from the appropriate governmental bodies and with personnel from internal assurance functions.

Stop and review! You have completed the outline for this subunit. Study multiple-choice questions 14 and 15 on page 35.

1.6 OTHER TOPICS

1. **Governance**

    a. Internal auditors evaluate and improve governance processes as part of their assurance function. This subunit addresses the overall role of internal auditing in governance. It also outlines more specific governance activities, such as the assessment of the internal audit activity's own performance.

Performance Standard 2110
Governance

The internal audit activity must assess and make appropriate recommendations for improving the governance process in its accomplishment of the following objectives:

- Promoting appropriate ethics and values within the organization;
- Ensuring effective organizational performance management and accountability;
- Communicating risk and control information to appropriate areas of the organization; and
- Coordinating the activities of and communicating information among the board, external and internal auditors, and management.

---

2. **Strategic Role of the Internal Audit Activity**

    a. According to Practice Advisory 2110-3, *Governance: Assessments*, "Internal auditors can act in a number of different capacities in assessing and contributing to the improvement of governance practices. Typically, internal auditors provide independent, objective assessments of the design and operating effectiveness of the organization's governance processes. They also may provide consulting services and advice on ways to improve those processes. In some cases, internal auditors may be called on to facilitate board self-assessments of governance practices" (para. 1).

    b. The internal audit activity therefore plays an important strategic role in the governance function of an organization. That role includes providing leadership, assessing the adequacy of performance measurement systems, making appropriate recommendations, and assessing the achievement of corporate objectives.

3. **Business Process Improvement**

    a. One of the strategic roles of internal auditors involves organizing and leading a team in mapping, analysis, and business process improvement.

        1) A process map is a simple flowchart or narrative description used to depict a process. It aids in assessing the effectiveness and efficiency of processes and controls.

    b. Internal auditors evaluate the whole management process of planning, organizing, and directing to determine whether reasonable assurance exists that objectives will be achieved.

    c. All business systems, processes, operations, functions, and activities within the organization are subject to the internal auditor's evaluations. Internal auditing provides reasonable assurance that management's

        1) Risk management activities are effective;

        2) Internal control is effective and efficient; and

        3) Governance process is effective by establishing and preserving values, setting goals, monitoring activities and performance, and defining the measures of accountability.

4. **Internal Audit Performance Measurements**

    a. Key performance measurements for the internal audit activity provide criteria against which it is judged.

b. The following guidance is provided by The IIA Practice Guide, *Measuring Internal Audit Effectiveness and Efficiency*:

1) Establishing performance measures is critical in determining whether an audit activity is meeting its objectives, consistent with the highest quality practices and standards.

2) The first step is to identify key performance measures for activities that stakeholders believe add value and improve the organization's operations.

3) Once key effectiveness and efficiency measurements and targets have been identified, a monitoring process and a method of reporting to stakeholders should be established (e.g., format, timing, and metrics). The frequency of reporting should be based on stakeholder needs.

4) It is important that the internal audit activity obtain feedback from key stakeholders on audit effectiveness and make adjustments when necessary.

5. **Performance Measurement Systems and Corporate Objectives**

a. An important element of corporate governance is the establishment of performance objectives. Internal auditors can use them as standards to measure performance.

b. Internal auditors can add value to an organization by assessing the adequacy of the performance measurement system and the achievement of corporate objectives.

c. Internal auditors may gather relevant information during multiple engagements. The results of these engagements provide a basis for assessing whether the current system is adequate.

Stop and review! You have completed the outline for this subunit. Study multiple-choice question 16 on page 35.

1.7 CHANGE MANAGEMENT

1. **Overview**

a. Change management is important to all organizations. An appropriate balance between change and stability is necessary for an organization to thrive.

1) Organizational change is conducted through change agents, who may include managers, employees, and consultants hired for the purpose.

2. **Interpersonal Skills**

a. The internal audit activity can add value to an organization by acting as a catalyst of change. According to The IIA competency framework, internal auditors need the following interpersonal skills to interact with others effectively. An internal auditor can do the following:

1) Champion the change, enlist others in its pursuit, and develop a change strategy that includes milestones and a timeline.

2) Model the change expected of others.

3) Accurately assess the potential barriers and resources for change initiatives.

4) Provide resources, remove barriers, and act as an advocate for those initiating change.

5) Maintain work efficiency and respond positively to a changing environment.

6) Promptly switch strategies if the current ones are not working.

7) Provide direction and focus during the change process.

8) Support new ideas, systems, and procedures.

9) Respond quickly to changing situations by having creative ideas and taking appropriate action.

10) Support the need for change.

    11) Take steps to understand reasons for change in environment and tasks.

    12) Operate even if decisions and actions are unclear.

    13) Cope with stress.

3. **Types of Change**

    a.   **Cultural change** is a change in attitudes and mindset, for example, when a total quality management approach is adopted.

    b.   A **product change** is a change in a product's physical attributes and usefulness to customers.

    c.   A **structural change** is a change in an organization's systems or structures.

4. **Resistance**

    a.   Organizational and procedural changes often are resisted by the individuals and groups affected. This response may be caused by simple surprise, inertia, or fear of failure. But it also may arise from the following:

        1) Misunderstandings or lack of needed skills

        2) Conflicts with, or lack of trust of, management

        3) Emotional reactions when change is forced

        4) Bad timing

        5) Insensitivity to employees' needs

        6) Perceived threats to employees' status or job security

        7) Dissolution of tightly knit work groups

        8) Interference with achievement of other objectives

    b.   Methods of coping with employee resistance include the following:

        1) Prevention through education and communication

        2) Participation in designing and implementing a change

        3) Facilitation and support through training and counseling

        4) Negotiation by providing a benefit in exchange for cooperation

        5) Manipulation of information or events

        6) Co-optation through allowing some participation but without meaningful input

        7) Coercion

5. **Models for Planned Change**

    a.   Change management has been studied by management experts. The following three models have emerged:

        1) Kurt Lewin's process model consists of three stages:

            a) **Unfreezing** is the diagnosis stage. It involves choosing a change strategy, preparing employees for the change, and offsetting resistance.

            b) **Change** is the intervention in (altering of) the status quo.

            c) **Refreezing** makes the change relatively permanent so that old habits will not reassert themselves. It is the follow-up stage.

        2) The **continuous-change process model** recognizes that change is ongoing and often requires a change agent to prevent the process from being haphazard. In this five-step model, the change agent coordinates steps b) through e) below.

            a) The forces for change accumulate.

            b) The organization recognizes that a problem exists and defines it.

            c) The problem is submitted to the organization's problem-solving process.

            d) The change is implemented.

            e) Success in implementation is measured and evaluated.

3) **Organizational development (OD)** provides a framework for managing change using the findings of the behavioral sciences.

   a) True OD has three distinctive characteristics:

      i) The change must be planned and deliberate.

      ii) The change must actually improve the organization. Changes forced by regulatory requirements or changes that merely attempt to follow management trends and fads are not included.

      iii) The change must be implemented using the findings of the behavioral sciences, such as organizational behavior and group psychology.

   b) The following are the objectives of OD:

      i) Deepen the sense of organizational purpose and align individuals with it

      ii) Promote interpersonal trust, communication, cooperation, and support

      iii) Encourage a problem-solving approach

      iv) Develop a satisfying work experience

      v) Supplement formal authority with authority based on expertise

      vi) Increase personal responsibility

      vii) Encourage willingness to change

Stop and review! You have completed the outline for this subunit. Study multiple-choice questions 17 through 19 on page 36.

1.8 ROLE OF INTERNAL AUDIT IN RISK MANAGEMENT

 At one time, audit professionals thought of risk only in the context of an audit (e.g., the probability of not discovering a material financial statement misstatement). Today, after extensive research and many scholarly publications, risk is recognized as something that must be examined and mitigated in every aspect of an organization's operations. Thus, CIA candidates should understand the distinct responsibilities of (1) the internal audit activity and (2) senior management and the board for enterprise-wide risk.

Performance Standard 2120
Risk Management

The internal audit activity must evaluate the effectiveness and contribute to the improvement of risk management processes.

---

1. **Overview**

   a. The IIA Position Paper: *The Role of Internal Auditing in Enterprise Wide Risk Management* states that "risk management is a fundamental element of corporate governance. Management is responsible for establishing and operating the risk management framework on behalf of the board.

   b. "Enterprise-wide risk management [ERM] brings many benefits as a result of its structured, consistent and coordinated approach. Internal auditor's core role in relation to ERM should be to provide assurance to management and to the board on the effectiveness of risk management.

   c. "When internal auditing extends its activities beyond this core role, it should apply certain safeguards, including treating the engagements as consulting services and, therefore, applying all relevant Standards. In this way, internal auditing will protect its independence and the objectivity of its assurance services. Within these constraints, ERM can help raise the profile and increase the effectiveness of internal auditing."

2. **Role of the Internal Audit Activity**

    a. Internal audit can add value to an organization by providing the board with objective assurance that

        1) The major business risks are being managed appropriately and
        2) The risk management and internal control framework is operating effectively.

    b. An organization can undertake a broad range of ERM activities. However, internal auditors should not undertake any activities that could threaten their independence and objectivity.

        1) The IIA Position Paper groups the internal audit activity's roles into three categories:

            a) <u>C</u>ore internal audit roles in regard to ERM
            b) <u>L</u>egitimate internal audit roles with safeguards
            c) <u>R</u>oles the internal audit activity should not undertake

        2) A helpful memory aid is

<u>C</u>	<u>C</u>atch
<u>L</u>	<u>L</u>ying
<u>R</u>	<u>R</u>ecords

3. **Core Internal Audit Activity Roles in ERM**

    a. Giving assurance on the risk management process
    b. Giving assurance that risks are correctly evaluated
    c. Evaluating risk management processes
    d. Evaluating the reporting of key risks
    e. Reviewing the management of key risks

4. **Legitimate Internal Audit Activity Roles Given Safeguards**

    a. Facilitating identification and evaluation of risks
    b. Coaching management in responding to risks
    c. Coordinating ERM activities
    d. Consolidating the reporting on risks
    e. Maintaining and developing the ERM framework
    f. Championing establishment of ERM
    g. Developing an ERM strategy for board approval

5. **Roles the Internal Audit Activity Should Not Undertake**

    a. Setting the risk appetite

        1) Risk appetite is the amount of risk an entity is willing to accept in pursuit of value. It reflects the risk management philosophy and influences the entity's culture and operating style.

    b. Imposing risk management processes
    c. Management assurance on risks
    d. Making decisions on risk responses
    e. Implementing risk responses on management's behalf
    f. Accountability for risk management

6. **Role in Risk Management**

   a. The following Interpretation clarifies the internal audit activity's role:

Interpretation of Standard 2120

Determining whether risk management processes are effective is a judgment resulting from the internal auditor's assessment that:

- Organizational objectives support and align with the organization's mission;
- Significant risks are identified and assessed;
- Appropriate risk responses are selected that align risks with the organization's risk appetite; and
- Relevant risk information is captured and communicated in a timely manner across the organization, enabling staff, management, and the board to carry out their responsibilities.

The internal audit activity may gather the information to support this assessment during multiple engagements. The results of these engagements, when viewed together, provide an understanding of the organization's risk management processes and their effectiveness.

Risk management processes are monitored through ongoing management activities, separate evaluations, or both.

---

   b. Two Implementation Standards link the assessment of risk to specific risk areas:

Implementation Standard 2120.A1

The internal audit activity must evaluate risk exposures relating to the organization's governance, operations, and information systems regarding the:

- Achievement of the organization's strategic objectives;
- Reliability and integrity of financial and operational information;
- Effectiveness and efficiency of operations and programs;
- Safeguarding of assets; and
- Compliance with laws, regulations, policies, procedures, and contracts.

Implementation Standard 2120.A2

The internal audit activity must evaluate the potential for the occurrence of fraud and how the organization manages fraud risk.

---

   c. Establishing a risk-based audit model and participating in the organization's risk management processes are ways for the internal audit activity to add value.

7. **Responsibility for Organizational Risk Management**

   a. The division of responsibility is described in Practice Advisory 2120-1, *Assessing the Adequacy of Risk Management Processes*.

      1) Risk management is a key responsibility of senior management and the board.

         a) **Management** ensures that sound **risk management processes** (RMPs) are in place and functioning.

         b) **Boards** have an oversight function. They determine that RMPs are in place, adequate, and effective.

         c) The **internal audit activity** may be directed to examine, evaluate, report, or recommend improvements.

            i) It also has a consulting role in identifying, evaluating, and implementing risk management methods and controls.

2) If the organization has no formal RMPs, the CAE has formal discussions with management and the board about their obligations for understanding, managing, and monitoring risks.

3) The CAE must understand management's and the board's expectations of the internal audit activity in risk management. The understanding is codified in the charters of the internal audit activity and the board.

4) Senior management and the board determine the internal audit activity's role in risk management based on factors such as (a) organizational culture, (b) abilities of the internal audit activity staff, and (c) local conditions and customs.

 a) That role may range from no role, to auditing the process as part of the audit plan, to active, continuous support and involvement in the process, to managing and coordinating the process.

  i) But assuming management responsibilities and the threat to internal audit activity independence must be fully discussed and board-approved.

5) RMPs may be formal or informal, quantitative or subjective, or embedded in business units or centralized. They are designed to fit the organization's culture, management style, and objectives. For example, a small entity may use an informal risk committee.

 a) The internal audit activity determines that the methods chosen are comprehensive and appropriate for the organization.

6) To form an opinion on the adequacy of RMPs, internal auditors should obtain sufficient, appropriate evidence regarding achievement of key objectives.

Stop and review! You have completed the outline for this subunit. Study multiple-choice questions 20 through 22 on page 37.

1.9 QUALITY ASSURANCE AND IMPROVEMENT PROGRAM (QAIP)

Attribute Standard 1300
Quality Assurance and Improvement Program

The chief audit executive must develop and maintain a quality assurance and improvement program that covers all aspects of the internal audit activity.

---

1. **Quality Assurance and Improvement Program (QAIP)**

 a. Practice Advisory 1300-1, *Quality Assurance and Improvement Program,* provides guidance for internal audit activities in the continuous examination of their processes and efforts to meet the needs of stakeholders.

 1) The CAE implements processes designed to provide reasonable assurance to stakeholders that the internal audit activity

  a) Performs in accordance with its charter, the Definition of Internal Auditing, the Code of Ethics, and the *Standards*

  b) Operates effectively and efficiently

  c) Is perceived as adding value and improving operations

 2) These processes include appropriate supervision, periodic internal and external assessments, and ongoing monitoring of quality assurance.

 3) The QAIP embraces all facets of the internal audit activity as reflected in the pronouncements of The IIA and **best practices** of the profession.

  a) Its processes are performed or supervised by the CAE.

  b) A large or complex entity has a formal, independent QAIP administered and monitored by an audit executive.

Attribute Standard 1310
Requirements of the Quality Assurance and Improvement Program

The quality assurance and improvement program must include both internal and external assessments.

---

    b.   Practice Advisory 1310-1, *Requirements of the Quality Assurance and Improvement Program*, provides detailed guidance:

        1)   A QAIP is an ongoing and periodic assessment of all work by the internal audit activity. These rigorous assessments include

            a)   Continuous supervision and testing of performance.

            b)   Periodic validation of conformance with mandatory IIA guidance.

            c)   Measurement and analysis of **performance metrics** (e.g., audit plan accomplishment and customer satisfaction).

        2)   Indicated improvements are implemented by the CAE through the QAIP.

        3)   Assessments evaluate and state conclusions about the **quality of the internal audit activity** and produce **recommendations**. QAIPs evaluate

            a)   Conformance with mandatory IIA guidance;

            b)   Adequacy of the internal audit activity's charter, objectives, policies, and procedures;

            c)   The contribution to risk management, control, and governance;

            d)   Compliance with laws, regulations, and government or industry standards;

            e)   Continuous improvement and adoption of best practices; and

            f)   Whether the internal audit activity adds value and improves operations.

        4)   QAIP efforts include follow-up involving appropriate and timely modification of resources, processes, procedures, and technology.

        5)   The **results** of assessments are communicated to stakeholders. The CAE reports to senior management and the board on QAIP efforts **at least annually**.

Attribute Standard 1311
Internal Assessments

Internal assessments must include:

- Ongoing monitoring of the performance of the internal audit activity; and
- Periodic self-assessments or assessments by other persons within the organization with sufficient knowledge of internal audit practices.

---

2.   **Internal Assessments**

    a.   Ongoing and periodic internal assessments are addressed in Practice Advisory 1311-1, *Internal Assessment*:

        1)   The processes and tools used in ongoing internal assessments include

            a)   Engagement supervision;

            b)   Checklists and procedures;

            c)   Feedback;

            d)   Peer reviews of working papers;

            e)   Budgets, timekeeping, and tracking of audit plan completion and cost recoveries; and

            f)   Analyses of other performance metrics.

2) The IIA's Quality Assessment Manual is a basis for **periodic** internal assessments. These may involve

    a) More thorough feedback from stakeholders (in interviews and surveys) than in an ongoing assessment,

    b) **Self-assessment**,

    c) Assessment by audit professionals (e.g., CIAs),

    d) A combination of self-assessment and preparation of materials to be reviewed by audit professionals, and

    e) Benchmarking against best practices.

3) A periodic internal assessment may facilitate and reduce the cost of an **external** assessment performed shortly afterward.

    a) But the results should not communicate assurances about the outcome of the external assessment, although the report may give recommendations to enhance practices.

    b) Moreover, the periodic internal assessment may be the self-assessment part of a **self-assessment with independent validation**.

4) After an ongoing or periodic internal assessment, conclusions about performance are reached, and appropriate action is begun to ensure improvements are made.

5) Those conducting internal assessments generally report directly to the CAE, who should establish a structure for reporting results that maintains credibility and objectivity.

6) At least annually, the CAE reports results, action plans, and implementation information to senior management and the board.

Attribute Standard 1312
External Assessments

External assessments must be conducted at least once every five years by a qualified, independent assessor or assessment team from outside the organization. The chief audit executive must discuss with the board:

- The form and frequency of external assessments; and
- The qualifications and independence of the external reviewer or assessment team, including any potential conflict of interest.

---

3. **External Assessments**

    a. External assessments provide an independent and objective evaluation of the internal audit activity's compliance with the *Standards* and Code of Ethics.

    b. Further specifics are provided in Practice Advisory 1312-1, *External Assessments*:

      1) An external assessment may be a full assessment by a qualified, independent external reviewer or review team. It also may be an internal **self-assessment with independent validation** by such a reviewer or team.

        a) An external assessment covers all work by the internal audit activity.

        b) The scope of work should include benchmarking, identification, and reporting of best practices.

        c) The scope must clearly state the **expected deliverables**.

2) **Individuals** who perform the external assessment should have no obligation to, or interest in, the organization assessed or its personnel. External assessors have no real or apparent **conflict of interest** due to current or past relationships with the organization.

    a) Matters relating to independence include conflicts of **former employees** or of **firms** providing (1) the financial statement audit, (2) significant consulting services, or (3) assistance to the internal audit activity.

    b) An individual in another part of the organization or in a related organization (e.g., a parent or an affiliate) is not independent.

    c) **Peer review** among three unrelated organizations (but not between two) may satisfy the independence requirement.

    d) Given concerns about independence, one or more **independent individuals** may provide separate validation.

3) **Integrity** is honesty and candor limited by confidentiality, with no subordination of service and the public trust to personal gain.

    a) **Objectivity** is impartiality, intellectual honesty, and freedom from conflicts of interest.

4) An external reviewer should be a certified audit professional well versed in the *Standards* and best practices with at least 3 years of management experience in internal auditing or related consulting.

    a) Leaders of independent review teams and those who validate a self-assessment must have additional competence and experience.

        i) Qualifications include prior external assessment work, quality assessment training, or service as a senior internal auditor.

5) The reviewer(s) should have relevant technical and industry experience, and other **specialists** may be needed.

6) Senior management and the board are involved in selecting (a) the approach and (b) the external quality assessment provider.

7) The **scope** of the review extends to conformance with mandatory guidance of The IIA, the internal audit activity's charter, laws, etc. It also extends to

    a) The expectations of management and the board,

    b) Integration of the internal audit activity with the **governance process**,

    c) The internal audit activity's tools and techniques,

    d) Competence (mix of the staff's knowledge, experience, and disciplines), and

    e) Whether the internal audit activity **adds value** and **improves operations**.

8) **Preliminary results** are discussed with the CAE. **Final results** are communicated to the CAE, and a formal communication is given to senior management and the board.

9) The communication includes an **opinion** on conformance with the mandatory guidance of The IIA. Conformance means the practices of the internal audit activity satisfy such guidance.

    a) Nonconformance means the internal audit activity's ability to discharge its responsibilities is impaired.

        i) The degree of partial conformance is expressed if relevant.

    b) Expression of an opinion requires sound business judgment, integrity, and due professional care.

      c) The communication also includes (1) an evaluation of the use of **best practices**, (2) recommendations, and (3) CAE responses regarding action plans and implementation dates.

    10) The **results**, including specific planned actions and information about their accomplishment, are communicated to stakeholders of the internal audit activity (e.g., senior management, the board, and external auditors).

      a) The purpose is to provide **accountability and transparency**.

4.   **Reporting Results**

   a.   Senior management and the board must be kept informed about the extent to which the internal audit activity achieves the degree of professionalism required by The IIA.

Attribute Standard 1320
Reporting on the Quality Assurance and Improvement Program

The chief audit executive must communicate the results of the quality assurance and improvement program to senior management and the board.

---

   b.   This excerpt from the Interpretation of Standard 1320 addresses the frequency of reporting on the QAIP:

> *To demonstrate conformance with the Definition of Internal Auditing, the Code of Ethics, and the* Standards, *the results of external and periodic internal assessments are communicated upon completion of such assessments and the results of ongoing monitoring are communicated at least annually.*

5.   **Importance of Conforming with the *Standards***

   a.   Compliance with the *Standards* requires an effective QAIP.

Attribute Standard 1321
Use of "Conforms with the *International Standards for the Professional Practice of Internal Auditing*"

The chief audit executive may state that the internal audit activity conforms with the *International Standards for the Professional Practice of Internal Auditing* only if the results of the quality assurance and improvement program support this statement.

---

6.   **Importance of Reporting Nonconformance**

   a.   The internal audit activity is a crucial part of a complex organization's governance processes. Senior management and the board must be informed when an assessment discovers significant nonconformance.

Attribute Standard 1322
Disclosure of Nonconformance

When nonconformance with the Definition of Internal Auditing, the Code of Ethics, or the *Standards* impacts the overall scope or operation of the internal audit activity, the chief audit executive must disclose the nonconformance and the impact to senior management and the board.

---

   b.   Nonconformance of this type refers to the overall internal audit activity and not to specific engagements.

Stop and review! You have completed the outline for this subunit. Study multiple-choice questions 23 through 25 on page 38.

QUESTIONS

1.1 Introduction to Internal Auditing

1. Internal auditing is an assurance and consulting activity. An example of an assurance service is a(n)

A. Advisory engagement.

B. Facilitation engagement.

C. Training engagement.

D. Compliance engagement.

Answer (D) is correct.

REQUIRED: The example of an assurance service.

DISCUSSION: According to The IIA Glossary, an assurance service is "an objective examination of evidence for the purpose of providing an independent assessment of governance, risk management, and control processes for the organization. Examples may include financial, performance, compliance, system security, and due diligence engagements."

Answer (A) is incorrect. An advisory engagement is a consulting service. Answer (B) is incorrect. A facilitation engagement is a consulting service. Answer (C) is incorrect. A training engagement is a consulting service.

2. What is the most accurate term for the procedures used by the board to oversee activities performed to achieve organizational objectives?

A. Governance.

B. Control.

C. Risk management.

D. Monitoring.

Answer (A) is correct.

REQUIRED: The most accurate term for the means of providing oversight of processes administered by management.

DISCUSSION: Governance is the "combination of processes and structures implemented by the board to inform, direct, manage, and monitor the activities of the organization toward the achievement of its objectives" (The IIA Glossary).

Answer (B) is incorrect. Control is "any action taken by management, the board, and other parties to manage risk and increase the likelihood that established objectives and goals will be achieved. Management plans, organizes, and directs the performance of sufficient actions to provide reasonable assurance that objectives and goals will be achieved" (The IIA Glossary). Answer (C) is incorrect. Risk management Is "a process to identify, assess, manage, and control potential events or situations to provide reasonable assurance regarding the achievement of the organization's objectives" (The IIA Glossary). Answer (D) is incorrect. Monitoring consists of actions taken by management and others to assess the quality of internal control performance over time. It is not currently defined in the *Standards* and The IIA Glossary.

1.2 Internal Audit Administrative Activities

3. The key factor in the success of an internal audit activity's human resources program is

A. An informal program for developing and counseling staff.

B. A compensation plan based on years of experience.

C. A well-developed set of selection criteria.

D. A program for recognizing the special interests of individual staff members.

Answer (C) is correct.

REQUIRED: The key factor in the success of an internal audit activity's human resources program.

DISCUSSION: Internal auditors should be qualified and competent. Because the selection of a superior staff is dependent on the ability to evaluate applicants, selection criteria must be well-developed. Appropriate questions and forms should be prepared in advance to evaluate, among other things, the applicant's technical qualifications, educational background, personal appearance, ability to communicate, maturity, persuasiveness, self-confidence, intelligence, motivation, and potential to contribute to the organization.

Answer (A) is incorrect. The human resources program should be formal. Answer (B) is incorrect. The quality of the human resources is more significant than compensation. Answer (D) is incorrect. The quality of the human resources is more significant than special interests of the staff.

4. A basic principle of governance is

A. Assessment of the governance process by an independent internal audit activity.

B. Holding the board, senior management, and the internal audit activity accountable for its effectiveness.

C. Exclusive use of external auditors to provide assurance about the governance process.

D. Separation of the governance process from promoting an ethical culture in the organization.

Answer (A) is correct.
REQUIRED: The basic principle of governance.
DISCUSSION: The internal audit activity must assess and make appropriate recommendations for improving the governance process (Perf. Std. 2110).
Answer (B) is incorrect. The internal audit activity is an assessor of the governance process. It is not accountable for that process. Answer (C) is incorrect. External parties and internal auditors may provide assurance about the governance process. Answer (D) is incorrect. The internal audit activity must assess and make appropriate recommendations for improving the governance process in its promotion of appropriate ethics and values within the organization.

5. Which of the following is most likely an internal audit role in a less structured governance process?

A. Designing specific governance processes.

B. Playing a consulting role in optimizing governance practices and structure.

C. Providing advice about basic risks to the organization.

D. Evaluating the effectiveness of specific governance processes.

Answer (C) is correct.
REQUIRED: The internal audit activity's likely role in a less structured governance process.
DISCUSSION: A less mature governance system will emphasize the requirements for compliance with policies, procedures, plans, laws, regulations, and contracts. It will also address the basic risks to the organization. Thus, the internal audit activity will provide advice about such matters. As the governance process becomes more structured, the internal audit activity's emphasis will shift to optimizing the governance structure and practices.
Answer (A) is incorrect. Internal auditors impair their objectivity by designing processes. However, evaluating the design and effectiveness of specific processes is a typical internal audit role. Answer (B) is incorrect. Playing a consulting role in optimizing governance practices and structure is typical of a more structured internal auditing governance maturity model. The emphasis shifts to considering best practices and adapting them to the specific organization. Answer (D) is incorrect. Evaluating the effectiveness of specific governance processes is typical of a more structured internal auditing governance maturity model.

6. Ensuring effective organizational performance management and accountability is most directly the proper function of

A. Control.

B. Governance.

C. Risk management.

D. A quality assurance program.

Answer (B) is correct.
REQUIRED: The process responsible for ensuring effective organizational performance management and accountability.
DISCUSSION: The internal audit activity must assess and make appropriate recommendations for improving the governance process in its accomplishment of the following objectives:

● Promoting appropriate ethics and values within the organization.
● Ensuring effective organizational performance management and accountability.
● Communicating risk and control information to appropriate areas of the organization.
● Coordinating the activities of and communicating information among the board, external and internal auditors and management. (Perf. Std. 2110)

Answer (A) is incorrect. Governance (not control) is directly responsible for ensuring effective organizational performance management and accountability. Answer (C) is incorrect. Governance (not risk management) is directly responsible for ensuring effective organizational performance management and accountability. Answer (D) is incorrect. A quality assurance program normally is implemented for an organizational unit, e.g., the internal audit activity.

7. Which of the following is most essential for guiding the internal audit staff?

    A. Quality program assessments.

    B. Position descriptions.

    C. Performance appraisals.

    D. Policies and procedures.

Answer (D) is correct.
    REQUIRED: The item most essential for guiding the internal audit staff.
    DISCUSSION: The chief audit executive must establish policies and procedures to guide the internal audit activity (Perf. Std. 2040).

8. Written policies and procedures relative to managing the internal audit activity should

    A. Ensure compliance with its performance standards.

    B. Give consideration to its structure and the complexity of the work performed.

    C. Result in consistent job performance.

    D. Prescribe the format and distribution of engagement communications and the classification of observations.

Answer (B) is correct.
    REQUIRED: The correct statement about written policies and procedures relative to the internal audit department.
    DISCUSSION: The form and content of policies and procedures are dependent upon the size and structure of the internal audit activity and the complexity of its work (Inter. Std. 2040). Thus, formal administrative and technical manuals may not be needed by all internal audit activities. A small internal audit activity may be managed informally (PA 2040-1, para. 1).
    Answer (A) is incorrect. No written policy or procedure can ensure compliance with standards. Answer (C) is incorrect. Consistent performance depends on various factors, especially adequate training and supervision. Answer (D) is incorrect. The format and distribution of engagement communications and the classification of observations may vary from engagement to engagement.

1.3 Stakeholder Relationships

9. Audit committees have been identified as a major factor in promoting the independence of both internal and external auditors. Which of the following is the most important limitation on the effectiveness of audit committees?

    A. Audit committees may be composed of independent directors. However, those directors may have close personal and professional friendships with management.

    B. Audit committee members are compensated by the organization and thus favor an owner's view.

    C. Audit committees devote most of their efforts to external audit concerns and do not pay much attention to the internal audit activity and the overall control environment.

    D. Audit committee members do not normally have degrees in the accounting or auditing fields.

Answer (A) is correct.
    REQUIRED: The most important limitation on the effectiveness of audit committees.
    DISCUSSION: The audit committee is a subcommittee made up of outside directors who are independent of management. Its purpose is to help keep external and internal auditors independent of management and to ensure that the directors are exercising due care. However, if independence is impaired by personal and professional friendships, the effectiveness of the audit committee may be limited.
    Answer (B) is incorrect. The compensation audit committee members receive is usually minimal. They should be independent and therefore not limited to an owner's perspective. Answer (C) is incorrect. Although audit committees are concerned with external audits, they also devote attention to the internal audit activity. Answer (D) is incorrect. Audit committee members do not need degrees in accounting or auditing to understand engagement communications.

10. The audit committee strengthens the control processes of an organization by

    A. Assigning the internal audit activity responsibility for interaction with governmental agencies.

    B. Using the chief audit executive as a major resource in selecting the external auditors.

    C. Following up on recommendations made by the chief audit executive.

    D. Approving internal audit activity policies.

Answer (C) is correct.
    REQUIRED: The way in which the audit committee strengthens control processes.
    DISCUSSION: Among the audit committee's functions are to ensure that engagement results are given due consideration and to receive distributions of final engagement communications by the internal auditors (PA 2440-1, para. 4). This enhancement of the position of internal auditing in turn strengthens control processes.

1.4 Ethical Climate

11. An accounting association established a code of ethics for all members. What is one of the association's primary purposes of establishing the code of ethics?

A. To outline criteria for professional behavior to maintain standards of integrity and objectivity.

B. To establish standards to follow for effective accounting practice.

C. To provide a framework within which accounting policies could be effectively developed and executed.

D. To outline criteria that can be used in conducting interviews of potential new accountants.

Answer (A) is correct.
REQUIRED: The primary purpose of establishing a code of ethics.
DISCUSSION: The primary purpose of a code of ethical behavior for a professional organization is to promote an ethical culture among professionals who serve others.
Answer (B) is incorrect. National standards-setting bodies, not codes of ethics, provide guidance for effective accounting practice. Answer (C) is incorrect. A code of ethics does not provide the framework within which accounting policies are developed. Answer (D) is incorrect. The primary purpose is not for interviewing new accountants.

12. The best reason for establishing a code of conduct within an organization is that such codes

A. Are typically required by governments.

B. Express standards of individual behavior for members of the organization.

C. Provide a quantifiable basis for personnel evaluations.

D. Have tremendous public relations potential.

Answer (B) is correct.
REQUIRED: The best reason for an organizational code of conduct.
DISCUSSION: An organization's code of ethical conduct is the established general value system the organization wishes to apply to its members' activities. It communicates organizational purposes and beliefs and establishes uniform ethical guidelines for members, which include guidance on behavior for members in making decisions. A code establishes high standards against which individuals can measure their own performance. It also communicates to those outside the organization the value system from which its members must not be asked to deviate.
Answer (A) is incorrect. Governments typically lack the power to impose ethical codes on nongovernment personnel (the Sarbanes-Oxley Act of 2002 contains a partial exception to this general rule). Answer (C) is incorrect. Codes of conduct provide qualitative, not quantitative, standards. Answer (D) is incorrect. Other purposes of a code of conduct are much more significant.

13. The code of ethics of a professional organization sets forth

A. Broad standards of conduct for the members of the organization.

B. The organizational details of the profession's governing body.

C. A list of illegal activities that are proscribed to the members of the profession.

D. A basis for the measurement of internal audit performance.

Answer (A) is correct.
REQUIRED: The content of a code of ethics of a professional organization.
DISCUSSION: An organization's code of ethical conduct is the established general value system the organization wishes to apply to its members' activities by communicating organizational purposes and beliefs and establishing uniform ethical guidelines for members, which include guidance on behavior for members in making decisions. A code establishes high standards against which individuals can measure their own performance and communicates to those outside the organization the value system from which the organization's members must not be asked to deviate.
Answer (B) is incorrect. The organizational details of the profession's governing body are stated in the by-laws of the professional organization. Answer (C) is incorrect. Certain actions may be legal but contrary to an organization's code of ethics. For example, an internal auditor may not perform a service for which (s)he does not possess the necessary knowledge, skills, and experience. Answer (D) is incorrect. The *Standards* establish a basis for the measurement of internal audit performance.

1.5 Coordination

14. A chief audit executive should include in regular evaluations of internal and external audit activity an assessment of which of the following?

    A. Only external audit cost.

    B. Efficiency of only internal audit activity.

    C. Aggregate audit cost.

    D. Effectiveness of only external audit activity.

Answer (C) is correct.
    REQUIRED: The assessment a CAE should include in evaluating a coordinated internal and external audit activity.
    DISCUSSION: The CAE is responsible for regular evaluations of the coordination between internal and external auditors. Such evaluations may also include assessments of the overall efficiency and effectiveness of internal and external audit activities, including aggregate audit cost (PA 2050-1, para. 7).
    Answer (A) is incorrect. Evaluation of internal audit cost is also included. Answer (B) is incorrect. The efficiency of external audit activity is also included. Answer (D) is incorrect. The effectiveness of internal audit activity is also included.

15. Which of the following is responsible for coordination of internal and external audit work?

    A. The board.

    B. The chief audit executive.

    C. Internal auditors.

    D. External auditors.

Answer (B) is correct.
    REQUIRED: The individual(s) responsible for coordination of internal and external audit work.
    DISCUSSION: Oversight of the work of external auditors, including coordination with the internal audit activity, is the responsibility of the board. Coordination of internal and external audit work is the responsibility of the chief audit executive (CAE). The CAE obtains the support of the board to coordinate audit work effectively.
    Answer (A) is incorrect. The board oversees but is not actually responsible for the coordination. Answer (C) is incorrect. Internal auditors carry out the coordinated directions from the CAE. Answer (D) is incorrect. External auditors perform their work in coordination with information provided by the CAE.

1.6 Other Topics

16. The internal audit activity has a role in an organization's governance process. The internal audit activity most directly contributes to this process by

    A. Identifying significant exposures to risk.

    B. Evaluating the effectiveness of the risk-management system.

    C. Promoting continuous improvement of controls.

    D. Evaluating the design of ethics-related activities.

Answer (D) is correct.
    REQUIRED: How the internal audit activity most directly contributes to an organization's governance process.
    DISCUSSION: Perf. Std. 2110 states, "The internal audit activity must assess and make appropriate recommendations for improving the governance process in its accomplishment of the following objectives:

- Promoting appropriate ethics and values within the organization;
- Ensuring effective organizational performance management and accountability;
- Communicating risk and control information to appropriate areas of the organization; and
- Coordinating the activities of and communicating information among the board, external and internal auditors and management."

Thus, in an assurance engagement, "The internal audit activity must evaluate the design, implementation, and effectiveness of the organization's ethics-related objectives, programs, and activities" (Impl. Std. 2110.A1).
    Answer (A) is incorrect. Identifying significant exposures to risk most directly relates to risk management rather than to governance. Answer (B) is incorrect. Evaluating the effectiveness of the risk-management system most directly relates to risk management rather than to governance. Answer (C) is incorrect. Promoting continuous improvement of controls relates to controls rather than to governance.

1.7 Change Management

17. Employee resistance to change may be caused by

A. Only simple surprise or inertia.

B. Manipulation of information or events.

C. Bad timing.

D. Coercion.

Answer (C) is correct.
  REQUIRED: The cause of employee resistance to change.
  DISCUSSION: Resistance may be caused by simple surprise or by inertia, but it also may arise from (1) misunderstandings or lack of the needed skills; (2) lack of trust of, or conflicts with, management; (3) emotional reactions when change is forced; (4) bad timing; (5) insensitivity to employees' needs; (6) perceived threats to employees' status or job security; (7) dissolution of tightly knit work groups; and (8) interference with achievement of other objectives.
  Answer (A) is incorrect. Simple surprise and inertia are not the only possible causes of resistance. Answer (B) is incorrect. Manipulation of information or events is a method of coping with employee resistance to change. Answer (D) is incorrect. Coercion is a method of coping with employee resistance.

18. Organizational change must be considered in the light of potential employee resistance. Resistance

A. May occur even though employees will benefit from the change.

B. Will be greatest when informal groups are weakest.

C. Will be insignificant if no economic loss by employees is expected.

D. Is centered mostly on perceived threats to psychological needs.

Answer (A) is correct.
  REQUIRED: The true statement about resistance to organizational change.
  DISCUSSION: Resistance to change may be caused by fear of the personal adjustments that may be required. Employees may have a genuine concern about the usefulness of the change, perceive a lack of concern for workers' feelings, fear the outcome, worry about downgrading of job status, and resent deviations from past procedures for implementing change (especially if new procedures are less participative than the old). Social adjustments also may be required that violate the behavioral norms of informal groups or disrupt the social status quo within groups. Economic adjustments may involve potential economic loss or insecurity based on perceived threats to jobs. In general, any perceived deterioration in the work situation that is seen as a threat to economic, social, and/or psychological needs will produce resistance. The various adjustments required are most likely to be resisted when imposed unilaterally by higher authority. However, employees who share in finding solutions to the problems requiring change are less likely to resist because they will have some responsibility for the change.

19. Co-optation is a

A. Method of coping with employee resistance.

B. Cause of resistance to change.

C. Model for categorizing organizational changes.

D. Way of allowing meaningful input by resistant employees.

Answer (A) is correct.
  REQUIRED: The definition of co-optation.
  DISCUSSION: Methods of coping with employee resistance include co-optation through allowing some participation but without meaningful input.
  Answer (B) is incorrect. Co-optation is a method of coping with employee resistance. Answer (C) is incorrect. Co-optation is a method of coping with employee resistance. Answer (D) is incorrect. Co-optation is a way of allowing some participation but without meaningful input.

1.8 Role of Internal Audit in Risk Management

20. The purpose of the internal audit activity's evaluation of the effectiveness of existing risk management processes is to determine that

A. Management has planned and designed so as to provide reasonable assurance of achieving objectives.

B. Management directs processes so as to provide reasonable assurance of achieving objectives.

C. The organization's objectives will be achieved efficiently and economically.

D. The organization's objectives will be achieved in an accurate and timely manner and with minimal use of resources.

Answer (B) is correct.
REQUIRED: The purpose of the evaluation of the effectiveness of risk management processes.
DISCUSSION: Risk management, control, and governance processes are effective if management directs processes to provide reasonable assurance of achieving the organization's objectives. In addition to accomplishing the objectives and planned activities, management directs by authorizing activities and transactions, monitoring resulting performance, and verifying that the organization's processes are operating as designed.

21. Internal auditors should review the means of physically safeguarding assets from losses arising from

A. Misapplication of accounting principles.

B. Procedures that are not cost justified.

C. Exposure to the elements.

D. Underusage of physical facilities.

Answer (C) is correct.
REQUIRED: The cause of losses giving rise to physical safeguards that should be reviewed by the auditor.
DISCUSSION: The internal audit activity must evaluate risk exposures relating to governance, operations, and information systems regarding the safeguarding of assets (Impl. Std. 2120.A1). For example, internal auditors evaluate risk exposure arising from theft, fire, improper or illegal activities, and exposure to the elements.
Answer (A) is incorrect. Misapplication of accounting principles relates to the reliability of information and not physical safeguards. Answer (B) is incorrect. Procedures that are not cost justified relate to efficiency, not effectiveness, of operations. Answer (D) is incorrect. Underusage of facilities relates to efficiency of operations.

22. If an organization has no formal risk management processes, the chief audit executive should

A. Establish risk management processes based on industry norms.

B. Formulate hypothetical results of possible consequences resulting from risks not being managed.

C. Inform regulators that the organization is guilty of an infraction.

D. Formally discuss with the directors their obligations for risk management processes.

Answer (D) is correct.
REQUIRED: The requirement for internal auditors if an organization has no established risk management process.
DISCUSSION: In situations where the organization does not have formal risk management processes, the chief audit executive formally discusses with management and the board their obligations to understand, manage, and monitor risks within the organization and the need to satisfy themselves that there are processes operating within the organization, even if informal, that provide the appropriate level of visibility into the key risks and how they are being managed and monitored (PA 2120-1, para. 3).
Answer (A) is incorrect. Internal auditors have no authority to establish risk management processes. They must seek direction from management and the board as to their role in the process. Answer (B) is incorrect. Internal auditors are not required to perform a risk analysis of the possible consequences of not establishing a risk management process. However, such a request might be made by management. Answer (C) is incorrect. In the absence of a specific legal requirement, internal auditors are not required to report to outside parties.

1.9 Quality Assurance and Improvement Program (QAIP)

23. The internal audit activity's quality assurance and improvement program is the responsibility of

    A. External auditors.

    B. The chief audit executive.

    C. The board.

    D. The audit committee.

Answer (B) is correct.
    REQUIRED: The individual(s) responsible for the quality assurance reviews of the internal audit activity.
    DISCUSSION: The chief audit executive must develop and maintain a quality assurance and improvement program that covers all aspects of the internal audit activity (Attr. Std. 1300).

24. At what minimal required frequency does the chief audit executive report the results of internal assessments in the form of ongoing monitoring to senior management and the board?

    A. Monthly.

    B. Quarterly.

    C. Annually.

    D. Biennially.

Answer (C) is correct.
    REQUIRED: The frequency of reporting by the CAE to the board and senior management.
    DISCUSSION: The CAE must communicate the results of the quality assurance and improvement program to senior management and the board (Attr. Std. 1320). To demonstrate conformance with the mandatory IIA guidance, the results of external and periodic internal assessments are communicated upon completion of such assessments and the results of ongoing monitoring are communicated at least annually (Inter. Std. 1320).

25. To demonstrate conformance of the internal audit activity with the mandatory guidance of The IIA,

    A. The chief audit executive determines the form and content of the results communicated without seeking input from senior management or the board.

    B. The results of external assessments are communicated upon their completion.

    C. The results of periodic internal assessments are communicated at least monthly.

    D. The results of ongoing monitoring are communicated upon their completion.

Answer (B) is correct.
    REQUIRED: The true statement about demonstrating conformance with the mandatory guidance of The IIA.
    DISCUSSION: "To demonstrate conformance with the Definition of Internal Auditing and the *Standards*, and application of the Code of Ethics, the results of external and periodic internal assessments are communicated upon completion of such assessments and the results of ongoing monitoring are communicated at least annually. The results include the reviewer's or review team's assessment with respect to the degree of conformance" (Inter. Std. 1320).
    Answer (A) is incorrect. The form, content, and frequency of communicating the results of the quality assurance and improvement program is established through discussions with senior management and the board and considers the responsibilities of the internal audit activity and chief audit executive as contained in the internal audit charter. Answer (C) is incorrect. The results of periodic internal assessments are communicated upon their completion. Answer (D) is incorrect. The results of ongoing monitoring are communicated at least annually.

Practice even more exam-emulating questions in **Gleim CIA Test Prep!**

STUDY UNIT TWO
ASSURANCE AND COMPLIANCE ENGAGEMENTS

(20 pages of outline)

This study unit is the second of four covering **Section I: Managing the Internal Audit Function** from The IIA's CIA Exam Syllabus. This section makes up 40% to 50% of Part 2 of the CIA exam and is tested at the **proficiency level**. The relevant portion of the syllabus is highlighted below. (The complete syllabus is in Appendix B.)

I. MANAGING THE INTERNAL AUDIT FUNCTION (40%–50%)

A. Strategic Role of Internal Audit

B. Operational Role of IA

C. Establish Risk-Based IA Plan

1. Use market, product, and industry knowledge to identify new internal audit engagement opportunities
2. Use a risk framework to identify sources of potential engagements (e.g., audit universe, audit cycle requirements, management requests, regulatory mandates)
3. Establish a framework for assessing risk
4. Rank and validate risk priorities to prioritize engagements in the audit plan
5. Identify internal audit resource requirements for annual IA plan
6. Communicate areas of significant risk and obtain approval from the board for the annual engagement plan
7. Types of engagements
   a. Conduct assurance engagements
      a.1 Risk and control self-assessments
         a) Facilitated approach
            (1) Client-facilitated
            (2) Audit-facilitated
         b) Questionnaire approach
         c) Self-certification approach
      a.2 Audits of third parties and contract auditing
      a.3 Quality audit engagements
      a.4 Due diligence audit engagements
      a.5 Security audit engagements
      a.6 Privacy audit engagements
      a.7 Performance audit engagements (key performance indicators)
      a.8 Operational audit engagements (efficiency and effectiveness)
      a.9 Financial audit engagements
   b. Compliance audit engagements
   c. Consulting engagements
      c.1 Internal control training
      c.2 Business process mapping
      c.3 Benchmarking
      c.4 System development reviews
      c.5 Design of performance measurement systems

2.1 ASSURANCE ENGAGEMENTS

The professional standards for internal auditors and external auditors differ significantly in the scope of their treatment of consulting services. For example, the AICPA's standards for financial statement auditing in the United States are extremely detailed, but its standards for consulting are limited. However, The IIA recognizes that consulting is a way for internal auditors to add significant value to the organization. Candidates for the CIA exam must be able to distinguish the requirements for consulting engagements from those for assurance engagements.

1. **Financial, Compliance, Operational, and IT Auditing**

   a. According to the Introduction to the *Standards*, "Assurance services involve the internal auditor's objective assessment of evidence to provide an independent opinion or conclusions regarding an entity, operation, function, process, system, or other subject matter."

   b. **Assurance services** are "an objective examination of evidence for the purpose of providing an independent assessment on governance, risk management, and control processes for the organization.

      1) Examples may include financial, performance, compliance, system security, and due diligence engagements" (The IIA Glossary).

      2) The nature and scope of the assurance engagement are determined by the internal auditor.

   c. The following overview of assurance services is based on various publications of The IIA:

      1) **Financial** assurance provides analysis of the economic activity of an entity as measured and reported by accounting methods.

         a) **Financial auditing** looks at the past to determine whether financial information was properly recorded and adequately supported. It also assesses whether the financial statement assertions about past performance are fair, accurate, and reliable.

      2) **Compliance** assurance is the review of financial and operating controls to assess conformance with established laws, standards, regulations, policies, plans, procedures, contracts, and other requirements.

         a) **Compliance auditing** looks at the past and examines the present to ask such questions as the following:

            i) Have we adhered to laws and regulations?

            ii) Are we currently complying with legal and regulatory requirements?

            iii) What are our organization's corporate standards of business conduct?

            iv) Do all members of our staff and management team consistently comply with internal policies and procedures?

      3) **Operational** assurance is the review of a function or process to appraise the efficiency and economy of operations and the effectiveness with which those functions achieve their objectives.

         a) **Operational auditing** focuses on the present and future. It is closely aligned with the organization's mission, vision, and objectives. It also evaluates the effectiveness (ensuring the right things are done), efficiency (ensuring things are done the right way), and economy (ensuring cost-effectiveness) of operations. This mindset includes such areas as (1) product quality, (2) customer service, (3) revenue maximization, (4) expense minimization, (5) fraud prevention, (6) asset safeguarding, (7) corporate social responsibility and citizenship, (8) streamlined workflows, (9) safety, and (10) planning. It concentrates on what is working and what is not as well as the opportunities for future improvement.

4) **IT** assurance is the review and testing of IT (for example, computers, technology infrastructure, IT governance, mobile devices, and cloud computing) to assure the integrity of information. Traditionally, IT auditing has been done in separate projects by IT audit specialists, but increasingly it is being integrated into all audits.

d. The three distinct categories of assurance services correspond to the three objectives of internal control defined in the control framework adopted by the Committee of Sponsoring Organizations (COSO).

1) Internal control is a process effected by an entity's board, management, and other personnel that is designed to provide reasonable assurance regarding the achievement of the following objectives:

a) **Reliability** of financial reporting, e.g., published financial information;

b) **Effectiveness and efficiency** of operations, e.g., achievement of performance and profit goals and the safeguarding of resources; and

c) **Compliance** with applicable laws and regulations.

Assurance Services

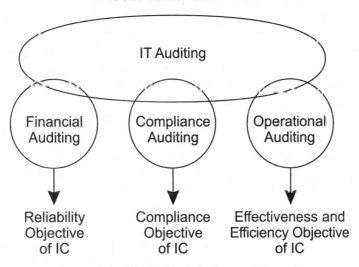

Figure 2-1

e. The services described also may be performed by external auditors, for example, in outsourcing or cosourcing engagements. Nevertheless, the traditional focus of external auditors is on the fair presentation of general purpose financial information.

1) By contrast, the traditional focus of internal auditors is on supporting management and governance authorities in performing their functions.

Stop and review! You have completed the outline for this subunit. Study multiple-choice questions 1 through 3 on page 59.

2.2 RISK AND CONTROL SELF-ASSESSMENT

1. **Control Self-Assessment (CSA)**

a. Control self-assessment (CSA) increases awareness of risk and control throughout the organization.

1) Risk assessment, business processes, and internal controls are not treated as exclusive concerns of senior management and the internal audit activity. Instead, CSA involves client personnel, asks for their input, and gives them a sense of participation.

b.   CSA's basic philosophy is that control is the responsibility of everyone in the organization. The people who work within the process, i.e., the employees and managers, are asked for their assessments of risks and controls in their process.

c.   CIA candidates should understand (1) the objectives of CSA, (2) its advantages to an organization, (3) its long-term objectives, and (4) the controls best evaluated by the program.

2.   **Elements of CSA**

a.   A typical CSA process has the following elements:

1)   Front-end planning and preliminary audit work.

2)   An in-person meeting, typically involving a facilitation seating arrangement (U-shaped table) and a meeting facilitator. The participants are process owners, i.e., management and staff who (a) are involved with the particular issues under examination, (b) know them best, and (c) are critical to the implementation of appropriate process controls.

3)   A structured agenda used by the facilitator to lead the group through an examination of the process's risks and controls. Frequently, the agenda is based on a well-defined framework or model so that participants can be sure to address all necessary issues. A model may focus on controls, risks, or a framework developed for that project.

4)   An option is the presence of a scribe to take an online transcription of the session and electronic voting technology to enable participants to state their perceptions of the issues anonymously.

5)   Reporting and the development of action plans.

b.   Accordingly, CSA typically employs a workshop-facilitation approach to self-assessment that is structured, documented, and repetitive. Thus, it should be contrasted with an approach that merely surveys employees regarding risks and controls.

c.   Senior management should oversee the establishment, administration, and evaluation of the processes of risk management and control.

1)   Operating managers' responsibilities include assessment of the risks and controls in their units.

2)   Internal and external auditors provide varying degrees of assurance about the state of effectiveness of the risk management and control processes of the organization.

3)   Managers and auditors have an interest in using methods that (a) improve the assessment of risk management and control processes and (b) identify ways to improve their effectiveness.

3.   **How Internal Auditors Use CSA**

a.   Internal auditing's investment in some CSA programs may be significant. It may (1) sponsor, design, implement, and own the process; (2) conduct the training; (3) supply the facilitators, scribes, and reporters; and (4) coordinate the participation of management and work teams.

1)   In other CSA programs, internal auditing may serve only as an interested party and consultant for the whole process and as the ultimate verifier of the evaluations produced by the teams.

2)   In most programs, the investment in the organization's CSA efforts is somewhere between the two extremes described above. As the level of involvement in the CSA program and individual workshop deliberations increases, the chief audit executive (CAE) (a) monitors the objectivity of the internal audit staff, (b) takes steps to manage that objectivity (if necessary), and (c) augments internal audit testing to ensure that bias or partiality does not affect the final judgments of the staff.

b. A CSA program augments the traditional role of the internal audit activity by assisting management in fulfilling its responsibilities to establish and maintain risk management and control processes and by evaluating the adequacy of that system. Through a CSA program, the internal audit activity and the business units and functions collaborate to produce better information about how well the control processes are working and how significant the residual risks are.

c. Although it provides staff support for the CSA program as facilitator and specialist, the internal audit activity often finds that it may reduce the effort spent in gathering information about control procedures and eliminate some testing. A CSA program (1) increases the coverage of assessments of control processes across the organization, (2) improves the quality of corrective actions made by the process owners, and (3) focuses the internal audit activity's work on reviewing high-risk processes and unusual situations. A CSA also can focus on (1) validating the evaluation conclusions produced by the CSA process, (2) synthesizing the information gathered from the components of the organization, and (3) expressing its overall judgment about the effectiveness of controls to senior management and the board.

4. **Key Features**

a. CSA includes self-assessment surveys and facilitated workshops. It is a useful and efficient approach for managers and internal auditors to collaborate in assessing and evaluating control procedures. In its purest form, CSA integrates business objectives and risks with control processes.

  1) CSA also is called control/risk self-assessment.

b. Although CSA practitioners use different methods and formats, most implemented programs share some key features and goals. An organization that uses self-assessment will have a formal, documented process that allows management and work teams who are directly involved in a business unit, function, or process to participate in a structured manner for the purpose of

  1) Identifying risks and exposures,
  2) Assessing the control processes that mitigate or manage those risks,
  3) Developing action plans to reduce risks to acceptable levels, and
  4) Determining the likelihood of achieving the business objectives.

5. **Outcomes**

a. People in the business units become trained and experienced in assessing risks and associating control processes with managing those risks and improving the chances of achieving business objectives.

b. Informal, soft controls are more easily identified and evaluated.

c. People are motivated to take ownership of the control processes in their units, and corrective actions taken by the work teams are often more effective and timely.

d. The entire objectives-risks-controls infrastructure of an organization is subject to greater monitoring and continuous improvement.

e. Internal auditors become involved in and knowledgeable about the self-assessment process by serving as facilitators, scribes, and reporters for the work teams and as trainers in risk and control concepts supporting the CSA program.

f. The internal audit activity acquires more information about the control processes within the organization and can leverage that additional information in allocating its scarce resources. The result is greater effort devoted to investigating and performing tests of business units or functions that have significant control weaknesses or high residual risks.

g. Management's responsibility for the risk management and control processes of the organization is reinforced, and managers will be less tempted to abdicate those activities to specialists, such as auditors.

h.   The primary role of the internal audit activity will continue to include validation of the evaluation process by the performance of tests and the expression of its professional judgment about the adequacy and effectiveness of the whole risk management and control system.

6.   **Approaches**

a.   The three primary approaches of CSA programs are (1) facilitation, (2) survey (questionnaire), and (3) self-certification. Organizations often combine approaches.

b.   The variety of approaches used for CSA processes in organizations reflects the differences in industry, geography, structure, organizational culture, degree of employee empowerment, dominant management style, and the manner of formulating strategies and policies. Thus, the success of a particular type of CSA program in one organization might not be replicated in another.

   1)   The CSA process should be customized to fit the unique characteristics of each organization. Also, a CSA approach needs to be dynamic and change with the continual development of the organization.

7.   **Facilitation Approach**

a.   The facilitation approach has four possible formats.

   1)   The **objective-based format** focuses on the best way to accomplish a business objective. The workshop begins by identifying the controls presently in place to support the objective and then determines the residual risks remaining.

      a)   The aim of the workshop is to decide whether the control procedures are working effectively and are resulting in residual risks within an acceptable level.

   2)   The **risk-based format** focuses on listing the risks to achieving an objective. The workshop begins by listing all possible barriers, obstacles, threats, and exposures that might prevent achieving an objective and then examines the control procedures to determine whether they are sufficient to manage the key risks.

      a)   The workshop's aim is to determine significant residual risks. This format takes the work team through the entire objective-risks-controls formula.

   3)   The **control-based format** focuses on how well the controls in place are working. This format is different from the two on the previous page because the facilitator identifies the key risks and controls before the beginning of the workshop. During the workshop, the work team assesses how well the controls mitigate risks and promote the achievement of objectives.

      a)   The aim of the workshop is to produce an analysis of the gap between how controls are working and how well management expects those controls to work.

   4)   The **process-based format** focuses on selected activities that are elements of a chain of processes. The processes are usually a series of related activities that go from some beginning point to an end, such as the various steps in purchasing, product development, or revenue generation. This type of workshop usually covers the identification of the objectives of the whole process and the various intermediate steps.

      a)   The workshop's aim is to evaluate, update, validate, improve, and even streamline the whole process and its component activities. This workshop format may have a greater breadth of analysis than a control-based approach by covering multiple objectives within the process and by supporting concurrent management efforts, such as reengineering, quality improvement, and continuous improvement initiatives.

8. **Survey Approach**

 a. The survey form of CSA uses a questionnaire that tends to ask mostly simple "yes/no" or "have/have not" questions that are carefully written to be understood by the target recipients.

 1) Surveys often are used if the desired respondents are too numerous or widely dispersed to participate in a workshop. They also are preferred if the culture in the organization may limit open, candid discussions in workshop settings or if management desires to minimize the time spent and costs incurred in gathering the information.

9. **Self-Certification Approach**

 a. This form of self-assessment is based on management-produced analyses to produce information about selected business processes, risk management activities, and control procedures. The analysis is often intended to reach an informed and timely judgment about specific characteristics of control procedures and is commonly prepared by a team in a staff or support role.

 1) The internal auditor may synthesize this analysis with other information to enhance the understanding about controls and to share the knowledge with managers in business or functional units as part of the organization's CSA program.

10. **Understanding of Risk and Control**

 a. All self-assessment programs assume that managers and members of the work teams understand risk and control concepts and use them in communications.

 1) For training sessions, to facilitate the orderly flow of workshop discussions, and as a check on the completeness of the overall process, organizations often use a control framework, such as the COSO (Committee of Sponsoring Organizations) model.

11. **Workshop Reports**

 a. In the typical CSA facilitated workshop, a report is substantially created during the deliberations. A consensus is recorded for the various segments of the discussions, and the group reviews the proposed final report before the end of the final session.

 1) Some programs use anonymous voting to ensure the free flow of information and opinions during the workshops and to aid in negotiating differences between interest groups.

Stop and review! You have completed the outline for this subunit. Study multiple-choice questions 4 through 6 on page 60.

2.3 AUDITS OF THIRD PARTIES AND CONTRACT AUDITING

1. **External Business Relationships**

 a. Organizations have multiple external (extended) business relationships (EBRs). The IIA's Practice Guide, *Auditing External Business Relationships*, contains extensive guidance.

 1) Each EBR has risks, and management is responsible for managing and monitoring the risks and achieving the benefits.

 2) Internal auditing assists management and validates its efforts.

    b.   EBRs may involve the following:

        1)   Service providers (e.g., for providing internal audit services, processing of payroll, sharing of services, or use of IT services)

        2)   Supply-side partners (e.g., outsourcing of production or R&D)

        3)   Demand-side partners (e.g., licensees or distributors)

        4)   Strategic alliances and joint ventures (e.g., cost-, revenue-, and profit-sharing in media production and development)

        5)   Intellectual property (IP) partners (e.g., licensing of software)

    c.   Among other things, EBR partners may offer lower costs, better operational efficiency, special expertise, new technology, a known brand, or economies of scale.

    d.   The internal audit activity helps management and the board identify, assess, and manage risks, including reputation risks as well as economic risks. The following are examples of significant risks of EBRs:

        1)   They may not be identified and therefore may not be (a) managed in accordance with relevant policies, (b) assessed, or (c) monitored.

        2)   EBRs may adversely affect the organization's reputation, e.g., by violating laws, committing fraud, or not complying with contracts.

        3)   EBRs may have inadequate insurance coverage.

        4)   Service levels or products may be unsatisfactory, e.g., because of inadequate definition in the contract.

        5)   Conflicts of interest may arise, e.g., when the work is affected by the EBR's contractual obligations to others.

        6)   Licensing of intellectual property may result in misuse, theft, or loss of revenue.

        7)   The organization may be overcharged for services.

        8)   The EBR partner may become insolvent.

        9)   The organization's confidential information (e.g., personally identifiable information) may be lost.

2. **Auditing EBRs**

    a.   Internal auditors need to understand all elements of an EBR:

        1)   Initiating the EBR

        2)   Contracting for and defining the EBR

        3)   Procurement

        4)   Managing and monitoring the EBR (including control environment considerations of objectivity and independence of managers)

        5)   Discontinuing the EBR

    b.   The internal auditors need to understand the expectations of the parties and the processes for managing and monitoring the EBR.

        1)   They then develop an appropriate audit program with relevant objectives.

            a)   Internal audit procedures may include evaluating compliance with the contract to determine whether monetary and nonmonetary obligations are met.

            b)   Audit procedures may discover missed revenue or cost savings, improve reporting, and add value to the EBR through the following:

                i)   Limiting fraud

                ii)   Increasing trust

                iii)   Fostering feedback

                iv)   Improving relationships

                v)   Helping management improve internal and external controls

    c.   The CAE decides whether to audit (1) each EBR separately, (2) certain EBRs, or (3) the total EBR process. The following is the cycle for an EBR audit:

        1)   **Understanding the organization, its environment, its processes, and the nature of each EBR**

            a)   The internal auditors need to understand (1) the reasons for, and the importance of, EBRs; (2) whether they have been identified; and (3) the risks of noncompliance by EBR partners.

        2)   **Assessing risks and controls**

            a)   The internal auditors need to (1) understand the EBR's inherent risks and the design of relevant controls; (2) determine the key controls; and (3) understand the EBR partner's environment, processes, and controls (including the work done by its auditors).

        3)   **Performing the audit**

            a)   The internal auditors need to determine whether to (1) do on-site work at the EBR, (2) evaluate results, (3) identify findings and their application (to one EBR, certain EBRs, or the total EBR process), and (4) reach conclusions.

        4)   **Reporting**

            a)   The internal auditors need to determine the frequency and content of reports to the board and senior management.

        5)   **Monitoring progress**

            a)   The internal auditors may determine whether findings (especially deficiencies) have been addressed. They also may assist in determining whether EBRs are well managed.

3.   **Third-Party Audits**

    a.   The organization may be audited. This is routine for organizations that issue general-use financial statements and for many EBRs.

        1)   For example, if the organization is a service provider, the external and internal auditors of the organization's clients must obtain assurance about the security of the organization's operations and the fulfillment of contractual obligations. Such audits are also common for joint ventures.

        2)   Another typical third-party audit is the audit performed by a qualified registrar as part of the ISO 9000 certification process.

    b.   In these cases, the internal auditors should coordinate their activities with those of the third-party auditor to share information and to prevent duplication of effort.

4.   **Contract Auditing**

    a.   Internal auditors often perform engagements to monitor and evaluate significant construction contracts and operating contracts that involve the provision of services. The usual types of arrangements for such contracts are lump-sum (fixed-price), cost-plus, and unit-price.

    b.   **Lump-sum contracts.** The internal auditor may have little to evaluate when the work is performed in accordance with the contract. However, reviewing such an agreement may call for consideration of the following:

        1)   Progress payments

        2)   Incentives (e.g., for early completion)

        3)   An escalator clause (e.g., one causing the entire price to be due in the event of some breach of the contract)

        4)   Adjustments for labor costs (e.g., premiums paid to obtain necessary labor)

        5)   Change orders

    c.   **Cost-plus contracts** are ways to cope with uncertainties about costs by setting a price equal to (1) cost plus a fixed amount or (2) cost plus a fixed percentage of cost. A problem is that the contractor may have little incentive for economy and efficiency, a reason for careful review by the internal auditors. These contracts may have provisions for

        1)   Maximum costs, with any savings shared by the parties, or
        2)   Incentives for early completion.

    d.   **Unit-price contracts** are often used when a convenient measure of work is available, such as acres of land cleared, cubic yards of earth moved, or square footage patrolled by a security service.

        1)   The key issue is the accurate measurement of the work performed.

    e.   To protect the organization, internal auditors should be involved throughout the contracting process, not merely in the performance phase. They should review the terms of the contract and the following:

        1)   Procedures for bidding (e.g., competitive bidding)
        2)   Procedures for cost estimation and control
        3)   Budgets and financial forecasts
        4)   The contractor's information and control systems
        5)   The contractor's financial position
        6)   Funding and tax matters
        7)   Progress of the project and costs incurred

Stop and review! You have completed the outline for this subunit. Study multiple-choice questions 7 through 10 beginning on page 60.

2.4 QUALITY AUDITING

1.   **Quality Auditing**

    a.   The internal audit activity's role is to provide assurance that the approved quality structures are in place and quality processes are functioning as intended.

2.   **Traditional vs. Modern Views of Quality**

    a.   The traditional view of quality emphasized the detection of products that do not meet standards.

        1)   This view involved the rejection or reworking of defective goods.

    b.   The modern view is that quality is a value-added activity performed throughout all processes, from product design to raw materials acquisition and final inspection.

        1)   It also extends to all of the organization's business processes, not just to the production of goods. This view of quality is the basis for total quality management (TQM).

3.   **Total Quality Management (TQM)**

    a.   TQM can increase revenues and decrease costs significantly. Thus, the internal audit activity's services with respect to the quality function may add substantial value. Indeed, the improvement of operations is part of the definition of internal auditing.

    b.   Quality is best viewed from multiple perspectives:

        1)   Attributes of the product (performance, serviceability, durability, etc.),
        2)   Customer satisfaction,
        3)   Conformity with manufacturing specifications, and
        4)   Value (relation of quality and price).

    c.   TQM is a comprehensive approach. It treats the pursuit of quality as a basic organizational function that is as important as production or marketing. It is also a strategic weapon because its cumulative effects cannot be easily duplicated by competitors.

        1)   TQM is the **continuous pursuit of quality** in every aspect of organizational activities through

            a)   A philosophy of doing it right the first time,
            b)   Employee training and empowerment,
            c)   Promotion of teamwork,
            d)   Improvement of processes, and
            e)   Attention to satisfaction of internal and external customers.

    d.   TQM emphasizes the supplier's relationship with the customer and identifies customer needs. It also recognizes that everyone in a process is at some time a customer or supplier of someone else, either within or outside the organization.

        1)   Thus, TQM begins with external customer requirements, identifies internal customer-supplier relationships and requirements, and establishes requirements for external suppliers.

    e.   The management of quality is not limited to quality management staff, engineers, production personnel, etc.

        1)   Given the organization-wide scope of TQM and of the internal audit activity, the role of the internal auditors is to evaluate the entire quality function.

            a)   The internal audit activity is well qualified to perform risk assessments and promote continuous improvement of controls.

                i)   The personnel involved in the technical improvements of processes may be unqualified with regard to risk management and control issues.

            b)   The internal audit activity performs procedures to provide **assurance** that the basic objectives of TQM are reached: customer satisfaction, continuous improvement, and promotion of teamwork.

            c)   TQM concepts also are applicable to the operations of the internal audit activity itself. For example, Practice Advisory 1311-1 states that periodic internal assessments of those operations may "include benchmarking of the internal audit activity's practices and performance metrics against relevant best practices of the internal audit profession."

Stop and review! You have completed the outline for this subunit. Study multiple-choice questions 11 through 13 beginning on page 61.

2.5 DUE DILIGENCE AUDITING

1.   **Due Diligence Auditing**

    a.   The term "due diligence" is applied to a service in which internal auditors and others (external auditors, tax experts, finance professionals, attorneys, etc.) determine the business justification for a major transaction (business combination, joint venture, divestiture, etc.) and whether that justification is valid.

        1)   Internal auditors might, for example, review operations (purchasing, shipping and receiving, inventory management, etc.), internal control over information systems, the compatibility of the organizational cultures, and finance and accounting issues.

        2)   The term "due diligence" also may be used for other engagements, for example, certain environmental audits.

    b.   The due diligence process establishes whether the expected benefits of the transaction (wider markets, more skilled employees, access to intellectual property, operating synergies, etc.) are likely to be realized. It also may facilitate the realization of those benefits by improving the effectiveness and efficiency of the implementation of the transaction.

    c.   One of the keys to the effectiveness and efficiency of the engagement is coordination among the groups involved. For example, the same software should be used for preparation of electronic working papers to facilitate sharing of information.

    d.   The final report should be factual, not subjective, with supporting information indexed and backed up on computer disks.

        1)   The report should contain an executive summary with key points highlighted.

        2)   The cycle approach used by the acquiring organization to organize its business is a desirable means of structuring the report.

Stop and review! You have completed the outline for this subunit. Study multiple-choice questions 14 and 15 beginning on page 62.

2.6 SECURITY AND PRIVACY AUDITS

NOTE: Physical security, such as safeguards against environmental risks and wrongful access to computers, must be audited even if software provides most of the protection for information.

    1.   **Information Security Auditing**

        a.   Information security auditing is an expansion of the assurance services performed by auditors. The creation of organization-wide computer networks with the potential for access by numerous outside parties has greatly increased risk. Thus, risk management and control processes may be inadequate.

        b.   The role of the internal audit activity in these circumstances is to assess risks, monitor the implementation of corrective action, and evaluate controls.

            1)   The internal audit activity also may act in a consulting capacity by identifying security issues and by working with users of information systems and with systems security personnel to devise and implement controls.

            2)   The internal audit activity works closely with senior management and the board to assist in the performance of the governance function with respect to information security.

Implementation Standard 2130.A1

The internal audit activity must evaluate the adequacy and effectiveness of controls in responding to the risks within the organization's governance, operations, and information systems regarding the:

- Achievement of the organization's strategic objectives;
- Reliability and integrity of financial and operational information;
- Effectiveness and efficiency of operations and programs;
- Safeguarding of assets; and
- Compliance with laws, regulations, policies, procedures, and contracts.

---

        c.   The following summarizes the provisions of Practice Advisory 2130.A1-1, *Information Reliability and Integrity*:

            1)   Information reliability and integrity includes accuracy, completeness, and security. The internal audit activity determines whether senior management and the board clearly understand that it is a management responsibility for all critical information regardless of its form.

2) The CAE determines whether the internal audit activity has competent audit resources for evaluating internal and external risks to information reliability and integrity.

3) The CAE determines whether senior management, the board, and the internal audit activity will be promptly notified about breaches and conditions that might represent a threat.

4) Internal auditors assess the effectiveness of preventive, detective, and mitigative measures against past and future attacks. They also determine whether the board has been appropriately informed.

5) Internal auditors periodically assess reliability and integrity practices and recommend new or improved controls. Such assessments can be made as separate engagements or as multiple engagements integrated with other elements of the audit plan.

    d.   Internal auditors also evaluate compliance with laws and regulations concerning privacy. Thus, they assess the adequacy of the identification of risks and the controls that reduce those risks.

2. **Security Auditing**

    a.   The most common use of the term "security" in an organizational setting is in connection with information technology (IT).

        1)   However, the organization must take a more comprehensive view of security.

        2)   One example is the protection of employees and visitors from workplace violence. Thus, security is an appropriate governance and risk management issue even in the absence of IT.

    b.   The internal audit activity evaluates the adequacy and effectiveness of controls designed and implemented by management in all areas of security.

3. **Privacy Auditing**

    a.   The amount of personal information stored on computers has greatly increased. The security risks involved also have increased because of the interconnections among computers permitted by the Internet.

    b.   The following summarizes the major provisions of Practice Advisory 2130.A1-2, *Evaluating an Organization's Privacy Framework*:

        1)   Protection of personal information prevents such negative organizational consequences as legal liability and loss of reputation.

        2)   The following are various definitions of privacy:

            a)   Personal privacy (physical and psychological)

            b)   Privacy of space (freedom from surveillance)

            c)   Privacy of communication (freedom from monitoring)

            d)   Privacy of information (collection, use, and disclosure of personal information by others)

        3)   Personal information is any information that can be associated with a specific individual or that might be combined with other information to do so. The following are examples:

            a)   Name, address, identification numbers, family relationships

            b)   Employee files, evaluations, comments, social status, or disciplinary actions

            c)   Credit records, income, financial status

            d)   Medical status

4) The board is ultimately accountable for identifying principal risks, implementing controls, and managing privacy risk, e.g., by establishing and monitoring a privacy framework.

5) The internal audit activity assesses the adequacy of (a) management's risk identification and (b) the controls that reduce those risks.

   a) Moreover, the internal audit activity evaluates the privacy framework, identifies significant risks, and makes recommendations. The internal audit activity also considers

      i) Laws, regulations, and practices in relevant jurisdictions;

      ii) The advice of legal counsel; and

      iii) The security efforts of IT specialists.

6) The internal audit activity's role depends on the level or maturity of the organization's privacy practices.

   a) Accordingly, the internal auditors may

      i) Facilitate the development and implementation of the privacy program,

      ii) Evaluate management's privacy risk assessment, or

      iii) Perform an assurance service regarding the effectiveness of the privacy framework.

   b) However, assumption of responsibility may impair independence.

7) The internal auditor identifies

   a) Personal information gathered,

   b) Collection methods, and

   c) Whether use of the information is in accordance with its intended use and applicable law.

8) Given the difficulty of the technical and legal issues, the internal audit activity needs the knowledge and competence to assess the risks and controls of the privacy framework.

c. The following summarizes the major provisions of Practice Advisory 2300-1, *Use of Personal Information in Conducting Engagements*:

1) Advances in IT and communications present privacy risks and threats. Thus, internal auditors need to consider the protection of personally identifiable information gathered during audits. Privacy controls are legal requirements in many jurisdictions.

2) Many jurisdictions require organizations to identify the purposes for which personal information is collected at or before collection. These laws also prohibit using and disclosing personal information for purposes other than those for which it was collected except with the individual's consent or as required by law.

3) Internal auditors must understand and comply with all laws regarding the use of personal information.

4) It may be inappropriate or illegal to access, retrieve, review, manipulate, or use personal information in conducting certain engagements. If the internal auditor accesses personal information, procedures may be necessary to safeguard this information. For example, the internal auditor may not record personal information in engagement records in some situations.

5) The internal auditor may seek advice from legal counsel before beginning audit work if questions arise about access to personal information.

    d.   Privacy engagements address the security of personal information, especially information stored in computer systems. An example is healthcare information in the files of insurers and providers.

        1)   The organization must comply with governmental statutory and regulatory mandates. Internal auditors consult the organization's legal counsel and then communicate the requirements to those responsible for designing and implementing the required safeguards.

            a)   Internal auditors determine that the requirements are incorporated into the information system and that compliance is achieved in its operation.

        2)   Personal information needs to be protected from both unauthorized intrusion and misuse by those who have authorized access.

        3)   Privacy is balanced with the need to allow appropriate and prompt availability of personal information to legitimate users.

        4)   The organization documents compliance with privacy and other legal requirements.

        5)   Benefits of the security arrangements should exceed the costs. For example, encryption techniques are an expensive way to address threats to the security of private information. Other methods, such as access controls, may be more appropriate relative to the assessed risk.

        NOTE: The IIA's Code of Ethics requires internal auditors to maintain the confidentiality of private information.

            a)   "Internal auditors shall be prudent in the use and protection of information acquired in the course of their duties" (Rule of Conduct 3.1).

            b)   "Internal auditors shall not use information for any personal gain or in any manner that would be contrary to the law or detrimental to the legitimate and ethical objectives of the organization" (Rule of Conduct 3.2).

Stop and review! You have completed the outline for this subunit. Study multiple-choice questions 16 through 18 on page 63.

2.7 PERFORMANCE AND OPERATIONAL AUDITING

1.   **Performance Auditing**

    a.   Internal auditors may conduct a performance audit to provide assurance about the organization's **key performance indicators**.

        1)   They also may conduct a consulting engagement to design such a performance measurement system.

    b.   Internal auditors assess an organization's ability to measure its performance, recognize deficiencies, and take corrective actions.

        1)   Effective management control requires performance measurement and feedback. This process affects allocation of resources to organizational subunits. It also affects decisions about managers' compensation, advancement, and future assignments.

        2)   Furthermore, evaluating their performance serves to motivate managers to optimize the measures in the performance evaluation model. However, that model may be inconsistent with the organization's model for managerial decision making.

            a)   To achieve consistency, the models should be synchronized. For example, if senior management wishes to maximize results over the long term, subordinates should be evaluated over the long term.

c.   The trend in performance measurement is the **balanced scorecard** approach. It is a report that connects critical success factors determined in a strategic analysis to financial and nonfinancial measures of the elements of performance vital to future success.

1)   A firm identifies its critical success factors by means of an analysis that addresses internal factors (<u>s</u>trengths and <u>w</u>eaknesses) and external factors (<u>o</u>pportunities and <u>t</u>hreats). This is called a **SWOT analysis**.

   a)   The firm's greatest strengths are its core competencies. These are the basis for its ability to compete successfully and its strategy.

   b)   **Strengths** and **weaknesses** are internal resources or a lack of resources. For example, strengths include technologically advanced products, a broad product mix, capable management, leadership in R&D, modern production facilities, and a strong marketing organization. Weaknesses result from the lack of such advantages.

   c)   **Opportunities** and **threats** arise from such factors external to the organization as government regulation, advances in technology, and demographic changes. They may be reflected in certain competitive conditions, including the following:

      i)   The number and strength of competitors in the firm's industry
      ii)   Changes in the intensity of rivalry within the industry, for example, because of excessive production capacity
      iii) The relative availability of substitutes for the firm's products or services
      iv)   Bargaining power of customers
      v)   Bargaining power of suppliers

   d)   The SWOT analysis helps the firm to determine its strategy by emphasizing the basic factors of cost, quality, and the speed of product development and delivery.

2)   Once the firm has identified its critical success factors, it must establish specific measures for each factor relevant to the success of the firm and reliably stated.

3)   Measures should be **nonfinancial** as well as financial, **long-term** as well as short-term, and **internal** as well as external. The balanced scorecard de-emphasizes short-term financial results and focuses attention on factors vital to future success.

4)   The development and implementation of a comprehensive balanced scorecard requires active participation by senior management.

   a)   The scorecard should contain detailed measures to permit everyone to understand how his or her efforts affect the firm's results.

   b)   The scorecard and the strategy it represents must be communicated to all managers and used as a basis for compensation decisions.

   c)   The scorecard should permit a determination of whether certain objectives are being achieved at the expense of others. For example, reduced spending on customer service may improve short-term financial results but cause a decline in customer satisfaction.

5) A typical balanced scorecard includes measures in four categories:

 a) **Financial.** These are measures of ultimate results provided to owners, e.g., sales, fair value of the firm's stock, profits, liquidity, and market share.

 b) **Customer.** These are measures of customer needs and satisfaction, e.g., customer retention rate, dealer and distributor relationships, marketing and selling performance, prompt delivery, and quality.

 c) **Internal.** These are measures of key processes that drive the business, e.g., quality, productivity (an input-output relationship), flexibility of response to changing conditions, operating readiness, and safety.

 d) **Learning, growth, and innovation.** These are measures of the basis for future success (people and infrastructure), e.g., development of new products, promptness of their introduction, human resource development, morale, and competence of the work force.

2. **Operational Audit Engagements**

 a. Internal auditors may conduct an operational audit to assess the efficiency and effectiveness of an organization's operations. The following are typical operational audit engagements:

 1) **Process (functional) engagements** are operational audit engagements that follow a process crossing organizational lines, service units, and geographical locations.

 a) The focus is on operations and how effectively and efficiently the organizational units affected will cooperate.

 b) These engagements tend to be challenging because of their scope and the need to deal with organizational units that may have conflicting objectives.

 c) Typical processes or functions are

 i) Purchasing and receiving
 ii) Distribution of services, materials, and supplies to users in the organization
 iii) Modification of products
 iv) Safety practices
 v) Scrap handling and disposal
 vi) Development of budgets
 vii) Marketing
 viii) Management of depreciable assets

 2) **Program-results engagements** are intended to obtain information about the costs, outputs, benefits, and effects of a program. They attempt to measure the accomplishment and relative success of the undertaking.

 a) Because benefits often cannot be quantified in financial terms, a special concern is the ability to measure effectiveness. Thus, clear definitions of objectives and standards should be provided at the outset of the program.

 b) A program is a funded activity not part of the normal, continuing operations of the organization, such as an expansion or a new information system.

Stop and review! You have completed the outline for this subunit. Study multiple-choice questions 19 through 21 on page 64.

2.8 COMPLIANCE AUDITING

 An internal audit activity can add value to its organization by performing many types of engagements. CIA candidates must know not only the requirements of these engagements but also when and where to perform each kind of engagement.

1. **Compliance**

    a. The IIA Glossary defines compliance as follows:

    Adherence to policies, plans, procedures, laws, regulations, contracts, or other requirements.

    b. Internal auditors assess compliance in specific areas as part of their role in organizational governance. They also conduct follow-up and report on management's response to regulatory body reviews. Given the scope of governmental regulation, these duties of internal auditors have great importance.

    Caution: Internal auditors are encouraged to consult legal counsel in all matters involving legal issues. Requirements may vary significantly in different jurisdictions.

    c. The internal audit activity's responsibilities with regard to compliance are addressed in two Implementation Standards.

    1) The internal audit activity must evaluate risk exposures relating to governance, operations, and information systems with regard to (a) compliance (Implementation Standard 2120.A1) and (b) the adequacy and effectiveness of controls responding to these risks (Implementation Standard 2130.A1).

2. **Programs**

    a. Compliance programs assist organizations in preventing unintended employee violations, detecting illegal acts, and discouraging intentional employee violations. They also help (1) prove insurance claims, (2) determine director and officer liability, (3) create or enhance corporate identity, and (4) decide the appropriateness of punitive damages.

    1) Internal auditors need to evaluate an organization's regulatory compliance programs.

    2) The CAE should meet with regulators to provide relevant information or receive advice on necessary compliance.

3. **Organizational Standards and Procedures**

    a. The organization establishes compliance standards and procedures to be followed by its employees and other agents who are reasonably capable of reducing the probability of criminal conduct. They include the following:

    1) A clearly written, straightforward, and fair business code of conduct that provides guidance to employees on relevant issues and is user-friendly

    2) An organizational chart identifying personnel responsible for compliance programs

    3) Financial incentives that do not reward misconduct

    4) For an international organization, a compliance program on a global basis that reflects local conditions and laws

4. **Responsibility**

    a.   Specific high-level personnel who are properly empowered and supplied with necessary resources should be responsible for the compliance program.

        1)   Senior management also should be involved.

        2)   High-level personnel should have substantial control of the organization or a substantial role in making policy.

        3)   Compliance personnel should have adequate access to senior management, and the chief compliance officer should report directly to the CEO.

5. **Applicant Screening**

    a.   Due care should be used to avoid delegating authority to those with a tendency to engage in illegal activities.

        1)   Applications should inquire about criminal convictions or discipline by licensing boards.

        2)   All applicants should be screened in a lawful manner that does not infringe upon privacy rights. The purpose is to detect evidence of past wrongdoing, especially that within the organization's industry.

6. **Communication**

    a.   Standards and procedures, including readily available ethics-related documents, should be communicated effectively, preferably in an interactive format and on multiple occasions.

        1)   Training programs and publications are typical methods. The best training allows employees to practice new techniques and use new information.

        2)   Compliance information should be conveyed through a variety of media. Moreover, it should be targeted to the areas important to each functional employee group and its job requirements.

            a)   For example, environmental compliance information should be directed to subunits, such as manufacturing, that are more likely to violate (or detect violations of) such laws and regulations.

        3)   New employees should receive basic compliance training as part of their orientation, and agents of the organization should be given a presentation specifically for them.

            a)   Agents should understand the organization's core values and that their actions will be monitored.

        4)   Organizations also should require employees to certify periodically that they have read, understood, and complied with the code of conduct. This information is relayed annually to senior management and the board.

7   **Monitoring and Reporting**

    a.   Monitoring and auditing systems for detecting illegal or unethical behavior and employee hotlines should be used. The best approach is to coordinate multiple monitoring and auditing systems.

        1)   For example, the internal audit plan should be given appropriate resources and applied to all of the organization's businesses. Also, it should include a review of the compliance program.

        2)   The compliance review considers (a) effectiveness of written materials, (b) employee receipt of communications, (c) handling of violations, (d) fairness of discipline, (e) observance of any protections given to informants, and (f) fulfillment of compliance unit responsibilities.

b.   Attorney-client and attorney work-product privileges protect certain information disclosed to (or produced by) an attorney from being used by an adverse party in a legal proceeding. An attorney monitoring the hotline is best able to protect the privileges.

1)   Employees may have little confidence in such hotlines or in write-in reports or an off-site person assigned to hear complaints. But they may have confidence in hotlines answered by an in-house representative and backed by a nonretaliation policy.

a)   However, a hotline cannot ensure anonymity.

c.   An on-site official may be assigned to receive and investigate complaints. This individual (an **ombudsperson**) is more effective if (s)he (1) reports directly to the chief compliance officer or the board, (2) keeps the names of informants secret, (3) provides guidance to informants, and (4) undertakes follow-up to ensure that retaliation has not occurred.

d.   An ethics questionnaire should be sent to each employee asking whether the employee is aware of kickbacks, bribes, or other wrongdoing.

e.   Organizational compliance standards should be consistently enforced by adequate, fair, case-specific discipline.

1)   Punishment should be appropriate to the offense, such as a warning, loss of pay, suspension, transfer, or termination.

2)   The program should provide for the discipline of managers and other responsible persons who knew or should have known of misconduct and did not report it. Failure to do so indicates a lack of due diligence.

a)   As a result, a court may rule that (1) the program is not effective and (2) the organization is therefore legally liable for giving authority to persons with a tendency to commit crimes.

f.   Termination or other discipline of employees may be limited by (1) whistleblower laws; (2) statutory exceptions to the employee-at-will doctrine (the right of an employer to fire an employee for any reason); (3) employee or union contracts; and (4) employer responsibilities with regard to discrimination, wrongful discharge, and requirements to act in good faith.

g.   Employee discipline should be thoroughly documented so that the organization will be able to prove that it made its best effort to collect information and took appropriate action.

h.   After detection, the response should be appropriate and designed to prevent other similar offenses.

1)   In some circumstances, an appropriate response may require self-reporting of violations to the government, cooperation with investigations, and the acceptance of responsibility.

a)   An effective compliance program and appropriate responses may result in more lenient punishment for committing the offense.

i.   Failure to detect or prevent a serious violation may indicate that the compliance program needs to be restructured. One change that may be required is the replacement or transfer of compliance personnel.

Stop and review! You have completed the outline for this subunit. Study multiple-choice questions 22 through 25 beginning on page 64.

QUESTIONS

2.1 Assurance Engagements

1. The chief executive officer wants to know whether the purchasing function is properly meeting its charge to "purchase the right materials at the right time in the right quantities." Which of the following types of engagements addresses this request?

- A. A financial engagement relating to the purchasing department.
- B. An operational engagement relating to the purchasing function.
- C. A compliance engagement relating to the purchasing function.
- D. A full-scope engagement relating to the manufacturing operation.

Answer (B) is correct.

REQUIRED: The type of engagement that determines whether the purchasing function is effective and efficient.

DISCUSSION: According to *Sawyer's Internal Auditing*, an operational engagement involves "the review of a function or process to appraise the efficiency and economy of operations and the effectiveness with which those functions achieve their objectives."

Answer (A) is incorrect. A financial engagement involves the analysis of the economic activity of an entity as measured and reported by accounting methods. Answer (C) is incorrect. A compliance engagement is a review of both financial and operating controls to assess conformance with established standards. It tests adherence to management's policies, procedures, and plans designed to ensure certain actions. Answer (D) is incorrect. A full-scale engagement relating to the manufacturing operation has financial, compliance, and operational aspects. It exceeds the chief executive officer's request.

2. The primary difference between operational engagements and financial engagements is that, in the former, the internal auditors

- A. Are not concerned with whether the client entity is generating information in compliance with financial accounting standards.
- B. Are seeking to help management use resources in the most effective manner possible.
- C. Start with the financial statements of the client entity and work backward to the basic processes involved in producing them.
- D. Can use analytical skills and tools that are not necessary in financial engagements.

Answer (B) is correct.

REQUIRED: The main distinction between operational and financial engagements.

DISCUSSION: Financial engagements are primarily concerned with forming an opinion on the fairness of the financial statements. Operational engagements evaluate accomplishment of established objectives and goals for operations or programs and economical and efficient use of resources.

Answer (A) is incorrect. The reliability and integrity of financial information are important in operational engagements. Information systems provide data for decision making, control, and compliance with external requirements. Answer (C) is incorrect. A financial engagement entails using financial statements as a starting point. Answer (D) is incorrect. Analytical skills are necessary in all types of engagements.

3. During an operational engagement, the internal auditors compare the current staffing of a department with established industry standards to

- A. Identify bogus employees on the department's payroll.
- B. Assess the current performance of the department and make appropriate recommendations for improvement.
- C. Evaluate the adequacy of the established internal controls for the department.
- D. Determine whether the department has complied with all laws and regulations governing its personnel.

Answer (B) is correct.

REQUIRED: The purpose of comparing the current staffing of a department with established industry standards.

DISCUSSION: According to *Sawyer's Internal Auditing*, an operational engagement involves "the review of a function or process to appraise the efficiency and economy of operations and the effectiveness with which those functions achieve their objectives."

Answer (A) is incorrect. The internal auditors would not be concerned with payroll processing during this type of testing and evaluation. Answer (C) is incorrect. Comparison of staffing levels with industry standards will not test the adequacy of internal controls. Answer (D) is incorrect. The internal auditors would be more concerned with legal requirements during a compliance engagement.

2.2 Risk and Control Self-Assessment

4. Which group is charged with overseeing the establishment, administration, and evaluation of the processes of risk management and control?

- A. Operating managers.
- B. Internal auditors.
- C. External auditors.
- D. Senior management.

Answer (D) is correct.
REQUIRED: The group charged with overseeing the establishment, administration, and evaluation of the processes of risk management and control.
DISCUSSION: Senior management is charged with overseeing the establishment, administration, and evaluation of the processes of risk management and control. Operating managers' responsibilities include assessment of the risks and controls in their units. Internal and external auditors provide varying degrees of assurance about the state of effectiveness of the risk management and control processes of the organization.

5. Which of the following statements about control self-assessment (CSA) is **false**?

- A. CSA is usually an informal and undocumented process.
- B. In its purest form, CSA integrates business objectives and risks with control processes.
- C. CSA is also known as control/risk self-assessment.
- D. Most implemented CSA programs share some key features and goals.

Answer (A) is correct.
REQUIRED: The false statement regarding CSA.
DISCUSSION: A methodology encompassing self-assessment surveys and facilitated workshops called CSA is a useful and efficient approach for managers and internal auditors to collaborate in assessing and evaluating control procedures. The process is a formal and documented way of allowing participation by those who are directly involved in the business unit, function, or process.

6. Which forms of control self-assessment assume that managers and members of work teams possess an understanding of risk and control concepts and use those concepts in communications?

- A. The self-certification approach.
- B. The self-certification approach and facilitated approach.
- C. The self-certification approach and questionnaire approach.
- D. All self-assessment programs.

Answer (D) is correct.
REQUIRED: The forms of CSA based on the assumption that managers and members of work teams possess an understanding of risk and control concepts and use them in communications.
DISCUSSION: All self-assessment programs assume that managers and members of the work teams possess an understanding of risk and control concepts and using those concepts in communications. For training sessions, to facilitate the orderly flow of workshop discussions and as a check on the completeness of the overall process, organizations often use a control framework, such as the COSO (Committee of Sponsoring Organizations) and CoCo (Canadian Criteria of Control Board) models.

2.3 Audits of Third Parties and Contract Auditing

7. In reviewing a cost-plus construction contract for a new catalog showroom, the internal auditor should be cognizant of the risk that

- A. The contractor could be charging for the use of equipment not used in the construction.
- B. Income taxes related to construction equipment depreciation may have been calculated erroneously.
- C. Contractor cash budgets could have been inappropriately compiled.
- D. Payroll taxes may have been inappropriately omitted from billings.

Answer (A) is correct.
REQUIRED: The risk inherent in a cost-plus construction contract.
DISCUSSION: Under a cost-plus contract, the contractor receives a sum equal to cost plus a fixed amount or a percentage of cost. The disadvantages of this arrangement are that the contractor's incentive for controlling costs is reduced and the opportunity to overstate costs is created. Consequently, internal auditors should be involved in monitoring economy and efficiency not only during the earliest phases of construction but also from the outset of the planning process.
Answer (B) is incorrect. Income tax provisions related to depreciation charges are not a risk; only those charges incurred under the terms of the contract constitute a risk. Answer (C) is incorrect. Budgets inappropriately prepared do not affect contract costs and therefore do not constitute a risk. Answer (D) is incorrect. The omission of taxes does not involve a risk of contract overcharges or inadequacies in construction. Possible delays in payment or underpayments from the omission are of less concern.

8. A company would like to contract for janitorial services for 1 year with 4 option years. The specifications require the potential contractor to perform certain cleaning services at specified intervals. Which of the following is the best contract type for this requirement?

    A. Cost-reimbursable.

    B. Indefinite delivery.

    C. Fixed-price.

    D. Time-and-materials.

Answer (C) is correct.

    REQUIRED: The appropriate type of contract for specific services at specified intervals.

    DISCUSSION: Fixed-price contracts are used when the requirements are well-defined, uncertainties can be identified and costs estimated, and there is adequate competition.

    Answer (A) is incorrect. Cost-reimbursable contracts are used when the requirements are complex and costs cannot be easily identified and estimated. Answer (B) is incorrect. Indefinite delivery contracts are used only when the supplies and/or service of future deliveries are not known at the time of contract award. Answer (D) is incorrect. Time-and-materials contracts are used when it is not possible at the time of placing the contract to estimate accurately the duration of the work.

9. An internal auditor is conducting an audit of environmental protection and alarm devices. Which is the most significant objective of such an assignment? To determine whether

    A. The devices are installed and operating properly.

    B. The costs of the devices were properly recorded.

    C. The device specification documents are complete.

    D. Acquisitions and disposals are properly authorized.

Answer (A) is correct.

    REQUIRED: The most significant audit objective in an audit of environmental protection and alarm devices.

    DISCUSSION: The objective should be to determine whether the devices are working properly. For this purpose, the internal auditor must observe an actual test of the operation.

    Answer (B) is incorrect. Recordkeeping is not as important as the effectiveness of such devices. Answer (C) is incorrect. Specification documents become important only when repairs are needed. Answer (D) is incorrect. Authorization is less important than effectiveness.

10. Which of the following does the internal auditor **not** have to review as thoroughly in a lump-sum contract?

    A. Progressive payments.

    B. Adjustments to labor costs.

    C. Work completed in accordance with the contract.

    D. Incentives associated with the contract.

Answer (C) is correct.

    REQUIRED: The item the internal auditor need not review thoroughly in a lump-sum contract.

    DISCUSSION: The internal auditor usually has little to evaluate when the work is performed in accordance with the contract. Further, the internal auditor may look the technical expertise to know if the contract is being completed according to the terms.

    Answer (A) is incorrect. The internal auditor should ensure that the contractor is receiving payment to meet expenses and complete the contract. Answer (B) is incorrect. Adjustments to labor cost may change the profitability of the contract and are of great importance to the internal auditor. Answer (D) is incorrect. Incentives such as a bonus for early completion affect the overall profitability of the contract and are frequently reviewed by the internal auditor.

2.4 Quality Auditing

11. Total quality management in a manufacturing environment is best exemplified by

    A. Identifying and reworking production defects before sale.

    B. Designing the product to minimize defects.

    C. Performing inspections to isolate defects as early as possible.

    D. Making machine adjustments periodically to reduce defects.

Answer (B) is correct.

    REQUIRED: The activity characteristic of TQM.

    DISCUSSION: Total quality management emphasizes quality as a basic organizational function. TQM is the continuous pursuit of quality in every aspect of organizational activities. One of the basic tenets of TQM is doing it right the first time. Thus, errors should be caught and corrected at the source, and quality should be built in (designed in) from the start.

12. Which of the following statements about TQM is **false**?

A. This approach can increase revenues and decrease costs significantly.

B. TQM is a comprehensive approach to quality.

C. TQM begins with internal suppliers' requirements.

D. TQM concepts are applicable to the operations of the internal audit activity itself.

Answer (C) is correct.

REQUIRED: The false statement about TQM.

DISCUSSION: The emergence of the total quality management (TQM) concept is one of the most significant developments in recent years because this approach can increase revenues and decrease costs significantly. TQM is a comprehensive approach to quality. It treats the pursuit of quality as a basic organizational function that is as important as production or marketing. TQM emphasizes the supplier's relationship with the customer. Thus, TQM begins with external customer requirements, identifies internal customer-supplier relationships and requirements, and establishes requirements for external suppliers. TQM concepts also are applicable to the operations of the internal audit activity itself. For example, periodic internal assessments of those operations may "include benchmarking of the internal audit activity's practices and performance metrics against relevant best practices of the internal audit profession" (PA 1311-1).

13. TQM is the continuous pursuit of quality in every aspect of organizational activities through a number of goals. Which of the following is **not** one of those goals?

A. A philosophy of doing it right the first time.

B. Promotion of individual work.

C. Employee training and empowerment.

D. Improvement of processes.

Answer (B) is correct.

REQUIRED: The answer choice that is not included in the definition of TQM.

DISCUSSION: TQM is the continuous pursuit of quality in every aspect of organizational activities through (1) a philosophy of doing it right the first time, (2) employee training and empowerment, (3) promotion of teamwork, (4) improvement of processes, and (5) attention to satisfaction of customers, both internal and external.

2.5 Due Diligence Auditing

14. An internal audit team is performing a due diligence audit to assess plans for a potential merger/acquisition. Which of the following would be the **least** valid reason for a company to merge with or acquire another company?

A. To diversify risk.

B. To respond to government policy.

C. To reduce labor costs.

D. To increase stock prices.

Answer (D) is correct.

REQUIRED: The least valid reason for a merger or acquisition.

DISCUSSION: A due diligence engagement is a service to determine the business justification for a major transaction, such as a business combination, and whether that justification is valid. Thus, the internal auditors and others may be part of a team that reviews the acquiree's operations, controls, financing, or disclosures of financial information. Increasing stock prices is not often a valid reason for a merger or acquisition. A business combination should be undertaken because it offers long-term fundamental competitive advantages. Increasing stock prices is an effect that can be achieved through other methods that directly improve the organization's performance.

Answer (A) is incorrect. The usual justifications for a combination include risk management through diversifying the businesses in which the organization is engaged. Answer (B) is incorrect. A change in governmental policy, for example, relaxation of antitrust laws, is also a valid reason for a business combination. A larger organization may be able to achieve greater economies of scale and competitive advantage. Answer (C) is incorrect. A business combination may result in cost synergies, for example, by eliminating duplicative functions.

15. An organization is considering purchasing a small toxic waste disposal business. The internal auditors are part of the team doing a due diligence review for the acquisition. The scope of the internal auditors' work will most likely **not** include

  A. An evaluation of the merit of lawsuits currently filed against the acquiree.

  B. A review of the acquiree's procedures for acceptance of waste material and comparison with legal requirements.

  C. Analysis of the acquiree's compliance with, and disclosure of, loan covenants.

  D. Assessment of the efficiency of the operations of the acquiree.

Answer (A) is correct.

    REQUIRED: The procedure not included in a due diligence review for an acquisition.

    DISCUSSION: An evaluation of the merit of lawsuits requires legal expertise.

2.6 Security and Privacy Audits

16. The reliability and integrity of all critical information of an organization, regardless of the media in which the information is stored, is the responsibility of

  A. Shareholders.

  B. IT department.

  C. Management.

  D. All employees.

Answer (C) is correct.

    REQUIRED: The responsibility for information reliability and integrity.

    DISCUSSION: Internal auditors determine whether senior management and the board have a clear understanding that information reliability and integrity is a management responsibility (PA 2130.A1-1, para. 1). Information reliability and integrity includes accuracy, completeness, and security.

17. Freedom from monitoring best defines

  A. Personal privacy.

  B. Privacy of space.

  C. Privacy of communication.

  D. Privacy of information.

Answer (C) is correct.

    REQUIRED: The type of privacy best defined as freedom monitoring.

    DISCUSSION: Privacy may encompass (1) personal privacy (physical and psychological), (2) privacy of space (freedom from surveillance), (3) privacy of communication (freedom from monitoring), and (4) privacy of information (collection, use, and disclosure of personal information by others) (PA 2130.A1-2, para. 2).

18. When evaluating management of the organization's privacy framework, the internal auditor considers

  A. The applicable laws relating to privacy.

  B. Conferring with in-house legal counsel.

  C. Conferring with information technology specialists.

  D. All of the answers are correct.

Answer (D) is correct.

    REQUIRED: The matters considered when evaluating management of the privacy framework.

    DISCUSSION: In an evaluation of the privacy framework, the internal auditor considers the following:

- The various laws, regulations, and policies relating to privacy in the jurisdictions where the organization operates.
- Conferring with in-house legal counsel to determine the exact nature of laws, regulations, and other standards and practices applicable to the organization and the countries where it operates.
- Conferring with information technology specialists to determine that information security and data protection controls are in place and regularly reviewed and assessed for appropriateness.
- The level or maturity of privacy practices (PA 2130.A1-2, para. 7).

2.7 Performance and Operational Auditing

19. Using the balanced scorecard approach, an organization evaluates managerial performance based on

- A. A single ultimate measure of operating results, such as residual income.
- B. Multiple financial and nonfinancial measures.
- C. Multiple nonfinancial measures only.
- D. Multiple financial measures only.

Answer (B) is correct.
REQUIRED: The nature of the balanced scorecard approach.
DISCUSSION: The trend in managerial performance evaluation is the balanced scorecard approach. Multiple measures of performance permit a determination as to whether a manager is achieving certain objectives at the expense of others that may be equally or more important. These measures may be financial or nonfinancial and usually include items in four categories: (1) financial; (2) customer; (3) internal business processes; and (4) learning, growth, and innovation.

20. Which type of engagement focuses on operations and how effectively and efficiently the organizational units affected will cooperate?

- A. Program-results engagement.
- B. Process engagement.
- C. Privacy engagement.
- D. Compliance engagement.

Answer (B) is correct.
REQUIRED: The engagement that focuses cooperation of operating subunits.
DISCUSSION: Process engagements tend to be challenging because of their scope and the need to deal with subunits that may have conflicting objectives.
Answer (A) is incorrect. A program-results engagement obtains information about the costs, outputs, benefits, and effects of a program. Answer (C) is incorrect. Privacy engagements address the security of personal information. Answer (D) is incorrect. Compliance engagements address compliance with all laws and regulations.

21. Which type of engagement attempts to measure the accomplishment and relative success of the undertaking?

- A. Program-results engagement.
- B. Privacy engagement.
- C. Process engagement.
- D. Compliance engagement.

Answer (A) is correct.
REQUIRED: The engagement to measure the accomplishment and relative success of the undertaking.
DISCUSSION: A program-results engagement obtains information about the costs, outputs, benefits, and effects of a program. It attempts to measure the accomplishment and relative success of the undertaking. Because benefits often cannot be quantified in financial terms, a special concern is the ability to measure effectiveness. A program is a funded activity not part of the normal, continuing operations of the organization.
Answer (B) is incorrect. A privacy engagement addresses the security of personal information. Answer (C) is incorrect. A process engagement addresses how effectively and efficiently operating units cooperate. Answer (D) is incorrect. A compliance engagement addresses compliance with related laws and regulations.

2.8 Compliance Auditing

22. Discipline of employees may be limited by all of the following **except**

- A. Whistleblower laws.
- B. A requirement to report certain employee violations to a governmental entity.
- C. Union contracts.
- D. Exceptions to the employee-at-will doctrine.

Answer (B) is correct.
REQUIRED: The item that does not limit the termination or other discipline of employees.
DISCUSSION: Termination or other discipline of employees may be limited by (1) whistleblower laws; (2) exceptions to the employee-at-will doctrine (the right of an employer to fire an employee for any reason); (3) employee or union contracts; and (4) employer responsibilities with regard to discrimination, wrongful discharge, and requirements to act in good faith. However, a governmental requirement that an entity report certain employee violations is not itself a limitation on the employer's power to discipline employees.

23. Compliance programs most directly assist organizations by doing which of the following?

1. Developing a plan for business continuity management.
2. Determining director and officer liability.
3. Planning for disaster recovery.

    A. 1 only.

    B. 2 only.

    C. 1 and 2 only.

    D. 1, 2, and 3.

Answer (B) is correct.

    REQUIRED: The way(s) in which compliance programs help organizations.

    DISCUSSION: Compliance is "adherence to policies, plans, procedures, laws, regulations, contracts, or other requirements" (The IIA Glossary). Such programs assist organizations in preventing inadvertent employee violations, detecting illegal activities, and discouraging intentional employee violations. They also can help (1) prove insurance claims, (2) determine director and officer liability, (3) create or enhance corporate identity, and (4) decide the appropriateness of punitive damages. However, developing a plan for business continuity management and planning for disaster recovery are operational activities not performed during a compliance program.

    Answer (A) is incorrect. Developing a plan for business continuity management is an operational activity, not part of a compliance program. E-commerce activities, not compliance programs, assist an organization. Answer (C) is incorrect. Determining director and officer liability is the only activity listed that is performed as part of a compliance program. Answer (D) is incorrect. Developing a plan for business continuity management and planning for disaster recovery are operational activities, not parts of a compliance program.

24. An organization establishes compliance standards and procedures and develops a written business code of conduct to be followed by its employees. Which of the following is true concerning business codes of conduct and the compliance standards?

    A. Compliance standards should be straightforward and reasonably capable of reducing the prospect of criminal conduct.

    B. The compliance standards should be codified in the charter of the audit committee.

    C. Companies with international operations should institute various compliance programs, based on selective geographic locations, that reflect appropriate local regulations.

    D. In order to prevent future legal liability, the code should consist of legal terms and definitions.

Answer (A) is correct.

    REQUIRED: The true statement regarding the code of conduct and compliance standards.

    DISCUSSION: The code of conduct should clearly identify prohibited activities, making compliance standards reasonably capable of reducing the prospect of criminal conduct (i.e., discouraging intentional employee violations). In addition, codes that are straightforward and fair tend to decrease the risk that employees will engage in unethical or illegal behavior.

    Answer (B) is incorrect. Among the items that must be included in the audit committee's charter is reviewing the process for communicating the code of conduct to company personnel and for monitoring compliance therewith; actually codifying the compliance standards is inappropriate. Answer (C) is incorrect. Companies with international operations should institute a compliance program on a global basis, not just for selective geographic locations. Such programs should reflect appropriate local conditions, laws, and regulations. Answer (D) is incorrect. The code should be written in a language that all employees can understand, avoiding legalese.

25. Employees have the most confidence in a hotline monitored by which of the following?

    A. An expert from the legal department, backed by a nonretaliation policy.

    B. An in-house representative, backed by a retaliation policy.

    C. An on-site ombudsperson, backed by a nonretaliation policy.

    D. An off-site attorney who can better protect attorney-client privilege.

Answer (C) is correct.

    REQUIRED: The hotline monitor that employees have the most confidence in.

    DISCUSSION: Although an attorney monitoring the hotline is better able to protect attorney-client and work-product privileges, one study observed that employees have little confidence in hotlines answered by the legal department or by an outside service. The same study showed that employees have even less confidence in write-in reports or an off-site ombudsperson, but have the most confidence in hotlines answered by an in-house representative (or an on-site ombudsperson) and backed by a nonretaliation policy.

    Answer (A) is incorrect. Employees have little confidence in hotlines answered by the legal department. Answer (B) is incorrect. A retaliation policy would dissuade whistleblowers from coming forth due to concern over possible backlash. Answer (D) is incorrect. Employees have little confidence in hotlines monitored by the legal department or by an external service provider. Thus, they would have even less confidence in an outside attorney.

> " I found in Gleim books a valuable support for preparing for the CIA exams: they are written in a very clear way, the method suggested for studying the content is very effective, and the information is organized in a rational way....Gleim material is an authoritative source for passing CIA exams at the first attempt and, even more important, is a reference for a "real life" auditor. "
>
> Alessandro Segalini, CISA, CIA, IIA 2014 Gold Medal Winner

> " I passed all CIA Exams on the first attempt within 6 months and I was pleasantly surprised to be notified by the IIA that I was the winner of the Kurt Riedener Bronze Medal Award...The Gleim CIA Review System enabled me to acquire the essential knowledge in a short time frame in a highly efficient and effective manner. "
>
> Drs. Mark de Jong, CIA, IIA 2014 Bronze Medal Winner

> " The Gleim CIA Review played an integral role in my passing of the CIA Exam part on the first try and earning the Silver Medalist Award... Gleim's study materials thoroughly covered each topic for every part of the exam, and reinforced those concepts with relevant multiple choice questions at the end of every study unit. Ironically, I also utilized Gleim materials 25 years ago when I passed all parts of the CPA Exam on the first try! Gleim materials have an excellent track record and are where I turn to for success in certifications. "
>
> Douglas S. Schmidt, CIA, CPA, IIA

> " I recently passed the CIA exam utilizing the Gleim Review System. I attribute my success to Gleim! I felt that the system provided me with a structured study plan and guidance throughout the process. My personal counselor was very knowledgeable and responsive. I would definitely recommend the Gleim system to anyone preparing for the CIA. "
>
> Ashley McWilliams, CIA

What our customers are saying

STUDY UNIT THREE
FINANCIAL, ENVIRONMENTAL,
AND CONSULTING ENGAGEMENTS

(24 pages of outline)

This study unit is the third of four covering **Section I: Managing the Internal Audit Function** from The IIA's CIA Exam Syllabus. This section makes up 40% to 50% of Part 2 of the CIA exam and is tested at the **proficiency level**. The relevant portion of the syllabus is highlighted below. (The complete syllabus is in Appendix B.)

I. MANAGING THE INTERNAL AUDIT FUNCTION (40%–50%)

A. **Strategic Role of Internal Audit**

B. **Operational Role of IA**

C. **Establish Risk-Based IA Plan**

1. Use market, product, and industry knowledge to identify new internal audit engagement opportunities
2. Use a risk framework to identify sources of potential engagements (e.g., audit universe, audit cycle requirements, management requests, regulatory mandates)
3. Establish a framework for assessing risk
4. Rank and validate risk priorities to prioritize engagements in the audit plan
5. Identify internal audit resource requirements for annual IA plan
6. Communicate areas of significant risk and obtain approval from the board for the annual engagement plan
7. Types of engagements
   a. Conduct assurance engagements
      - a.1 Risk and control self-assessments
      - a.2 Audits of third parties and contract auditing
      - a.3 Quality audit engagements
      - a.4 Due diligence audit engagements
      - a.5 Security audit engagements
      - a.6 Privacy audit engagements
      - a.7 Performance audit engagements (key performance indicators)
      - a.8 Operational audit engagements (efficiency and effectiveness)
      - a.9 Financial audit engagements
   b. Compliance audit engagements
   c. Consulting engagements
      - c.1 Internal control training
      - c.2 Business process mapping
      - c.3 Benchmarking
      - c.4 System development reviews
      - c.5 Design of performance measurement systems

3.1 ENVIRONMENTAL AUDITING

1. **Environmental Risks**

   a. The CAE includes **environmental, health, and safety (EHS)** risks in any organization-wide risk management assessment. These activities are assessed in a balanced manner relative to other types of risk associated with an organization's operations. Among the risk exposures to be evaluated are the following:

      1) Organizational reporting structures
      2) Likelihood of causing environmental harm, fines, and penalties
      3) Expenditures mandated by governmental agencies
      4) History of injuries and deaths
      5) History of losing customers
      6) Episodes of negative publicity and loss of public image and reputation

2. **Environmental Audit Function**

   a. If the CAE finds that the management of these risks largely depends on an environmental audit function, the CAE needs to consider the implications of that structure and its effects on operations and reporting.

      1) If the CAE finds that the exposures are not adequately managed and residual risks exist, changes in the internal audit activity's plan of engagements and further investigations are normal results.

      2) The typical environmental audit function reports to the organization's environmental component or general counsel. The common models for environmental auditing are the following:

         a) The CAE and environmental audit executive are in separate functional units and have little contact.

         b) The CAE and environmental audit executive are in separate functional units and coordinate their activities.

         c) The CAE has responsibility for auditing environmental issues.

3. **Research Findings**

   a. A research study of EHS auditing found the following risk and independence issues:

      1) The EHS audit function is isolated from other auditing activities. It is (a) organized separately from internal auditing, (b) only tangentially related to external audits of financial statements, and (c) reports to an EHS executive, not to the board or senior management.

         a) This structure suggests that management believes EHS auditing to be a technical field that is best placed within the EHS function. In this position, auditors could be unable to maintain their independence.

      2) EHS audit managers usually report administratively to the executives who are responsible for the physical facilities being audited. Because poor EHS performance reflects badly on the facilities management team, these executives have an incentive to influence (a) audit findings, (b) how audits are conducted, or (c) what is included in the audit plan.

         a) This potential subordination of the auditors' professional judgment, even when only apparent, violates auditor independence and objectivity.

      3) It is also common for written audit reports to be distributed no higher in the organization than to senior environmental executives.

         a) Those executives may have a potential conflict of interest, and they may prevent or limit further distribution of EHS audit results to senior management and the board.

        4)   Audit information is often classified as either (a) subject to the attorney-client privilege or attorney work-product doctrine (if available in the relevant jurisdiction); (b) secret and confidential; or (c) if not confidential, then closely held.

           a)   The effect is severely restricted access to EHS audit information.

4. **Role of the CAE**

    a.   The CAE fosters a close working relationship with the chief environmental officer and coordinates activities with the plan for environmental auditing.

        1)   When the environmental audit function reports to someone other than the CAE, the CAE offers to review the audit plan and the performance of engagements.

        2)   Periodically, the CAE schedules a quality assurance review of the environmental audit function if it is organizationally independent of the internal audit activity. That review determines whether environmental risks are being adequately addressed.

        3)   An EHS audit program may be

           a)   **Compliance-focused** (verifying compliance with laws, regulations, and the organization's own EHS policies, procedures, and performance objectives),

           b)   **Management systems-focused** (providing assessments of management systems intended to ensure compliance with legal and internal requirements and the mitigation of risks), or

           c)   A **combination** of both approaches.

    b.   The CAE evaluates whether the environmental auditors, who are not part of the CAE's organization, are conforming with recognized professional auditing standards and a recognized code of ethics.

    c.   The CAE evaluates the organizational placement and independence of the environmental audit function to ensure that significant matters resulting from serious risks to the organization are reported up the chain of command to the board.

        1)   The CAE also facilitates the reporting of significant EHS risk and control issues to the board.

    NOTE: The internal audit activity has an established place in the organization and normally has a broad scope of work permitting ready assimilation of the new function. Thus, it is an advantage to conduct environmental audits under the direction of the internal audit activity because of its position within the organization.

5. **Environmental Auditing**

    a.   An organization subject to environmental laws and regulations having a significant effect on its operations should establish an environmental management system.

        1)   One feature of this system is environmental auditing, which includes reviewing the adequacy and effectiveness of the controls over hazardous waste. It also extends to review of the reasonableness of contingent liabilities accrued for environmental remediation.

    b.   According to a research report prepared for The IIA Research Foundation,

        An environmental management system is an organization's structure of responsibilities and policies, practices, procedures, processes, and resources for protecting the environment and managing environmental issues. Environmental auditing is an integral part of an environmental management system whereby management determines whether the organization's environmental control systems are adequate to ensure compliance with regulatory requirements and internal policies.

c.   The report describes seven types of environmental audits:

1)   **Compliance audits** are the most common form for industrial organizations. Their extent depends on the degree of risk of noncompliance.

    a)   They are detailed, site-specific audits of current operations, past practices, and planned future operations.

    b)   They usually involve a review of all environmental media the site may contaminate, including air, water, land, and wastewater. Moreover, they have quantitative and qualitative aspects and should be repeated periodically.

    c)   Compliance audits range from preliminary assessments to (1) performance of detailed tests, (2) installation of groundwater monitoring wells, and (3) laboratory analyses.

2)   Environmental issues may arise from practices that were legal when they were undertaken. **Environmental management systems audits** determine whether systems are in place and operating properly to manage future environmental risks.

3)   **Transactional audits** assess the environmental risks and liabilities of land or facilities prior to a property sale or purchase. Current landowners may be responsible for contamination whether or not they caused it.

    a)   Transactional audits require due diligence (a reasonable level of research) from the auditor. What constitutes due diligence for each phase of a transactional audit and the definitions of the phases are questions for debate. These phases are often characterized as follows:

        i)   Phase I – qualitative site assessments involving a review of records and site reconnaissance

        ii)   Phase II – sampling for potential contamination

        iii)   Phase III – confirming the rate and extent of contaminant migration and the cost of remediation

    b)   A transactional audit addresses all media exposures and all hazardous substances, e.g., radon, asbestos, PCBs, operating materials, and wastes.

4)   **Treatment, storage, and disposal facility (TSDF) audits.** The law may require that hazardous materials be tracked from their acquisition or creation to disposal by means of a document (a manifest). All owners in the chain of title may be liable.

    a)   For example, if an organization contracts with a transporter to dispose of hazardous waste in a licensed landfill and the landfill owner contaminates the environment, all the organizations and their officers may be financially liable for cleanup.

    b)   TSDF audits are conducted on facilities the organization owns, leases, or manages, or on externally owned facilities where the organization's waste is treated, stored, or disposed. Thus, when an outside vendor is used for these purposes, the audit should consist of such procedures as

        i)   Reviewing the vendor's documentation on hazardous material,

        ii)   Reviewing the financial solvency of the vendors,

        iii)   Reviewing the vendor's emergency response planning,

        iv)   Determining that the vendor is approved by the governmental organization that is responsible for environmental protection,

        v)   Obtaining the vendor's permit number, and

        vi)   Inspecting the vendor's facilities.

5) A **pollution prevention audit** determines how waste can be minimized and pollution can be eliminated at the source. The following is a pollution prevention hierarchy from most desirable (recovery) to least (release without treatment):

   a) Recovery as a usable product
   b) Elimination at the source
   c) Recycling and reuse
   d) Energy conservation
   e) Treatment
   f) Disposal
   g) Release without treatment

6) **Environmental liability accrual audits.** Recognizing, quantifying, and reporting liability accruals may require redefinition of what is probable, measurable, and estimable. When an environmental issue becomes a liability is also unclear.

   a) The internal auditors may be responsible for assessing the reasonableness of cost estimates for environmental remediation. Due diligence may require assistance from independent experts, such as engineers.

7) **Product audits** determine whether products are environmentally friendly and whether product and chemical restrictions are being met. This process may result in the development of

   a) Fully recyclable products,
   b) Changes in the use and recovery of packaging materials, and
   c) The phaseout of some chemicals.

Stop and review! You have completed the outline for this subunit. Study multiple-choice questions 1 through 7 beginning on page 91.

3.2 FINANCIAL ENGAGEMENTS

1. **Financial Statements and Corporate Governance**

   a. Internal auditors provide assurance regarding financial reporting to management and the board. For example, in many countries, laws require that management certify that the general-purpose financial statements are fairly stated in all material respects.

Implementation Standard 2120.A1

The internal audit activity must evaluate risk exposures relating to the organization's governance, operations, and information systems regarding the:

- Achievement of the organization's strategic objectives;
- Reliability and integrity of financial and operational information;
- Effectiveness and efficiency of operations and programs;
- Safeguarding of assets; and
- Compliance with laws, regulations, policies, procedures, and contracts.

---

2. **Management's Assertions**

   a. Management implicitly or explicitly makes assertions about the measurement, presentation, and disclosure of information in financial statements.

      1) Part of any engagement may involve testing these assertions to determine whether they are supported by the evidence.

      2) Determining whether these assertions are supported by the evidence also can help the auditor to determine whether controls are working as designed.

    b.   The following are assertions generally made by management:

        1)   All transactions and events that should have been recorded were recorded.

        2)   Amounts and other data were recorded appropriately.

        3)   Assets, liabilities, and other interests are reported at appropriate amounts, and any valuation or allocation adjustments are appropriately recorded.

        4)   Assets, liabilities, and equity interests actually exist.

        5)   Transactions and events were recorded in the proper period.

        6)   The entity holds or controls the rights to assets, and liabilities are its obligations.

        7)   Recorded events and transactions actually occurred.

        8)   Transactions and events were recorded in the proper accounts and are presented and described clearly.

3.   **Assessment of Internal Control**

    a.   Many countries also require management to provide an assessment of the organization's internal control over financial reporting. Internal auditors assist management in meeting these responsibilities.

Performance Standard 2130
Control

The internal audit activity must assist the organization in maintaining effective controls by evaluating their effectiveness and efficiency and by promoting continuous improvement.

---

    b.   Guidance on assessing control is provided by Practice Advisory 2130-1, *Assessing the Adequacy of Control Processes*:

        1)   The purpose of control is to support risk management and achievement of objectives.

            a)   Control processes should meet the requirements of Implementation Standard 2130.A1 (below).

Implementation Standard 2130.A1

The internal audit activity must evaluate the adequacy and effectiveness of controls in responding to risks within the organization's governance, operations, and information systems regarding the:

- Achievement of the organization's strategic objectives;
- Reliability and integrity of financial and operational information;
- Effectiveness and efficiency of operations and programs;
- Safeguarding of assets; and
- Compliance with laws, regulations, policies, procedures, and contracts.

---

        2)   Senior management oversees the establishment, administration, and assessment of risk management and control processes.

            a)   Line managers assess control in their areas.

        3)   Internal auditors provide assurance about the effectiveness of risk management and control.

        4)   The CAE obtains sufficient audit evidence to form an overall opinion on the adequacy and effectiveness of control. This opinion is communicated to senior management and the board.

5) The CAE should develop a flexible internal audit plan to provide sufficient evidence to evaluate control. It should permit adjustments during the year. The plan

    a) Covers all major operations, functions, and controls

    b) Gives special consideration to operations most affected by recent or unexpected changes

    c) Considers relevant work performed by others, including management's assessments of risk management, control, and quality processes and the work completed by external auditors

6) The CAE evaluates the plan's coverage.

    a) If the scope of the plan is insufficient to permit expression of an opinion about risk management and control, the CAE informs senior management and the board about gaps in audit coverage.

7) The evaluation of control combines many individual assessments (e.g., from internal audits, self-assessments, and the work of other assurance providers).

    a) Communication of findings to appropriate managers needs to be timely.

8) The overall evaluation of control considers whether

    a) Significant weaknesses or discrepancies exist,

    b) Corrections or improvements were made, and

    c) A pervasive condition exists leading to unacceptable risk.

9) Whether unacceptable risk exists depends on the nature and extent of risk exposure and level of consequences.

    a) Thus, a significant discrepancy or weakness may not indicate an unacceptable risk.

10) The CAE's report on control processes is usually presented annually to senior management and the board. It describes

    a) The role of control processes,

    b) The work performed, and

    c) Any reliance on other assurance providers.

c. Reports of governance failures emphasize the need for greater accountability and transparency by all organizations. Senior management, boards, internal auditors, and external auditors are the basis of effective governance.

1) The internal audit activity has a key role in improving operations by evaluating and improving the effectiveness of governance, risk management, and control.

2) Senior management has become more accountable (for example, as a result of legislation) for the information contained in financial reports. Thus, senior management and the board now tend to request more services from the internal audit activity.

    a) These requests include evaluations of internal controls over financial reporting and the reliability and integrity of financial reports.

4. **Reporting on Internal Control**

a. The board and internal audit activity have shared goals. The core role of the CAE is to ensure that the board receives the support and assurance services it requests.

b. A primary objective of the board is oversight of financial reporting processes to ensure their reliability and fairness. The board and senior management typically request the internal audit activity to perform sufficient audit work and gather other available information during the year to form an opinion on the adequacy and effectiveness of internal control.

1) The CAE normally communicates this overall evaluation, on a timely basis, to the board. The board evaluates the CAE's report.

    c.   The internal audit activity's work plans and specific assurance engagements begin with careful identification of the exposures facing the organization. Thus, the work plan is based on the risks and the assessments of the risk management and control processes maintained by management to mitigate those risks. Among the events and transactions included in the identification of risks are the following:

        1)   New businesses, including mergers and acquisitions
        2)   New products and systems
        3)   Joint ventures and partnerships
        4)   Restructuring
        5)   Management estimates, budgets, and forecasts
        6)   Environmental matters
        7)   Regulatory compliance

5.   **A Framework for Internal Control**

    a.   The assessment of internal control uses a broad definition of control. One source of effective internal control guidance is *Internal Control – Integrated Framework*, published by the Committee of Sponsoring Organizations (COSO).

        1)   The COSO model is widely accepted, but it may be appropriate to use some other model recognized worldwide. Also, regulatory or legal requirements may specify a particular model or control design.

    b.   In the COSO framework, control has five interrelated components:

        1)   **Control activities** are the policies and procedures applied to ensure that management directives are executed and actions are taken to address risks affecting achievement of objectives. Whether automated or manual, they have various objectives and are applied at all levels and functions of the organization. They include

            a)   Performance reviews by top managers,
            b)   Performance reviews at the functional or activity level,
            c)   Analysis of performance indicators,
            d)   Controls over information processing (e.g., application controls and general controls),
            e)   Physical controls, and
            f)   Segregation of duties (separation of the functions of authorization, recordkeeping, and asset custody).

        2)   **Risk assessment** is based on a set of complementary operational, financial reporting, and compliance objectives linked across all levels of the organization. Risk assessment identifies and analyzes external or internal risks affecting achievement of the objectives at the activity level and the entity level.

        3)   **Information and communication.** Relevant internal and external information should be identified, captured, and communicated in a timely manner and in appropriate forms.

        4)   **Monitoring** assesses the quality of a system's performance over time.

        5)   The **control environment** reflects the attitude and actions of the board and management regarding the significance of control within the organization.

        6)   A common memory aid is **CRIME**.

    c.   The following conclusions by the COSO are relevant:

        1)   Internal control is defined broadly. It is not limited to accounting controls or financial reporting.

        2) Accounting and financial reports are important. However, other matters also are important, such as (a) resource protection; (b) operational efficiency and effectiveness; and (c) compliance with rules, regulations, and organization policies.

            a) These factors affect financial reporting.

        3) Internal control is management's responsibility. The participation of all persons within an organization is required if it is to be effective.

        4) The control framework should relate to business objectives and be adaptable.

6. **Reporting on the Effectiveness of Internal Control**

    a. The CAE provides the board an assessment of the effectiveness of the organization's controls, including the adequacy of the control model or design. The board must rely on management to maintain adequate and effective internal control. It reinforces this reliance with independent oversight.

        1) Controls are effective if management directs processes to provide reasonable assurance that objectives are achieved.

        2) Controls are adequate if management has designed them to provide reasonable assurance that (a) risks are managed effectively and (b) objectives are achieved effectively (The IIA Glossary).

    b. However, even effective internal controls cannot ensure success. Bad decisions, poor managers, or environmental factors can negate controls. Also, dishonest management may override controls and discourage, ignore, or conceal communications from subordinates.

        1) An active and independent board needs open and truthful communications from all components of management. Moreover, the board needs to be assisted by capable financial, legal, and internal audit functions.

            a) In these circumstances, the board can identify problems and provide effective oversight.

    c. The board or other governance body should request evaluations of internal controls as part of its oversight function. Those evaluations by the internal audit activity depend on answers to the following questions:

        1) Is the **ethical environment and culture** strong?

            a) Do board members and senior executives set examples of high integrity?

            b) Are performance and incentive targets realistic, or do they create excessive pressure for short-term results?

            c) Is the organization's code of conduct reinforced with training and top-down communication? Does the message reach the employees in the field?

            d) Are the organization's communication channels open? Do all levels of management get the information they need?

            e) Does the organization have zero tolerance for fraudulent financial reporting at any level?

        2) How does the organization **identify and manage risks**?

            a) Does the organization have a risk management process, and is it effective?

            b) Is risk managed throughout the organization?

            c) Are major risks candidly discussed with the board?

        3) Is the **control system** effective?

            a) Are the organization's controls over the financial reporting process comprehensive, including preparation of financial statements, related notes, and the other required and discretionary disclosures that are an integral part of the financial reports?

        b)   Do senior and line management demonstrate that they accept control responsibility?

        c)   Is the frequency of surprises increasing at the senior management, board, or public levels from the organization's reported financial results or in the accompanying financial disclosures?

        d)   Is communication and reporting good throughout the organization?

        e)   Are controls seen as enhancing the achievement of objectives or as a necessary evil?

        f)   Are qualified people hired promptly, and do they receive adequate training?

        g)   Are problems fixed quickly and completely?

    4)   Is **monitoring** strong?

        a)   Is the board independent of management, free of conflicts of interest, well informed, and inquisitive?

        b)   Does internal auditing have the support of senior management and the board?

        c)   Do the internal and external auditors have and use open lines of communication and private access to all members of senior management and the board?

        d)   Is line management monitoring the control process?

        e)   Does the organization have a program to monitor outsourced processes?

7.   **Roles for the Internal Auditor**

    a.   Adequate resources need to be committed to helping senior management, the board, and the external auditor with their responsibilities in the upcoming year's financial reporting regimen. Furthermore, the CAE needs to review internal audit's risk assessment and audit plans for the year.

        1)   The financial reporting process encompasses the steps to create information and prepare financial statements, related notes, and other accompanying disclosures in the organization's financial reports.

    b.   The CAE's allocation of the internal audit activity's resources to the financial reporting, governance, and control processes is consistent with the organization's risk assessment.

        1)   The CAE performs procedures that provide a level of assurance to senior management and the board that controls over the processes supporting the development of financial reports are adequately designed and effectively executed.

        2)   Controls need to be adequate to ensure the prevention and detection of (a) significant errors; (b) fraud; (c) incorrect assumptions and estimates; and (d) other events that could result in inaccurate or misleading financial statements, related notes, or other disclosures.

    c.   The following are lists of suggested topics that the CAE considers in supporting the organization's governance process and the oversight responsibilities of the board:

        1)   **Financial Reporting**

            a)   Providing information relevant to the appointment of the independent accountants.

            b)   Coordinating audit plans, coverage, and scheduling with the external auditors.

      c) Sharing audit results with the external auditors.

      d) Communicating pertinent observations to the external auditors and board about (1) accounting policies and policy decisions (including accounting decisions for discretionary items and off-balance-sheet transactions), (2) specific components of the financial reporting process, and (3) unusual or complex financial transactions and events (e.g., related party transactions, mergers and acquisitions, joint ventures, and partnership transactions).

      e) Participating in the financial reports and disclosures review process with the board, external auditors, and senior management.

      f) Evaluating the quality of financial reports, including those filed with regulatory agencies.

      g) Assessing the adequacy and effectiveness of the organization's internal controls, specifically those controls over the financial reporting process. This assessment considers the organization's susceptibility to fraud and the effectiveness of programs and controls to mitigate or eliminate those exposures.

      h) Monitoring management's compliance with the organization's code of conduct and ensuring that ethical policies and other procedures promoting ethical behavior are being followed. An important factor in establishing an effective ethical culture in the organization is that members of senior management set a good example of ethical behavior and provide open and truthful communications to employees, the board, and outside stakeholders.

2) **Governance**

      a) Reviewing the organization's policies relating to (1) compliance with laws and regulations, (2) ethics, (3) conflicts of interest, and (4) the timely and thorough investigation of misconduct and fraud allegations.

      b) Reviewing pending litigation or regulatory proceedings bearing upon organizational risk and governance.

      c) Providing information on employee conflicts of interest, misconduct, fraud, and other outcomes of the organization's ethical procedures and reporting mechanisms.

3) **Corporate Control**

      a) Reviewing the reliability and integrity of the operating and financial information compiled and reported by the organization.

      b) Performing an analysis of the controls over critical accounting policies and comparing them with preferred practices. For example, transactions that raise questions about revenue recognition or off-balance-sheet accounting treatment are reviewed for compliance with appropriate standards, such as International Financial Reporting Standards.

      c) Evaluating the reasonableness of estimates and assumptions used in preparing operating and financial reports.

      d) Ensuring that estimates and assumptions included in disclosures or comments are consistent with underlying organizational information and practices and with similar items reported by other organizations, if appropriate.

      e) Evaluating the process of preparing, reviewing, approving, and posting journal entries.

      f) Evaluating the adequacy of controls in the accounting function.

8. **Accounting Cycles**

    a. An audit of financial information may follow the cycle approach to internal accounting control (a cycle is a functional grouping of transactions).

    b. **Sales, Receivables, and Cash Receipts Cycle**

        1) Processing customer orders
        2) Customer acceptance and granting credit
        3) Shipping goods
        4) Recording sales and receivables (including observing a proper cutoff)
        5) Billing customers
        6) Receiving, processing, and recording cash receipts
        7) Providing for, and writing off, bad debts
        8) Receiving, processing, and recording sales returns
        9) Providing for adjustments, allowances, warranties, and other credits

    c. **Purchases, Payables, and Cash Payments Cycle**

        1) Processing purchase requests
        2) Issuing purchase orders
        3) Receiving goods and services
        4) Processing vendor invoices, receiving reports, and purchase orders
        5) Disbursing cash
        6) Accounting for and documenting receipts, liabilities, cash payments, and accrued expenses

    d. **Production or Conversion Cycle**

        1) Inventory planning
        2) Receipt and storage of goods
        3) Production or conversion of goods or provision of services
        4) Accounting for costs, deferred costs, and property
        5) Storage of produced or converted goods
        6) Shipment

    e. **Financial Capital and Payment Cycle**

        1) Issuing long-term debt and stock
        2) Paying interest and dividends
        3) Repurchase of equity and debt securities and payment at maturity
        4) Maintaining detailed records for payment of interest, dividends, and taxes
        5) Purchases and sales of investments
        6) Recording receipts of interest and dividends
        7) Recording stock options and treasury stock
        8) Accounting for investing and financing transactions

    f. **Personnel and Payroll Cycle**

        1) Personnel department's hiring of employees
        2) Personnel department's authorization of payroll rates, deductions, etc.
        3) Timekeeping
        4) Payroll preparation and payment
        5) Filing payroll tax returns and paying the taxes

    g. **External Financial Reporting Cycle**

        1) Preparation of financial statements
        2) Disclosure of related information
        3) Controls over financial reporting
        4) Selection of accounting principles
        5) Unusual or nonrecurring items
        6) Contingencies

The IIA has consistently tested candidates on the aspects of internal control in different accounting cycles. Appendix E is dedicated to reviewing the most significant accounting cycles. This review is needed for an understanding of basic internal controls. Other accounting cycles and controls may be tested. Thus, the subject of a control question on the exam may not be covered. However, an understanding of (1) basic control principles, (2) accounting cycles, and (3) how the controls help prevent or detect fraud or error should enable candidates to handle any other cycles and controls that are tested. For example, authorizations required by a health insurer before a claim is paid are not significantly different from those required for a debtor's payment of interest on a note payable. Both require the auditor to trace the payment to documentation about authorization as well as supporting documentation.

Furthermore, candidates should not necessarily be concerned about memorizing every control in every cycle. Rather, they should understand control concepts.

    h.   In Appendix E are five flowcharts and accompanying tables describing the steps in five basic accounting cycles and the controls in each step for an organization large enough to have an optimal segregation of duties.

        1)   In small- and medium-sized organizations, some duties must be combined. The internal auditor must assess whether organizational segregation of duties is adequate.

9. **Fraud Risk**

    a.   The auditor plans and performs the audit to obtain reasonable assurance about whether the financial statements are free of material misstatement, whether caused by fraud or error.

    b.   The types of fraud relevant to the financial statement auditor include misstatements arising from

        1)   Fraudulent financial reporting. These are intentional misstatements or omissions to deceive users, such as altering accounting records or documents, misrepresenting or omitting significant information, and misapplying accounting principles.

        2)   Misappropriation of assets. These result from theft, embezzlement, or an action that causes payment for items not received.

    c.   **Fraud** is fully covered in Study Unit 7.

Stop and review! You have completed the outline for this subunit. Study multiple-choice questions 8 through 15 beginning on page 93.

3.3 CONSULTING ENGAGEMENTS -- OVERVIEW

1. **Definition**

    a.   **Consulting services** are "advisory and related client service activities, the nature and scope of which are agreed with the client, are intended to add value and improve an organization's governance, risk management, and control processes without the internal auditor assuming management responsibility. Examples include counsel, advice, facilitation, and training" (The IIA Glossary).

Implementation Standard 1000.C1

The nature of consulting services must be defined in the internal audit charter.

---

        1)   The nature and scope of the consulting engagement are subject to agreement with the engagement client.

        2)   The IIA's Consulting Implementation Standards describe the requirements of consulting engagements. The related outlines are based on publications of The IIA.

2. **Principles Applied to Internal Auditors' Consulting Activities**

    a. **Value Proposition** – The value proposition of the internal audit activity is realized within every organization that employs internal auditors in a manner that suits the culture and resources of that organization. That value proposition is captured in the definition of internal auditing and includes assurance and consulting activities designed to add value to the organization by bringing a systematic, disciplined approach to the areas of governance, risk, and control.

    b. **Consistency with Internal Audit Definition** – A disciplined, systematic evaluation methodology is incorporated in each internal audit activity. The list of services can generally be incorporated into the broad categories of assurance and consulting. However, the services also may include evolving forms of value-adding services that are consistent with the broad definition of internal auditing.

    c. **Audit Activities beyond Assurance and Consulting** – Assurance and consulting are not mutually exclusive and do not preclude other internal audit services, such as investigations and nonaudit roles. Many audit services will have both an assurance and consultative (advising) role.

    d. **Interrelationship between Assurance and Consulting** – Internal audit consulting enriches value-adding internal auditing. While consulting is often the direct result of assurance services, assurance also could result from consulting engagements.

    e. **Empower Consulting through the Internal Audit Charter** – Internal auditors have traditionally performed many types of consulting services, including the analysis of controls built into developing systems, analysis of security products, serving on task forces to analyze operations and make recommendations, and so forth. The board empowers the internal audit activity to perform additional services if they do not represent a conflict of interest or detract from its obligations to the board. That empowerment is reflected in the internal audit charter.

    f. **Objectivity** – Consulting services may enhance the auditor's understanding of business processes or issues related to an assurance engagement and do not necessarily impair the auditor's or the internal audit activity's objectivity. Internal auditing is not a management decision-making function. Decisions to adopt or implement recommendations made as a result of an internal audit advisory service are made by management. Therefore, internal audit objectivity is not impaired by the decisions made by management.

    g. **Internal Audit Foundation for Consulting Services** – Much of consulting is a natural extension of assurance and investigative services and may represent informal or formal advice, analysis, or assessments. The internal audit activity is uniquely positioned to perform this type of consulting work based on (1) its adherence to the highest standards of objectivity and (2) its breadth of knowledge about organizational processes, risk, and strategies.

    h. **Communication of Fundamental Information** – A primary internal audit value is to provide **assurance** to senior management and the board. Consulting engagements cannot be performed in a manner that masks information that, in the judgment of the chief audit executive (CAE), should be presented to senior executives and board members. All consulting is to be understood in that context.

    i. **Principles of Consulting Understood by the Organization** – Organizations must have ground rules for the performance of consulting services that are understood by all members of an organization. These rules are codified in the audit charter approved by the board and issued within the organization.

    j. **Formal Consulting Engagements** – Management often engages external consultants for formal consulting engagements that last a significant period of time. However, an organization may find that the internal audit activity is uniquely qualified for some formal consulting tasks. If an internal audit activity undertakes to perform a formal consulting engagement, the internal audit group brings a systematic, disciplined approach to the conduct of the engagement.

k. **CAE Responsibilities** – Consulting services permit the CAE to enter into dialogue with management to address specific managerial issues. In this dialogue, the breadth of the engagement and time frames are made responsive to management needs. However, the CAE retains the prerogative of setting the audit techniques and the right of reporting to senior executives and the board when the nature and materiality of results pose significant risks to the organization.

l. **Criteria for Resolving Conflicts or Evolving Issues** – An internal auditor is first and foremost an internal auditor. Thus, in the performance of all services, the internal auditor is guided by The IIA Code of Ethics and the Attribute and Performance Standards of the *International Standards for the Professional Practice of Internal Auditing*. The resolution of any unforeseen conflicts of activities needs to be consistent with the Code of Ethics and *Standards*.

3. **Classification of Engagements**

Implementation Standard 2010.C1

The chief audit executive should consider accepting proposed consulting engagements based on the engagement's potential to improve management of risks, add value, and improve the organization's operations. Accepted engagements must be included in the plan.

Implementation Standard 2120.C1

During consulting engagements, internal auditors must address risk consistent with the engagement's objectives and be alert to the existence of other significant risks.

Implementation Standard 2120.C2

Internal auditors must incorporate knowledge of risks gained from consulting engagements into their evaluation of the organization's risk management processes.

Implementation Standard 2120.C3

When assisting management in establishing or improving risk management processes, internal auditors must refrain from assuming any management responsibility by actually managing risks.

Implementation Standard 2130.C1

Internal auditors must incorporate knowledge of controls gained from consulting engagements into evaluation of the organization's control processes.

---

a. The chief audit executive determines the methodology to use for classifying engagements within the organization.

1) In some circumstances, it may be appropriate to conduct a blended engagement that incorporates elements of both consulting and assurance activities into one consolidated approach.

2) In other cases, it may be appropriate to distinguish between the assurance and consulting components of the engagement.

b. Internal auditors may conduct consulting services as part of their normal or routine activities as well as in response to requests by management. Each organization considers the type of consulting activities to be offered and determines whether specific policies or procedures need to be developed for each type of activity. Possible categories could include the following:

1) **Formal consulting** engagements are planned and subject to written agreement.

2) **Informal consulting** engagements involve routine activities, such as (a) participation on standing committees, (b) limited-life projects, (c) ad-hoc meetings, and (d) routine information exchange.

3) **Special consulting** engagements include participation on a merger and acquisition team or system conversion team.

4) **Emergency consulting** engagements include participation on a team (a) established for recovery or maintenance of operations after a disaster or other extraordinary business event or (b) assembled to supply temporary help to meet a special request or unusual deadline.

c.   Auditors generally should not agree to conduct a consulting engagement simply to circumvent, or to allow others to circumvent, requirements that would normally apply to an assurance engagement if the service in question is more appropriately conducted as an assurance engagement. This does not preclude adjusting methods if services once conducted as assurance engagements are deemed more suitable to being performed as a consulting engagement.

4.   **Governmental Internal Auditing**

a.   A governmental internal audit activity's provision of consulting services may be limited by local law, audit standards, etc. The parameters of these services are defined in its charter and supported by its policies and procedures.

b.   Assurance services help ensure management's accountability. These services include an assistance dimension when auditors recommend operational improvements. But auditors jeopardize their independence and objectivity by being responsible for implementing or authorizing improvements, even those arising from consulting.

c.   When consulting, auditors stay within the bounds of the core elements of the audit function. These give credibility to the auditors' attestation to management assertions. **Core** elements support the principle that an objective third party is providing assurance about the assertions. The core elements that protect auditors' ability to give assurance are

1) Independence,
2) Objectivity,
3) Not auditing one's own work, and
4) Not performing functions or making decisions that are managerial.

d.   Other threats to auditor independence include consulting work that (1) creates a mutuality of interest or (2) positions auditors as advocates for the organization.

e.   Governing rules may restrict the internal audit activity's consulting services. These rules may apply to external auditors or all auditors. They may be based on law, regulation, a code of ethics, or audit standards. The CAE ensures that the internal audit activity's charter, policies, and procedures comply with the governing rules.

f.   Even if restrictive governing rules do not apply, the quality assurance system should minimize threats to auditor independence or objectivity posed by consulting. Otherwise, the internal audit activity's assurance role and the ability of other auditors to rely on its work may be compromised. Avoiding these threats depends in part on distinguishing between (1) merely advising and (2) assuming management responsibilities.

g.   The internal audit activity documents procedures for review of threats to independence and objectivity. The documentation is available to external quality control reviewers.

h.   The internal audit activity implements controls to reduce the potential threats to auditor independence or objectivity posed by consulting. These controls may include the following:

1) Charter language defining consulting service parameters
2) Policies and procedures limiting type, nature, or level of participation in consulting
3) Screening consulting projects, with limits on engagements threatening objectivity
4) Segregation of consulting units from assurance units in the audit function
5) Rotation of auditors

6) Employing external service providers for (a) consulting or (b) assurance engagements involving activities subject to prior consulting work that impaired objectivity or independence

7) Disclosure in audit reports when objectivity was impaired by participation in a prior consulting project

5. **Independence and Objectivity**

> ### Implementation Standard 1130.C1
>
> Internal auditors may provide consulting services relating to operations for which they had previous responsibilities.
>
> ### Implementation Standard 1130.C2
>
> If internal auditors have potential impairments to independence or objectivity relating to proposed consulting services, disclosure must be made to the engagement client prior to accepting the engagement.

    a. Internal auditors are sometimes requested to provide consulting services relating to operations for which they had previous responsibilities or had conducted assurance services. Prior to offering consulting services, the CAE confirms that the board understands and approves the concept of providing consulting services. Once approved, the internal audit charter is amended to include authority and responsibilities for consulting activities, and the internal audit activity develops appropriate policies and procedures for conducting such engagements.

    b. Internal auditors maintain their objectivity when drawing conclusions and offering advice to management. If impairments to independence or objectivity exist prior to commencement of the consulting engagement, or subsequently develop during the engagement, disclosure is made immediately to management.

    c. Independence and objectivity may be impaired if assurance services are provided within 1 year after a formal consulting engagement. Steps can be taken to minimize the effects of impairment by (1) assigning different auditors to perform each of the services, (2) establishing independent management and supervision, (3) defining separate accountability for the results of the projects, and (4) disclosing the presumed impairment. Management is responsible for accepting and implementing recommendations.

    d. Care is taken, particularly involving consulting engagements that are ongoing or continuous in nature, so that internal auditors do not inappropriately or unintentionally assume management responsibilities that were not intended in the original objectives and scope of the engagement.

6. **Due Professional Care**

> ### Implementation Standard 1210.C1
>
> The chief audit executive must decline the consulting engagement or obtain competent advice and assistance if the internal auditors lack the knowledge, skills, or other competencies needed to perform all or part of the engagement.
>
> ### Implementation Standard 1220.C1
>
> Internal auditors must exercise due professional care during a consulting engagement by considering the:
>
> - Needs and expectations of clients, including the nature, timing, and communication of engagement results;
> - Relative complexity and extent of work needed to achieve the engagement's objectives; and
> - Cost of the consulting engagement in relation to potential benefits.

a.   The internal auditor exercises due professional care in conducting a formal consulting engagement by understanding the following:

1)   Needs of management officials, including the nature, timing, and communication of engagement results

2)   Possible motivations and reasons of those requesting the service

3)   Extent of work needed to achieve the engagement's objectives

4)   Skills and resources needed to conduct the engagement

5)   Effect on the scope of the audit plan previously approved by the audit committee

6)   Potential impact on future audit assignments and engagements

7)   Potential organizational benefits to be derived from the engagement

b.   In addition to the independence and objectivity evaluation and due professional care considerations, the internal auditor

1)   Conducts appropriate meetings and gathers necessary information to assess the nature and extent of the service to be provided.

2)   Confirms that those receiving the service understand and agree with (a) the relevant guidance contained in the internal audit charter, (b) internal audit activity's policies and procedures, and (c) other related guidance for consulting engagements. The internal auditor declines to perform consulting engagements that (a) are prohibited by the charter, (b) conflict with the policies and procedures of the internal audit activity, or (c) do not add value and promote the best interests of the organization.

3)   Evaluates the consulting engagement for compatibility with the internal audit activity's overall plan of engagements. The risk-based plan of engagements may incorporate and rely on consulting engagements, to the extent deemed appropriate, to provide necessary audit coverage.

4)   Documents general terms, understandings, deliverables, and other key factors of the formal consulting engagement in a written agreement or plan. It is essential that the internal auditor and those receiving the consulting engagement understand and agree with the reporting and communication requirements.

7.   **Scope of Work**

Implementation Standard 2201.C1

Internal auditors must establish an understanding with consulting engagement clients about objectives, scope, respective responsibilities, and other client expectations. For significant engagements, this understanding must be documented.

Implementation Standard 2210.C1

Consulting engagement objectives must address governance, risk management, and control processes to the extent agreed upon with the client.

Implementation Standard 2210.C2

Consulting engagement objectives must be consistent with the organization's values, strategies, and objectives.

Implementation Standard 2220.C1

In performing consulting engagements, internal auditors must ensure that the scope of the engagement is sufficient to address the agreed-upon objectives. If internal auditors develop reservations about the scope during the engagement, these reservations must be discussed with the client to determine whether to continue with the engagement.

a. Internal auditors need to have an understanding about the objectives and scope of the consulting engagement with the client. Any reservations about the value, benefit, or possible negative implications of the engagement are communicated to the client.

   1) Internal auditors design the scope of work to ensure that the professionalism, integrity, credibility, and reputation of the internal audit activity will be maintained.

b. In planning formal consulting engagements, internal auditors design objectives to meet the appropriate needs of management officials receiving these services. If management makes special requests and the internal auditor believes the objectives that need to be pursued go beyond those requested by management, the internal auditor may consider

   1) Persuading management to include the additional objectives in the consulting engagement or

   2) Documenting the failure to pursue the objectives, disclosing that observation in the final communication of consulting engagement results, and including the objectives in a separate and subsequent assurance engagement.

Implementation Standard 2240.C1

Work programs for consulting engagements may vary in form and content depending upon the nature of the engagement.

---

c. Work programs for formal consulting engagements document the objectives and scope of the engagement and the methods to be used in satisfying the objectives.

   1) In establishing the scope of the engagement, internal auditors may expand or limit the scope to satisfy management. However, the internal auditor needs to be satisfied that the projected scope of work will be adequate to meet the objectives of the engagement.

   2) The objectives, scope, and terms of the engagement are periodically reassessed and adjusted during the course of the work.

Implementation Standard 2220.C2

During consulting engagements, internal auditors must address controls consistent with the engagement's objectives and be alert to significant control issues.

---

d. Internal auditors are observant of the effectiveness of risk management and control processes during formal consulting engagements. Substantial risk exposures or material control weaknesses are reported to management.

   1) In some situations, the auditor's concerns also are communicated to senior management or the board. (According to The IIA Glossary, the board includes any "designated body of the organization, including the audit committee.")

   2) Auditors determine (a) the significance of exposures or weaknesses and the actions taken or contemplated to mitigate or correct and (b) the expectations of senior management and the board about reporting.

8. **Communicating Results**

Implementation Standard 2410.C1

Communication of the progress and results of consulting engagements will vary in form and content depending upon the nature of the engagement and the needs of the client.

Implementation Standard 2440.C1

The chief audit executive is responsible for communicating the final results of consulting engagements to clients.

Implementation Standard 2440.C2

During consulting engagements, governance, risk management, and control issues may be identified. Whenever these issues are significant to the organization, they must be communicated to senior management and the board.

---

    a.   Reporting requirements are generally determined by those requesting the consulting service and meet the objectives as determined and agreed to with management.

        1)   However, the format for communicating the results clearly describes the nature of the engagement and any limitations, restrictions, or other factors about which users of the information need to be made aware.

    b.   In some circumstances, the internal auditor may communicate results beyond those who received or requested the service. In such cases, the internal auditor expands the reporting so that results are communicated to the appropriate parties. The auditor therefore takes the following steps until satisfied with the resolution of the matter:

        1)   Determine what direction is provided in the agreement concerning the consulting engagement and related communications.

        2)   Attempt to persuade those receiving or requesting the service to expand the communication to the appropriate parties.

        3)   Determine what guidance is provided in the internal audit charter or the internal audit activity's policies and procedures concerning consulting communications.

        4)   Determine what guidance is provided in the organization's code of conduct, code of ethics, and other related policies, administrative directives, or procedures.

        5)   Determine what guidance is provided by The IIA's *Standards* and Code of Ethics, other standards or codes applicable to the auditor, and any legal or regulatory requirements that relate to the matter under consideration.

    c.   Internal auditors disclose to management, the board, or other governing body of the organization the nature, extent, and overall results of formal consulting engagements along with other reports of internal audit activities. Internal auditors keep management and the board informed about how audit resources are being deployed.

        1)   Neither detail reports of these consulting engagements nor the specific results and recommendations are required to be communicated. But an appropriate description of these types of engagements and their significant recommendations are communicated. This communication is essential in satisfying the CAE's responsibility to comply with Performance Standard 2060, *Reporting to Senior Management and the Board*.

9.   **Documentation**

Implementation Standard 2330.C1

The chief audit executive must develop policies governing the custody and retention of consulting engagement records, as well as their release to internal and external parties. These policies must be consistent with the organization's guidelines and any pertinent regulatory or other requirements.

---

    a.   Documentation requirements for assurance engagements do not necessarily apply to consulting engagements.

    b.   In formal consulting engagements, auditors adopt appropriate record retention policies and address such related issues as ownership of the engagement records. Legal, regulatory, tax, and accounting matters may require special treatment in the records.

10. **Monitoring**

Implementation Standard 2500.C1

The internal audit activity must monitor the disposition of results of consulting engagements to the extent agreed upon with the client.

---

    a. The internal audit activity monitors the results of consulting engagements to the extent agreed upon with the client. Varying types of monitoring may be appropriate for differing types of consulting engagements.

    b. The monitoring effort may depend on various factors, such as management's explicit interest in the engagement or the internal auditor's assessment of the project's risks or value to the organization.

Stop and review! You have completed the outline for this subunit. Study multiple-choice questions 16 through 20 beginning on page 96.

3.4 CONSULTING ENGAGEMENTS -- SPECIFIC TYPES

1. This subunit covers five specific consulting services listed in the CIA 2013 Exam Syllabus.

2. **Internal Control Training**

    a. Internal auditors may perform consulting engagements to provide internal control training to the employees of the organization.

        1) Such training may involve instruction about the organization's objectives, policies, standards, procedures, performance measurements, and feedback methods.

        2) In addition to providing courses for client personnel, the internal audit activity may offer internships to some new managers. Among other things, these managers gain experience in assessing controls.

    b. As part of their coordination with external auditors, the internal auditors may provide opportunities for joint control training and other matters.

    c. Internal auditors also should undergo internal control training, for example, with regard to control frameworks, specific controls and control objectives, standards, technological developments, and new professional literature.

    d. Control self-assessment provides training for people in business units. Participants gain experience in assessing risks and associating control processes with managing those risks and improving the chances of achieving business objectives.

    e. The ethical culture of an organization is linked to the governance process and is the most important soft control.

        1) Internal auditors have many roles in supporting the ethical culture, including those of ethics counselor and ethics expert.

3. **Business Process Mapping**

    a. One approach to business process mapping (review) is reengineering (also called business process reengineering). It involves process innovation and core process redesign. Instead of improving existing procedures, it finds new ways of doing things.

        1) The emphasis is on simplification and elimination of nonvalue-adding activities. Thus, reengineering is not continuous improvement, it is not simply downsizing or modifying an existing system, and it should be reserved for the most important processes.

        2) An organization may need to adapt quickly and radically to change. Thus, reengineering is usually a cross-departmental process of innovation requiring substantial investment in information technology and retraining. Successful reengineering may bring dramatic improvements in customer service and the speed with which new products are introduced.

b.   One well-known tool useful in reengineering is work measurement, a process that involves analysis of activities. The nature and extent of a task, the procedures needed for its execution, and the efficiency with which it is carried out are determined by work measurement.

1)   This technique is appropriate when management takes an engineered-cost approach to control. Such an approach is indicated when the workload is divisible into control-factor units, for example, accounting entries made, lines of text word processed, or number of packages shipped. The cost of a control-factor unit is treated as a variable cost for budgeting purposes.

2)   One method used for work measurement is micromotion study, which requires videotaping the performance of a job, e.g., assembly-line activities.

3)   Another method is work sampling, making many random observations of an activity to determine what steps it normally requires.

c.   Reengineering and total quality management (TQM) techniques (as discussed in Study Unit 2, Subunit 4) eliminate many traditional controls. They exploit modern technology to improve productivity and decrease the number of clerical workers. Thus, the emphasis is on developing controls that are automated and self-correcting and that require minimal human intervention.

1)   The emphasis shifts to monitoring internal control so management can determine when an operation may be out of control and corrective action is needed.

a)   Most reengineering and TQM techniques also assume that humans will be motivated to work actively in improving operations when they are full participants in the process.

2)   Monitoring assesses the quality of internal control over time. Management considers whether internal control is properly designed and operating as intended and modifies it to reflect changing conditions. Monitoring may be in the form of separate, periodic evaluations or of ongoing monitoring.

a)   Ongoing monitoring occurs as part of routine operations. It includes management and supervisory review, comparisons, reconciliations, and other actions by personnel as part of their regular activities.

d.   Internal auditors may perform the functions of determining whether the reengineering process has senior management's support, recommending areas for consideration, and developing audit plans for the new system. However, they should not become directly involved in the implementation of the process. This involvement would impair their independence and objectivity.

4.   Benchmarking

a.   Benchmarking is one of the primary tools used in TQM. It is a means of helping organizations with productivity management and business process review. It is therefore a source of consulting engagements for internal auditors.

b.   Benchmarking is a continuous evaluation of the practices of the best organizations in their class and the adaptation of processes to reflect the best of these practices. It involves (1) analyzing and measuring key outputs against those of the best organizations and (2) identifying the underlying key actions and causes that contribute to the performance difference.

1)   **Best practices** are recognized by authorities in the field and by customers for generating outstanding results. They are generally innovative technically or in their management of human resources.

2)   Benchmarking is an ongoing process that involves quantitative and qualitative measurement of the difference between the organization's performance of an activity and the performance by the benchmark organization.

c.   The following are kinds of benchmarking:

1)   **Competitive** benchmarking studies an organization in the same industry.
2)   **Process (function)** benchmarking studies operations of organizations with similar processes regardless of industry. Thus, the benchmark need not be a competitor or even a similar organization.

a)   This method may introduce new ideas that provide a significant competitive advantage.

3)   **Strategic** benchmarking is a search for successful competitive strategies.
4)   **Internal** benchmarking is the application of best practices in one part of the organization to its other parts.
5)   **Generic** benchmarking observes a process in one operation and compares it with a process having similar characteristics but in a different industry.

d.   The first phase in the benchmarking process is to select and prioritize benchmarking projects.

1)   An organization must understand its critical success factors and business environment to identify key business processes and drivers and to develop parameters defining what processes to benchmark. The criteria for selecting what to benchmark are based mostly on satisfaction of customer needs.

e.   The next phase is to organize benchmarking teams. A team organization is appropriate because it permits a fair division of labor, participation by those responsible for implementing changes, and inclusion of a variety of functional expertise and work experience.

1)   The benchmarking team must thoroughly investigate and document the organization's internal processes.

a)   The team must develop a family of measures that are true indicators of process performance.
b)   The development of key indicators for performance measurement in a benchmarking context is an extension of the basic evaluative function of internal auditors.

f.   Researching and identifying best-in-class performance is often the most difficult phase. The critical steps are

1)   Setting up databases,
2)   Choosing information-gathering methods (internal sources, external public domain sources, and original research),
3)   Formatting questionnaires (lists of questions prepared in advance), and
4)   Selecting benchmarking partners.

g.   Data analysis involves identifying performance gaps, understanding the reasons, and prioritizing the key activities that will facilitate the behavioral and process changes needed to implement recommendations.

h.   Leadership is most important in the implementation phase because the team must justify its recommendations. Moreover, the process improvement teams must manage the implementation of approved changes.

5.   **System Development Reviews**

    a.   Internal auditor involvement throughout the systems development life cycle can ensure that the appropriate internal controls and audit trails are included in the application. According to The IIA's *GTAG 12: Auditing IT Projects,* "Internal auditing can bring the value of their experience and methodology to review projects in the early stages to also help increase the likelihood of success." Benefits of internal audit involvement may include

        1)   Providing independent, ongoing advice throughout the project and

        2)   Identifying key risks or issues early, which enables project teams to operate proactively to mitigate risks.

    b.   The section for systems development and acquisition controls in *GTAG 1: Information Technology Risks and Controls* is useful for understanding the role of the internal auditor. It states that "the IT auditor should assess whether the organization uses a controlled method to develop or acquire application systems and whether it delivers effective controls over and within the applications and data they process. By examining application development procedures, the auditor can gain assurance that application controls are adequate. Some basic control issues should be addressed in all systems development and acquisition work. For example,

        1)   User requirements should be documented, and their achievement should be measured.

        2)   Systems design should follow a formal process to ensure that user requirements and controls are designed into the system.

        3)   Systems development should be conducted in a structured manner to ensure that requirements and approved design features are incorporated into the finished product.

        4)   Testing should ensure that individual system elements work as required, system interfaces operate as expected, and that the system owner has confirmed that the intended functionality has been provided.

        5)   Application maintenance processes should ensure that changes in application systems follow a consistent pattern of control. Change management should be subject to structured assurance validation processes."

    c.   If "systems development is outsourced, the outsourcer or provider contracts should require similar controls. Project management techniques and controls should be part of the development process—whether developments are performed in-house or are outsourced. Management should know whether projects are on time and within budget and that resources are used efficiently. Reporting processes should ensure that management understands the current status of development projects and does not receive any surprises when the end product is delivered."

6.   **Design of Performance Measurement Systems**

    a.   As an assurance engagement, internal auditors conduct performance audits to measure how well an organization is achieving its targets for its key performance indicators. As a consulting engagement, internal auditors work with clients to improve the performance measured by the key performance indicators.

Stop and review! You have completed the outline for this subunit. Study multiple-choice questions 21 through 25 beginning on page 97.

QUESTIONS

3.1 Environmental Auditing

1. In any organization-wide risk management assessment, the CAE should include risks associated with which of the following activities?

   A. Environmental.

   B. Health.

   C. Safety.

   D. All of the answers are correct.

Answer (D) is correct.
   REQUIRED: The risks assessed by the CAE that should be included in any organization-wide risk assessment.
   DISCUSSION: The CAE includes environmental, health, and safety (EHS) risks in any organization-wide risk management assessment and assesses the activities in a balanced manner relative to other types of risk associated with an organization's operations.

2. An organization is considering purchasing a commercial property. Because of the location of the property and the known recent history of activities on the property, management has asked the internal audit activity, in cooperation with legal counsel, to provide a preliminary identification of any environmental liability. The strongest reason supporting management's decision to request such an investigation is

   A. The potential for future liability may outweigh any advantages achieved by obtaining the property.

   B. Management will be able to pay a lower price for the property if environmental contamination can be identified.

   C. The current owner would be required by law to clean up all identified contamination before the sale is closed.

   D. Regulatory agencies require a purchaser to identify and disclose all actual and potential instances of contamination.

Answer (A) is correct.
   REQUIRED: The strongest reason for management to request the internal audit activity to investigate a land purchase for any environmental liability.
   DISCUSSION: The internal auditors should conduct a transactional audit prior to the acquisition of property. A current landowner may be held responsible for environmental contamination by previous owners. Thus, a buyer (or lender) can attempt to identify and quantify a problem, determine its extent, and estimate the potential liability and cost of cleanup. This information can then be reflected in the terms of the transaction.
   Answer (B) is incorrect. Although the price of contaminated property may be lower, management may want to avoid the potential liability altogether by not purchasing the property. Answer (C) is incorrect. The current owner may agree to clean up the site but may be under no legal obligation to do so. Answer (D) is incorrect. Purchasers are not required to disclose any instances of contamination, whether actual or potential.

3. Which of the following suggestions for the CAE related to EHS auditing is **false**?

   A. The CAE should foster a close working relationship with the chief environmental officer and coordinate activities with the plan for environmental auditing.

   B. At least once every three years, the CAE should schedule a quality assurance review of the environmental audit function if it is organizationally independent of the internal audit function.

   C. The CAE should evaluate the organizational placement and independence of the environmental audit function to ensure that significant matters resulting from serious risks to the enterprise are reported up the chain of command.

   D. The CAE should evaluate whether the environmental auditors, who are not part of the CAE's organization, are in compliance with recognized professional auditing standards and a recognized code of ethics.

Answer (B) is correct.
   REQUIRED: The CAE suggestion that is falsely stated.
   DISCUSSION: The CAE should foster a close working relationship with the chief environmental officer and coordinate activities with the plan for environmental auditing. If the environmental audit function reports to someone other than the CAE, the CAE should offer to review the audit plan and the performance of engagements. Periodically, the CAE schedules a quality assurance review of the environmental audit function if it is organizationally independent of the internal audit activity. The review determines whether the environmental risks are being adequately addressed. The CAE evaluates whether the environmental auditors, who are not part of the CAE's organization, conform with recognized professional auditing standards and a recognized code of ethics. The CAE evaluates the organizational placement and independence of the environmental audit function to ensure that significant matters resulting from serious risks to the organization are reported up the chain of command to the board.

4. Internal auditors are increasingly called on to perform audits related to an organization's environmental stewardship. Which of the following does **not** describe the objectives of a type of environmental audit?

    A. Determine whether environmental management systems are in place and operating properly to manage future environmental risks.

    B. Determine whether environmental issues are considered as part of economic decisions.

    C. Determine whether the organization's current actions are in compliance with existing laws.

    D. Determine whether the organization is focusing efforts on ensuring that its products are environmentally friendly, and confirm that product and chemical restrictions are met.

Answer (B) is correct.
    REQUIRED: The item that does not describe the objectives of an environmental audit.
    DISCUSSION: Determining whether environmental issues are considered as part of economic decisions is an audit procedure. It does not describe the objectives of an environmental audit.
    Answer (A) is incorrect. An environmental management system audit determines whether environmental management systems are in place and operating properly to manage future environmental risks. Answer (C) is incorrect. A compliance audit determines whether the organization's current actions are in compliance with existing laws. Answer (D) is incorrect. A product audit determines whether the organization focuses efforts on ensuring that its products are environmentally friendly and confirms that product and chemical restrictions are met.

5. What type of audit assesses the environmental risks and liabilities of land or facilities prior to a property transaction?

    A. Pollution prevention audit.

    B. Compliance audit.

    C. Transactional audit.

    D. Product audit.

Answer (C) is correct.
    REQUIRED: The type of audit used prior to property transactions.
    DISCUSSION: Transactional audits (also called acquisition and divestiture audits, property transfer site assessments, property transfer evaluations, and due diligence audit) assess the environmental risks and liabilities of land or facilities prior to a property transaction.
    Answer (A) is incorrect. A pollution prevention audit determines how waste can be minimized and pollution can be eliminated at the source. Answer (B) is incorrect. A compliance audit is most common for industries. They are detailed site-specific audits of current operations. Answer (D) is incorrect. A product audit determines whether products are environmentally friendly and whether product and chemical restrictions are being met.

6. Smith Ice Plant (SIP) is located on the Mississippi River. SIP has a history of leaking pollutants into the Mississippi. Among the following environmental risk exposures, which one does SIP **not** have to evaluate as part of its organization-wide environmental risk management assessment?

    A. History of financial distress.

    B. Likelihood of water pollution fines.

    C. History of employee injuries.

    D. Likelihood of loss of public reputation.

Answer (A) is correct.
    REQUIRED: The environmental risk exposures that need to be evaluated during an organization-wide assessment.
    DISCUSSION: As part of an environmental risk assessment, the CAE evaluates the following risk exposures: (1) organizational reporting structures; (2) likelihood of environmental harm, fines, and penalties; (3) expenditures mandated by governmental agencies; (4) history of injuries and deaths; (5) history of losing customers; and (6) episodes of negative publicity and loss of public image and reputation. The history of financial distress is not included in the list of environmental risk exposures.
    Answer (B) is incorrect. The likelihood of environmental harm, fines, and penalties is included in the list of environmental risk exposures to be evaluated. Answer (C) is incorrect. The history of deaths and injuries is included in the list of environmental risk exposures to be evaluated. Answer (D) is incorrect. Episodes of negative publicity and loss of public image and reputation are included in the list of environmental risk exposures to be evaluated.

7. Which of the following is true about the interaction of the internal audit function and the environmental audit function?

A. If the environmental audit function reports to someone other than the CAE, the CAE should not offer to review the audit plan since (s)he was not consulted to do so.

B. It is not advantageous for the internal audit function to conduct environmental audits since it is too busy with its current responsibilities.

C. The CAE should evaluate whether the environmental auditors are conforming to recognized professional auditing standards and a recognized code of ethics.

D. The CAE should not evaluate the organizational placement and independence of the environmental audit function since the internal function has no control over a separate environmental audit function.

Answer (C) is correct.
    REQUIRED: The role of the CAE in the environmental audit function.
    DISCUSSION: This is a proper interaction between the environmental audit function and the internal audit function.
    Answer (A) is incorrect. When the environmental audit function reports to someone other than the CAE, the CAE offers to review the audit plan and the performance of engagements. Answer (B) is incorrect. The internal audit activity has an established place in the organization and normally has a broad scope of work permitting ready assimilation of the new function. Thus, it is advantageous to conduct environmental audits under the direction of the internal audit activity because of its position within the organization. Answer (D) is incorrect. The CAE evaluates the organizational placement and independence of the environmental audit function to ensure that matters resulting from serious risks to the organization are reported up the chain of command to the board.

3.2 Financial Engagements

8. An engagement objective is to determine if a company's accounts payable contain all outstanding liabilities. Which of the following audit procedures would **not** be relevant for this objective?

A. Examine supporting documentation of subsequent (after-period) cash disbursements and verify period of liability.

B. Send confirmations, including zero-balance accounts, to vendors with whom the company normally does business.

C. Select a sample of accounts payable from the accounts payable listing and verify the supporting receiving reports, purchase orders, and invoices.

D. Trace receiving reports issued before the period end to the related vendor invoices and accounts payable listing.

Answer (C) is correct
    REQUIRED: The audit procedure not relevant to testing the completeness assertion for accounts payable.
    DISCUSSION: The assertion being tested here is completeness: Are all legitimate liabilities recorded as such? Thus, the auditor's procedures must address whether all accounts payable that should have been recorded were recorded. Vouching a sample of payables, which by definition have already been recorded, to supporting documentation will not accomplish this.
    Answer (A) is incorrect. This procedure identifies payments for liabilities not included in the prior period but paid in the subsequent period. Answer (B) is incorrect. This procedure identifies amounts not included in accounts payable. Zero-balance accounts should be verified as part of the process. Answer (D) is incorrect. Tracing receiving reports from before the end of the period to invoices and the payables listing ensures that liabilities for these shipments are included in accounts payable.

9. Which of the following engagement procedures provides the best information about the collectibility of notes receivable?

A. Confirmation of note receivable balances with the debtors.

B. Examination of notes for appropriate debtors' signatures.

C. Reconciliation of the detail of notes receivable and the provision for uncollectible amounts to the general ledger control.

D. Examination of cash receipts records to determine promptness of interest and principal payments.

Answer (D) is correct.
    REQUIRED: The engagement procedure that provides the best information about the collectibility of notes receivable.
    DISCUSSION: The best information about the collectibility (valuation) of notes receivable lies in actual cash collections. Nonpayment or late payment may bear unfavorably on the possibility of collection. An internal auditor also normally sends positive confirmations to the makers and holders and inspects the notes to verify maturity dates and other terms.
    Answer (A) is incorrect. Confirmation establishes existence, not collectibility. Answer (B) is incorrect. Inspection helps verify the validity (not collectibility) of the notes. Answer (C) is incorrect. Reconciliation merely tests bookkeeping procedures.

10. Shipments are made from the warehouse based on customer purchase orders. The matched shipping documents and purchase orders are then forwarded to the billing department for sales invoice preparation. The shipping documents are neither accounted for nor prenumbered. Which of the following substantive tests should be extended as a result of this control weakness?

   A. Select sales invoices from the sales register and examine the related shipping documents.

   B. Select bills of lading from the warehouse and trace the shipments to the related sales invoices.

   C. Foot the sales register and trace the total to the general ledger.

   D. Trace quantities and prices on the sales invoice to the customer purchase order and test extensions and footings.

Answer (B) is correct.
   REQUIRED: The substantive test extended when shipping documents are neither accounted for nor prenumbered.
   DISCUSSION: When shipping documents are neither accounted for nor prenumbered, unrecorded sales are likely to result. Selecting bills of lading and tracing them to sales invoices will test that goods shipped were billed.

11. An engagement to review payroll is **least** likely to include

   A. Tests of computations for gross and net wages.

   B. Comparison of payroll costs to budget.

   C. Tracing a sample of employee names to employment records in the personnel department.

   D. Observing the physical distribution of paychecks.

Answer (D) is correct.
   REQUIRED: The least likely procedure in a review of payroll.
   DISCUSSION: Most organizations large enough to have an internal audit activity do not physically distribute paychecks on a regular basis. Moreover, observing the physical distribution of paychecks is usually regarded as an extended procedure most applicable to fraud engagements.
   Answer (A) is incorrect. Tests of computations for gross and net wages are standard. Answer (B) is incorrect. Comparison of payroll costs to budget is standard. Answer (C) is incorrect. Tracing a sample of employees to personnel records is standard.

12. An internal auditor fails to discover an employee fraud during an assurance engagement. The nondiscovery is most likely to suggest a violation of the International Professional Practices Framework if it was the result of a

   A. Failure to perform a detailed review of all transactions in the area.

   B. Determination that any possible fraud in the area would not involve a material amount.

   C. Determination that the cost of extending procedures in the area would exceed the potential benefits.

   D. Presumption that the internal controls in the area were adequate and effective.

Answer (D) is correct.
   REQUIRED: The most likely reason that failure to detect fraud is a violation of the *Standards*.
   DISCUSSION: The internal audit activity evaluates the adequacy and effectiveness of controls (Impl. Std. 2130.A1). Moreover, the internal audit activity must assist the organization in maintaining effective controls by evaluating their effectiveness and efficiency and by promoting continuous improvement (Perf. Std. 2130). Thus, an internal auditor must not simply assume that controls are adequate and effective.
   Answer (A) is incorrect. Due professional care does not require detailed reviews of all transactions. Answer (B) is incorrect. The relative complexity, materiality, or significance of matters to which assurance procedures are applied should be considered. Answer (C) is incorrect. The internal auditor should consider the cost of assurance in relation to potential benefits.

13. Controls should be designed to ensure that

A. Operations are performed efficiently.

B. Management's plans have not been circumvented by worker collusion.

C. The internal audit activity's guidance and oversight of management's performance is accomplished economically and efficiently.

D. Management's planning, organizing, and directing processes are properly evaluated.

Answer (A) is correct.
REQUIRED: The purpose of controls.
DISCUSSION: The purpose of control processes is to support the organization in the management of risks and the achievement of its established and communicated objectives. The control processes are expected to ensure, among other things, that operations are performed efficiently and achieve established results (PA 2130-1, para. 1).

Answer (B) is incorrect. Collusion is an inherent limitation of internal control. Answer (C) is incorrect. The board provides oversight of risk management and control processes administered by management. Answer (D) is incorrect. Controls are actions by management, the board, and others to manage risk and increase the likelihood that established goals and objectives will be achieved (The IIA Glossary). The internal audit activity evaluates the effectiveness of control processes. Thus, controls do not directly address management's planning, organizing, and directing processes. Internal auditors evaluate management processes to determine whether reasonable assurance exists that objectives and goals will be achieved.

14. The chief audit executive's responsibility for assessing and reporting on control processes includes

A. Communicating to senior management and the board an annual judgment about internal control

B. Overseeing the establishment of internal control processes.

C. Maintaining the organization's governance processes.

D. Arriving at a single assessment based solely on the work of the internal audit activity.

Answer (A) is correct.
REQUIRED: The chief audit executive's responsibility for assessing and reporting on control processes.
DISCUSSION: The CAE's report on the organization's control processes is normally presented once a year to senior management and the board (PA 2130-1, para. 11).

Answer (B) is incorrect. Senior management is responsible for overseeing the establishment of internal control processes. Answer (C) is incorrect. The board is responsible for establishing and maintaining the organization's governance processes. Answer (D) is incorrect. The challenge for the internal audit activity is to evaluate the effectiveness of the organization's system of controls based on the aggregation of many individual assessments. Those assessments are largely gained from internal auditing engagements, management's self assessments, and external assurance providers' work.

15. What should the CAE do if the scope of the internal audit plan is insufficient to permit expression of an opinion about risk management and control?

A. Design more procedures to ensure the audit plan becomes sufficient.

B. The CAE should inform senior management and the board about gaps in audit coverage.

C. Make the decision to outsource the internal audit function so the scope of the audit plan can be sufficient.

D. Hire more internal auditors to increase the scope of the engagement.

Answer (B) is correct.
REQUIRED: The action the CAE should take if the internal audit plan is insufficient.
DISCUSSION: In the event that the audit plan is insufficient, the CAE should inform senior management and the board about gaps in audit coverage.

Answer (A) is incorrect. In the event that the audit plan is insufficient, the CAE should inform senior management and the board. Answer (C) is incorrect. In the event that the audit plan is insufficient, the CAE should inform senior management and the board. Also, the CAE does not have the authority to make this type of decision. Answer (D) is incorrect. In the event that the audit plan is insufficient, the CAE should inform senior management and the board. Also, the CAE does not have the authority to make this type of decision.

3.3 Consulting Engagements -- Overview

16. Internal auditors may provide consulting services that add value and improve an organization's operations. The performance of these services

    A. Impairs internal auditors' objectivity with respect to an assurance service involving the same engagement client.

    B. Precludes generation of assurance from a consulting engagement.

    C. Should be consistent with the internal audit activity's empowerment reflected in the charter.

    D. Imposes no responsibility to communicate information other than to the engagement client.

Answer (C) is correct.
    REQUIRED: The internal auditors' responsibility regarding consulting services.
    DISCUSSION: According to Impl. Std. 1000.C1, the nature of consulting services must be defined in the charter.
    Answer (A) is incorrect. Consulting services do not necessarily impair objectivity. Decisions to implement recommendations made as a result of a consulting service are made by management. Thus, decision making by management does not impair the internal auditors' objectivity. Answer (B) is incorrect. Assurance and consulting services are not mutually exclusive. One type of service may be generated from the other. Answer (D) is incorrect. A primary internal audit value is to provide assurance to senior management and audit committee directors. Consulting engagements cannot be rendered in a manner that masks information that in the judgment of the chief audit executive (CAE) should be presented to senior executives and board members.

17. Which of the following statements is **false**?

    A. A disciplined, systematic evaluation methodology is incorporated in each internal audit activity. The list of services can generally be incorporated into two broad categories of assurance and consulting.

    B. Assurance and consulting are mutually exclusive and do preclude other auditing services such as investigations and nonauditing roles.

    C. Many audit services will have both an assurance and consultative role.

    D. Internal audit consulting enriches value-adding internal auditing.

Answer (B) is correct.
    REQUIRED: The false statement regarding consulting and assurance services.
    DISCUSSION: Certain principles guide the performance of consulting activities of internal auditors. For example, assurance and consulting are not mutually exclusive and do not preclude other auditing services such as investigations and nonauditing roles.

18. Who is responsible for determining the methodology to use for classifying engagements within the organization?

    A. The chief audit executive.

    B. Management.

    C. The board.

    D. The audit committee.

Answer (A) is correct.
    REQUIRED: The person/group responsible for determining the methodology to use for classifying engagements within the organization.
    DISCUSSION: The chief audit executive determines the methodology to use for classifying engagements within the organization. In some circumstances, it may be appropriate to conduct a blended engagement that incorporates elements of both consulting and assurance activities into one consolidated approach. In other cases, it may be appropriate to distinguish between the assurance and consulting components of the engagement.

19. An internal auditor performed a formal consulting engagement for XYZ Corporation on June 1, Year 1. When is the earliest time the auditor can perform assurance services for XYZ Corporation and be considered independent and objective?

    A. January 1, Year 2.

    B. June 1, Year 2.

    C. July 1, Year 1.

    D. June 2, Year 1.

Answer (B) is correct.
    REQUIRED: The earliest date the internal auditor can perform assurance services and be considered independent and objective.
    DISCUSSION: Independence and objectivity may be impaired if assurance services are provided within 1 year after a formal consulting engagement. Steps can be taken to minimize the effects of impairment by assigning different auditors to perform each of the services, establishing independent management and supervision, defining separate accountability for the results of the projects, and disclosing the presumed impairment.

20. Internal auditors should design the scope of work in a consulting engagement to ensure that all of the following will be maintained **except**

    A. Independence.

    B. Integrity.

    C. Credibility.

    D. Professionalism.

Answer (A) is correct.
    REQUIRED: The attribute of the internal audit activity that need not be maintained in a consulting engagement.
    DISCUSSION: Internal auditors need to reach an understanding of the objectives and scope of the consulting engagement with those receiving the service. During a consulting engagement, the internal auditor is acting as an advocate for management, and independence is not required.

3.4 Consulting Engagements -- Specific Types

21. Reengineering is the thorough analysis, fundamental rethinking, and complete redesign of essential business processes. The intended result is a dramatic improvement in service, quality, speed, and cost. An internal auditor's involvement in reengineering should include all of the following **except**

    A. Determining whether the process has senior management's support.

    B. Recommending areas for consideration.

    C. Developing audit plans for the new system.

    D. Directing the implementation of the redesigned process.

Answer (D) is correct.
    REQUIRED: The item not included in an internal auditor's involvement in reengineering.
    DISCUSSION: Internal auditors should not become directly involved in the implementation of the redesign process. This involvement would impair their independence and objectivity. Staff assignments of internal auditors should be rotated periodically whenever it is practicable to do so.

22. Monitoring is an important component of internal control. Which of the following items would **not** be an example of monitoring?

    A. Management regularly compares divisional performance with budgets for the division.

    B. Data processing management regularly generates exception reports for unusual transactions or volumes of transactions and follows up with investigation as to causes.

    C. Data processing management regularly reconciles batch control totals for items processed with batch controls for items submitted.

    D. Management has asked internal auditing to perform regular audits of the controls over cash processing.

Answer (C) is correct.
    REQUIRED: The item not an example of monitoring.
    DISCUSSION: Monitoring assesses the quality of internal control over time. Management considers whether internal control is properly designed and operating as intended and modifies it to reflect changing conditions. Reconciling batch control totals is a processing control over a single instance of accounting activity.
    Answer (A) is incorrect. Budgetary comparison is a typical example of a monitoring control. Answer (B) is incorrect. Investigation of exceptions is a monitoring control used by lower-level management to determine when their operations may be out of control. Answer (D) is incorrect. Internal auditing is a form of monitoring. It serves to evaluate management's other controls.

23. What is the first phase in the benchmarking process?

    A. Organize benchmarking teams.

    B. Select and prioritize benchmarking projects.

    C. Researching and identifying best-in-class performance.

    D. Data analysis.

Answer (B) is correct.
    REQUIRED: The first phase in the benchmarking process.
    DISCUSSION: The first phase in the benchmarking process is to select and prioritize benchmarking projects. The next phase is to organize benchmarking teams. Researching and identifying best-in-class is the third phase in the benchmarking process. The fourth phase is data analysis, and the final phase is the implementation phase.
    Answer (A) is incorrect. Organizing benchmarking teams is a subsequent phase. Answer (C) is incorrect. Researching and identifying best-in-class performance is a subsequent phase. Answer (D) is incorrect. Data analysis is a subsequent phase.

24. Which of the following statements regarding benchmarking is **false**?

A. Benchmarking involves continuously evaluating the practices of best-in-class organizations and adapting company processes to incorporate the best of these practices.

B. Benchmarking, in practice, usually involves a company's formation of benchmarking teams.

C. Benchmarking is an ongoing process that entails quantitative and qualitative measurement of the difference between the company's performance of an activity and the performance by the best in the world or the best in the industry.

D. The benchmarking organization against which a firm is comparing itself must be a direct competitor.

Answer (D) is correct.
　REQUIRED: The false statement about benchmarking.
　DISCUSSION: Benchmarking is an ongoing process that entails quantitative and qualitative measurement of the difference between the company's performance of an activity and the performance by a best-in-class organization. The benchmarking organization against which a firm is comparing itself need not be a direct competitor. The important consideration is that the benchmarking organization be an outstanding performer in its industry.

25. Which of the following is an example of business process reengineering?

A. Adding a new machine to the existing production line to speed up production.

B. Redesigning the production line to speed up production.

C. Repairing a machine on the process line to speed up production.

D. Updating the computer systems involved on the production line to speed up production.

Answer (B) is correct.
　REQUIRED: The example of business process reengineering.
　DISCUSSION: One approach to business process mapping is reengineering. It involves process innovation and core process redesign. Instead of improving existing procedures, it finds new ways of doing things. Redesigning the production line is an example of this.
　Answer (A) is incorrect. One approach to business process mapping is reengineering. It involves process innovation and core process redesign. Instead of improving existing procedures, it finds new ways of doing things. Adding a new machine is an example of improving existing procedures. Answer (C) is incorrect. One approach to business process mapping is reengineering. It involves process innovation and core process redesign. Instead of improving existing procedures, it finds new ways of doing things. Repairing a machine is an example of improving existing procedures. Answer (D) is incorrect. One approach to business process mapping is reengineering. It involves process innovation and core process redesign. Instead of improving existing procedures, it finds new ways of doing things. Updating the computer systems is an example of improving existing procedures.

Practice even more exam-emulating questions in **Gleim CIA Test Prep!**

STUDY UNIT FOUR
ENGAGEMENT PLANNING

(13 pages of outline)

This study unit is the fourth of four covering **Section I: Managing the Internal Audit Function** from The IIA's CIA Exam Syllabus. This section makes up 40% to 50% of Part 2 of the CIA exam and is tested at the **proficiency level**. This study unit also covers parts of **Section II: Managing Individual Engagements.** The relevant portion of the syllabus is highlighted below. (The complete syllabus is in Appendix B.)

I. **MANAGING THE INTERNAL AUDIT FUNCTION (40%–50%)**

    A. **Strategic Role of Internal Audit**

    B. **Operational Role of IA**

    C. **Establish Risk-Based IA Plan**

       1. Use market, product, and industry knowledge to identify new internal audit engagement opportunities

       2. Use a risk framework to identify sources of potential engagements (e.g., audit universe, audit cycle requirements, management requests, regulatory mandates)

       3. Establish a framework for assessing risk

       4. Rank and validate risk priorities to prioritize engagements in the audit plan

       5. Identify internal audit resource requirements for annual IA plan

       6. Communicate areas of significant risk and obtain approval from the board for the annual engagement plan

       7. Types of engagements

II. **MANAGING INDIVIDUAL ENGAGEMENTS (40%–50%)**

    A. **Plan Engagements**

       1. Establish engagement objectives/criteria and finalize the scope of the engagement

       2. Plan engagement to assure identification of key risks and controls

       3. Complete a detailed risk assessment of each audit area (prioritize or evaluate risk/control factors)

       5. Determine the level of staff and resources needed for the engagement

       6. Construct audit staff schedule for effective use of time

    B. **Supervise Engagement**

    C. **Communicate Engagement Results**

    D. **Monitor Engagement Outcomes**

4.1 ENGAGEMENT OBJECTIVES, SCOPE, AND CRITERIA

    1. **Engagements**

        a. An **engagement** is a "specific internal audit assignment, task, or review activity, such as an internal audit, control self-assessment review, fraud examination, or consultancy. An engagement may include multiple tasks or activities designed to accomplish a specific set of related objectives" (The IIA Glossary). An engagement consists of planning, performing procedures, communicating results, and monitoring progress. The internal auditor's responsibility is to plan and perform the engagement, subject to review and approval by supervisors. This study unit concerns the planning phase of the engagement.

Performance Standard 2200
Engagement Planning

Internal auditors must develop and document a plan for each engagement, including the engagement's objectives, scope, timing, and resource allocations.

---

2. **Engagement Objectives**

   a. After the preliminary survey and preliminary risk assessment are complete, the internal auditor sets objectives for the engagement. The objectives should explain why this activity is being audited and should be clear about which assurances the audit will provide.

Performance Standard 2210
Engagement Objectives

Objectives must be established for each engagement.

---

   b. Engagement objectives are "broad statements developed by internal auditors that define intended engagement accomplishments" (The IIA Glossary).

   c. Relevant guidance is in Practice Advisory 2210-1, *Engagement Objectives*:

   1) Internal auditors establish objectives to address the risks associated with the activity under review.

      a) For planned engagements, the objectives should be consistent with those initially identified during the risk assessment process from which the internal audit plan is derived.

      b) For unplanned engagements, the objectives are established prior to the start of the engagement. They are designed to address the specific risk that prompted the engagement.

   2) The risk assessment during the planning phase is used to further define the initial objectives and identify other significant areas of concern.

   3) After identifying the risks, the auditor determines the procedures to be performed and the scope (nature, timing, and extent) of those procedures. Procedures performed within the appropriate scope are the means to derive conclusions related to the objectives.

Implementation Standard 2210.A2

Internal auditors must consider the probability of significant errors, fraud, noncompliance, and other exposures when developing the engagement objectives.

---

3. **Engagement Scope**

Performance Standard 2220
Engagement Scope

The established scope must be sufficient to achieve the objectives of the engagement.

Implementation Standard 2220.A1

The scope of the engagement must include consideration of relevant systems, records, personnel, and physical properties, including those under the control of third parties.

4. **Criteria**

    a. Criteria are needed to measure the effectiveness of internal control. Management and internal audit also have different responsibilities regarding this process.

Implementation Standard 2210.A3

Adequate criteria are needed to evaluate governance, risk management, and controls. Internal auditors must ascertain the extent to which management and/or the board has established adequate criteria to determine whether objectives and goals have been accomplished. If adequate, internal auditors must use such criteria in their evaluation. If inadequate, internal auditors must work with management and/or the board to develop appropriate evaluation criteria.

---

        1) Acceptable industry standards, standards developed by professions or associations, standards in law and government regulations, and other sound business practices are usually deemed to be appropriate criteria.

Stop and review! You have completed the outline for this subunit. Study multiple-choice questions 1 through 4 beginning on page 111.

4.2 PLANNING AND RISK ASSESSMENT

Performance Standard 2201
Planning Considerations

In planning the engagement, internal auditors must consider:

- The objectives of the activity being reviewed and the means by which the activity controls its performance;
- The significant risks to the activity, its objectives, resources, and operations and the means by which the potential impact of risk is kept to an acceptable level;
- The adequacy and effectiveness of the activity's governance, risk management, and control processes compared to a relevant framework or model; and
- The opportunities for making significant improvements to the activity's governance, risk management, and control processes.

---

1. **Engagement Planning**

    a. Relevant guidance is in Practice Advisory 2200-1, *Engagement Planning*:

        1) The formality and documentation of planning (e.g., of planning meetings, risk assessments, and detail in the work program) should be appropriate to the organization. The following are factors to consider:

            a) Whether the work or its results will be relied upon by others (e.g., in litigation)

            b) The size of the internal audit activity, experience of the auditors, and direct supervision required

            c) Whether staffing is internal, by guest auditors, or by external service providers

            d) The project's complexity and scope

            e) The value of documentation (e.g., whether it will be used in subsequent years)

        2) Other requirements to be determined are the period covered, completion dates, and the communication format.

        3) Managers are informed on a need-to-know basis.

4) Meetings are held with managers responsible for the audited activity, and summaries of discussions and conclusions are distributed and documented. Topics of discussion may include

a) Engagement objectives and scope,

b) Resources,

c) Timing of work,

d) Key factors (including the external environment) affecting business conditions and operations, and

e) Management concerns or requests.

5) The CAE determines how, when, and to whom results are communicated. If appropriate, these documented determinations are communicated to management during planning.

a) Subsequent changes that affect the timing or reporting of engagement results also are communicated.

2. **Identify Key Risks and Controls**

a. During the planning of the engagement, internal auditors must identify key business risks and controls, especially the client's inherent risks. This risk assessment should include both the impact (effect) of the risk and its likelihood.

1) The controls that are most critical to reducing business risks to acceptably low levels must be identified.

3. **Risk**

a. Risk is the possibility that an event will occur having an impact on the achievement of objectives. It is measured in terms of impact and likelihood (The IIA Glossary).

Implementation Standard 2210.A1

Internal auditors must conduct a preliminary assessment of the risks relevant to the activity under review. Engagement objectives must reflect the results of this assessment.

---

4. **Risk Assessment**

a. After completing the preliminary survey, the internal auditor performs a preliminary risk assessment.

b. Relevant guidance is in Practice Advisory 2210.A1-1, *Risk Assessment in Engagement Planning*:

1) Internal auditors consider

a) Management's **assessment of risks**.

b) Its reliability;

c) The process for addressing risk and control matters;

d) The reporting about, and the responses to, events exceeding the **risk appetite**; and

e) Risks in related activities.

2) Internal auditors obtain **background** information about the activities reviewed to determine their effect on the objectives and scope.

3) A **survey** is usually performed to

a) Become familiar with the client's activities, risks, and controls;

b) Identify areas of emphasis; and

c) Invite comments from the client.

4)   A **summary** of results is prepared that includes

- a)   Significant issues;
- b)   Objectives and procedures;
- c)   Critical control points, deficiencies, or excess controls;
- d)   Methods, such as those that are technology-based; and
- e)   Reasons for modifying objectives or not continuing the engagement.

Stop and review! You have completed the outline for this subunit. Study multiple-choice questions 5 through 11 beginning on page 112.

4.3 RISK-BASED AUDIT PLAN

1.   **Determining Priorities Based on the Risk Assessment**

a.   The large, complex, interconnected organizations in the modern economy require sophisticated assessment of many diverse risks. Thus, the work plan of any internal audit activity must reflect the organization's assessment of these risks.

1)   The knowledge, skills, and other competencies of the internal auditors affect what engagements can be performed without using external service providers.

2)   However, the knowledge, skills, and other competencies of the internal auditors do not affect the risk assessment.

b.   The audit plan must be logically related to identified risks of the organization. These are in turn related to its strategic and operational goals. Making this connection between identified risks and how they relate to strategic and operational goals is the primary advantage of risk-based audit planning. This requirement is codified in the following standard:

Performance Standard 2010
Planning

The chief audit executive must establish a risk-based plan to determine the priorities of the internal audit activity, consistent with the organization's goals.

---

1)   The importance of basing the audit work plan on a systematic assessment of risk is emphasized in the following Interpretation and Implementation Standards:

Interpretation of Standard 2010

The chief audit executive is responsible for developing a risk-based plan. The chief audit executive takes into account the organization's risk management framework, including using risk appetite levels set by management for the different activities or parts of the organization. If a framework does not exist, the chief audit executive uses his/her own judgment of risks after consideration of input from senior management and the board. The chief audit executive must review and adjust the plan, as necessary, in response to changes in the organization's business, risks, operations, programs, systems, and controls.

Implementation Standard 2010.A1

The internal audit activity's plan of engagements must be based on a documented risk assessment, undertaken at least annually. The input of senior management and the board must be considered in this process.

c.   Planning also involves considering what services stakeholders want.

Implementation Standard 2010.A2

The chief audit executive must identify and consider the expectations of senior management, the board, and other stakeholders for internal audit opinions and other conclusions.

---

d.   Planning for consulting services involves considering what benefits these engagements may offer.

Implementation Standard 2010.C1

The chief audit executive should consider accepting proposed consulting engagements based on the engagement's potential to improve management of risks, add value, and improve the organization's operations. Accepted engagements must be included in the plan.

---

2.   **Specific Guidance**

a.   Practice Advisory 2010-1, *Linking the Audit Plan to Risk and Exposures*, provides specific guidance regarding planning and risk.

1)   Developing the internal audit activity's audit plan often follows developing or updating the audit universe.

a)   The **audit universe** (all possible audits) may include the organization's strategic plan. Thus, it may reflect

i)   Overall business objectives,
ii)   The attitude toward risk,
iii)   The difficulty of reaching objectives,
iv)   The results of risk management, and
v)   The operating environment.

b)   The audit universe should be assessed **at least annually** to reflect the most current strategies and direction of the organization.

i)   But more frequent updating of audit plans may be needed to respond to changes in circumstances.

NOTE: The audit universe includes all units, processes, or operations that can be evaluated and defined. They include accounts, divisions, functions, procedures, products, systems, and many other possibilities. Thus, the audit plan includes audits requested by management or required by regulators, e.g., as a condition of receiving government contracts. Moreover, many entity operations or functions are audited cyclically. Accordingly, the priority of an audit may depend on how recently a specific operation or function has been audited.

2)   The internal audit activity's **audit plan** is based on

a)   The audit universe,
b)   Input from senior management and the board, and
c)   Assessed risk and exposures.

3)   Key audit objectives are to provide assurance and information to senior management and the board.

a)   Assurance includes an assessment of **risk management activities.**

4) **Work schedules** are based on an assessment of risk priority and exposure.

    a) Most **risk models** used to prioritize engagements are based on risk factors, e.g., quality of and adherence to controls, degree of change, timing and results of last engagement, impact, likelihood, materiality, asset liquidity, management competence, complexity, and employee and government relations.

NOTE: An unexpected, significant change in an account that cannot be explained raises the assessed risk for that account.

b. Practice Advisory 2010-2, *Using the Risk Management Process in Internal Audit Planning*, provides specific guidance regarding planning and risk management.

    1) **Risk management (RM)** is critical to sound governance of all organizational activities. Consistent RM should be fully integrated into management at all levels.

        a) Management typically uses a framework to conduct the assessment and document the results.

    2) Effective RM assists in identifying key controls related to significant inherent risks. **Enterprise risk management (ERM)** is a common term. It has been defined as a process, effected by the board, management, and others, applied in setting strategy across the entity. It identifies events that may affect the entity and manages risks within the risk appetite. Its ultimate purpose is to provide reasonable assurance of achieving entity objectives.

        a) Control is often used to manage risk within the risk appetite. Internal auditors audit key controls and provide assurance on the management of significant risks.

    3) Inherent risk and residual risk (also known as current risk) are basic concepts.

        a) Financial (external) auditors define **inherent risk** as the susceptibility of information or data to a material misstatement given no related mitigating controls.

        b) Current risk is the risk managed within existing controls or control systems.

    4) Key controls reduce an otherwise unacceptable risk to a tolerable level. Controls are processes that address risks.

        a) Effective RM identifies key controls based on the difference between inherent and residual risk across all affected systems. Key controls are relied upon to reduce the rating of significant risks.

        b) When identifying key controls (and if RM is mature and reliable), the internal auditor looks for

            i) Individual risk factors when the reduction from inherent to residual risk is significant (particularly if inherent risk was very high).

            ii) Controls that mitigate a large number of risks.

    5) Audit planning uses the organizational RM process if one exists. The internal auditor considers the significant risks of the activity and the means by which management mitigates the risks.

        a) Risk assessment methods are used to develop the audit plan and to determine priorities for allocating audit resources.

        b) Risk assessment examines auditable units and selects areas for review that have the greatest risk exposure.

      6)   The following factors affect the internal audit plan:

          a)   Inherent and residual risks should be identified and assessed.

          b)   Mitigating controls, contingency plans, and monitoring activities should be linked to events or risks.

          c)   Risk registers should be systematic, complete, and accurate.

              i)   A **risk register** (risk log) is used to identify and analyze risks. The register describes each risk, its impact and likelihood, and the risk score (impact × likelihood). The register also records planned responses if the event occurs, preventive measures, and a risk ranking.

          d)   Risks and activities should be documented.

      7)   The internal auditor also coordinates with other assurance providers and considers planned reliance on their work.

      8)   The internal audit activity needs to identify high inherent and residual risks and key control systems, and management needs to be notified about unacceptable residual risk.

          a)   Strategic audit planning identifies the following activities to include in the plan:

              i)   Control reviews to provide assurance

              ii)   Inquiry activities to gain a better understanding of the residual risk

              iii)   Consulting activities to give advice on controls to mitigate unacceptable risks

          b)   Internal auditors also identify controls with costs exceeding benefits.

      9)   Risk registers may document risks below the strategic level. They address (a) significant risks, (b) inherent and residual risk ratings, (c) key controls, and (d) mitigating factors.

          a)   The auditors then can identify more direct links between

              i)   Risk categories and aspects described in the risk registers and,
              ii)   If applicable, the items already in the audit universe.

     10)   Lower-risk audits need to be included in the audit plan to give them coverage and confirm that their risks have not changed.

          a)   Also, priorities should be set for outstanding risks not yet subject to audit.

     11)   An internal audit plan normally focuses on the following:

          a)   Unacceptable current risks requiring management action
          b)   Control systems on which the organization is most reliant
          c)   Areas where the difference between inherent risk and residual risk is great
          d)   Areas where inherent risk is very high

     12)   When planning individual audits, the internal auditor identifies and assesses risks relevant to the area under review.

3.   **AICPA Audit Risk Model**

   a.   **Overview**

      1)   Internal auditors must establish a framework for assessing risk.

      2)   The American Institute of Certified Public Accountants (AICPA) is the private sector body that establishes standards for external audits of financial statements in the United States.

     a) The following is the audit risk model used by the AICPA:

Audit risk = Risk of material misstatement × Detection risk

        i) The risk of material misstatement is the combined inherent risk and control risk.

   3) This model is used by an independent auditor engaged to report on whether financial statements are fairly presented, in all material respects, in accordance with the applicable financial reporting framework.

     a) The IIA does not officially define audit risk or its components. However, internal auditors can adapt the model to other audit and assurance engagements.

b. **Audit Risk and Its Components**

   1) **Audit risk** is "the risk that the auditor expresses an inappropriate audit opinion when the financial statements are materially misstated."

     a) In an internal audit context, audit risk is the risk that the auditor will provide senior management and the board with flawed or incomplete information about governance, risk management, and control.

   2) **Inherent risk** is "the susceptibility of an assertion . . . to a misstatement that could be material . . . before consideration of any related controls."

     a) In an internal audit context, inherent risk is the risk arising from the nature of the account or activity under review. For example, a uranium mine is inherently riskier than an accounts payable function.

   3) **Control risk** is "the risk that a misstatement that could occur In an assertion . . . and that could be material . . . will not be prevented, or detected and corrected, on a timely basis by the entity's internal control."

     a) In an internal audit context, control risk is the risk that the system of internal control designed and implemented by management will fail to achieve management's goals and objectives for the account or activity under review.

   4) **Detection risk** is "the risk that the procedures performed by the auditor to reduce audit risk to an acceptably low level will not detect a misstatement that exists and that could be material . . . ."

     a) In an internal audit context, detection risk is the risk that the auditor will fail to discover conditions relevant to the established audit objectives for the account or activity under review.

c. **Auditor Response to Assessed Risk**

   1) Of the three components, only detection risk is under the auditor's direct control.

   2) The internal auditor must first determine the levels of inherent and control risk for the account or activity under review. Detection risk is then adjusted to achieve an overall acceptable level of audit risk.

     a) If inherent risk, control risk, or both is(are) determined to be high, detection risk must be set at a low level to compensate, and the nature, timing, and extent of engagement procedures are changed.

   3) All three components may be assessed in quantitative (e.g., scale of 1 to 10, with 10 being maximum risk) or nonquantitative (e.g., high, medium, low) terms.

     a) For example, the auditor may determine during the preliminary survey that the account or activity under review has high inherent risk but that internal control is effective. The auditor then may assess detection risk at a moderate level.

4.   **Rank and Validate Risk Priorities**

    a.   Risk modeling is an effective method used to rank and validate risk priorities when prioritizing engagements in the audit plan.

    b.   **Risk** is the possibility that an event will occur having an impact on the achievement of objectives. Risk is measured in terms of impact and likelihood.

        1)   Risk factors may be weighted based on professional judgments to determine their relative significance, but the weights need not be quantified.

        2)   This simple model and the resulting risk assessment process can be depicted as follows:

EXAMPLE

A chief audit executive is reviewing the following enterprise-wide **risk map**:

I M P A C T		LIKELIHOOD		
		Remote	Possible	Likely
	Critical	Risk A	Risk C	Risk D
	Major		Risk B	
	Minor			

In establishing the appropriate priorities for the deployment of limited internal audit resources, the CAE undertakes the following analysis:

- Risk D clearly takes precedence over Risk C because D has a higher likelihood.
- Risk C also clearly has a higher priority than Risk A because C has a higher likelihood and the same impact.

Choosing the higher priority between Risk B and Risk A is a matter of professional judgment based on the organizational risk assessment and the stated priorities of senior management and the board.

- If the more likely threat is considered the greater risk, Risk B will rank higher in the internal audit work plan.
- Likewise, if the threat with the greater possible impact causes senior management and the board more concern, the internal audit activity will place a higher priority on Risk A.

---

    c.   Open channels of communication with senior management and the board are necessary to ensure the audit plan is based on the appropriate risk assessments and audit priorities. The audit plan should be reevaluated as needed.

    d.   Risk modeling in a consulting service can be accomplished by ranking the engagement's potential to improve management of risks, add value, and improve the organization's operations as identified in Implementation Standard 2010.C1. Senior management assigns different weights to each of these items based on organizational objectives. The engagements with the appropriate weighted value would be included in the annual audit plan.

Stop and review! You have completed the outline for this subunit. Study multiple-choice questions 12 through 16 beginning on page 114.

4.4 INTERNAL AUDIT RESOURCE REQUIREMENTS

Performance Standard 2030
Resource Management

The chief audit executive must ensure that internal audit resources are appropriate, sufficient, and effectively deployed to achieve the approved plan.

> ### Interpretation of Standard 2030
>
> Appropriate refers to the mix of knowledge, skills, and other competencies needed to perform the plan. Sufficient refers to the quantity of resources needed to accomplish the plan. Resources are effectively deployed when they are used in a way that optimizes the achievement of the approved plan.

1. **Managing Internal Audit Resources**

   a. Practice Advisory 2030-1, *Resource Management,* provides guidance.

      1) The CAE is primarily responsible for the sufficiency and management of resources, including communication of needs and status to senior management and the board. These parties ultimately must ensure the adequacy of resources.

         a) **Resources** may include employees, service providers, financial support, and IT-based audit methods.

         NOTE: To determine the sufficiency of resource allocation, the CAE must consider all relevant factors, including

         - Communications received from management and the board;
         - Information about ongoing and new engagements;
         - Consequences of not completing an engagement on time; and
         - Knowledge, skills, and competencies of the internal audit staff.

      2) The **skills, capabilities, and technical knowledge** of the internal audit staff should be appropriate for the planned activities. The CAE conducts a **periodic skills assessment** based on the needs identified in the risk assessment and audit plan.

         NOTE: A job description summarizes the duties and qualifications required for a job. Properly formulated job descriptions provide a basis for identifying job qualifications such as training and experience. They also facilitate recruiting the appropriate internal audit staff with the necessary attributes for the planned activities.

      3) Resources need to be sufficient for audit activities to be performed in accordance with the expectations of senior management and the board. **Resource planning** considers

         a) The audit universe,
         b) Relevant risk levels,
         c) The internal audit plan,
         d) Coverage expectations, and
         e) An estimate of unanticipated activities.

      4) Resources must be effectively **deployed** by assigning qualified auditors and developing an appropriate resourcing approach and organizational structure.

      5) The CAE considers succession planning, staff evaluation and development, and other human resource disciplines.

         a) The CAE also addresses **resourcing needs**, including whether those skills are present.

         b) Other ways to meet needs include external service providers, specialized consultants, or other employees of the organization.

      6) The CAE's ongoing communications with senior management and the board include periodic summaries of resource status and adequacy, e.g., the effect of temporary vacancies and comparison of resources with the audit plan.

    b.   When selecting the appropriate audit staff, the CAE must consider these factors:

        1)   Complexity of the engagement
        2)   Experience levels of the auditors
        3)   Training needs of the auditors
        4)   Available resources

2.   **Outsourcing the Internal Audit Activity**

    a.   An organization's governing body may decide that an external service provider is the most effective means of obtaining internal audit services.

        1)   In such cases, the following Performance Standard requires those performing internal audit services to remind the organization of where ultimate responsibility for maintaining an effective internal audit activity lies.

Performance Standard 2070
External Service Provider and Organizational Responsibility for Internal Auditing

When an external service provider serves as the internal audit activity, the provider must make the organization aware that the organization has the responsibility for maintaining an effective internal audit activity.

Stop and review! You have completed the outline for this subunit. Study multiple-choice questions 17 through 22 beginning on page 116.

4.5 STAFF AND RESOURCES

Performance Standard 2230
Engagement Resource Allocation

Internal auditors must determine appropriate and sufficient resources to achieve engagement objectives based on an evaluation of the nature and complexity of each engagement, time constraints, and available resources.

---

1.   **Resources at the Engagement Level**

    a.   This standard imposes a responsibility on **internal auditors**, not on the CAE. Standards that impose responsibilities on the CAE address management of the internal audit activity, organizational independence, and certain other matters.

    b.   Relevant guidance is in Practice Advisory 2230-1, *Engagement Resource Allocation*:

        1)   Engagement resource allocation is based on evaluation of

            a)   The number and experience of staff;
            b)   The knowledge, skills, and competencies of the staff;
            c)   Training needs; and
            d)   Whether external resources are required.

2.   **Audit Staff Schedules**

    a.   Audit staff schedules should be prepared to achieve effective use of time.

        1)   Audit teams are selected based on their knowledge, skills, and other competencies to meet engagement objectives efficiently and effectively. Any training opportunities also should be considered.

        2)   All engagements should be under budgetary control. Project budgets and schedules should be developed for each engagement.

            a)   Budgets are derived by carefully analyzing the time spent in the prior year on the same or a comparable engagement.

      b) Because no projects are precisely the same (even those covering the same activity), budgets are reevaluated after the preliminary survey.

         i) The CAE reduces excessive budgets, increases insufficient budgets, or changes the scope of the engagements.

         ii) Adjustments and the reasons for them are documented.

      c) Time budgets for engagements are usually prepared in employee-hours or employee-days. Time estimates are given to each internal auditor to help with time management.

   3) Budget adjustments need to be justified and approved at a level higher than the engagement supervisor. Requests for adjustment should include the following:

      a) The operational activities to be reviewed,
      b) The activities actually being performed, and
      c) The employee-days or hours attributable to the difference.

   4) Monitoring time budgets and schedules allows the CAE to control projects and avoid overruns.

      a) Staff auditors submit periodic time sheets that indicate time spent and the status of the job.

Stop and review! You have completed the outline for this subunit. Study multiple-choice questions 23 through 25 beginning on page 117.

QUESTIONS

4.1 Engagement Objectives, Scope, and Criteria

1. The established scope of the engagement must be sufficient to satisfy the objectives of the engagement. When developing the objectives of the engagement, the internal auditor considers the

  A. Probability of significant noncompliance.

  B. Information included in the engagement work program.

  C. Results of engagement procedures.

  D. Resources required.

Answer (A) is correct.
    REQUIRED: The factor the internal auditor considers when developing the objectives of the engagement.
    DISCUSSION: Internal auditors must consider the probability of significant errors, fraud, noncompliance, and other exposures when developing assurance engagement objectives (Impl. Std. 2210.A2).
    Answer (B) is incorrect. Engagement objectives must be determined before the engagement work program is written. Answer (C) is incorrect. The objectives determine the procedures to be performed. Answer (D) is incorrect. Internal auditors determine the resources required to achieve the engagement objectives.

2. Documentation required to plan an internal audit engagement includes information that

  A. Resources needed to complete the engagement were considered.

  B. Planned engagement work will be completed on a timely basis.

  C. Intended engagement observations have been clearly identified.

  D. Internal audit activity resources are efficiently and effectively employed.

Answer (A) is correct.
    REQUIRED: The information included in the documentation required to plan an engagement.
    DISCUSSION: Internal auditors must develop and document a plan for each engagement, including the engagement's objectives, scope, timing, and resource allocations (Perf. Std. 2200).
    Answer (B) is incorrect. Whether the planned work will actually be completed on time cannot be known in the planning phase. Answer (C) is incorrect. Observations are what is actually found by performing procedures. Auditors must not anticipate the results of the work. To do so indicates a lack of objectivity. Answer (D) is incorrect. Documenting the economic and efficient use of resources can be done only upon completion of the engagement.

3. In the planning phase, the scope of an internal audit engagement is defined by the

- A. Engagement objectives.
- B. Scheduling and time estimates.
- C. Preliminary survey.
- D. Engagement work program.

Answer (A) is correct.
REQUIRED: The factor initially defining the scope of an internal audit engagement.
DISCUSSION: The established scope must be sufficient to satisfy the objectives of the engagement (Perf. Std. 2220).
Answer (B) is incorrect. The scheduling and time estimates are based on the objectives and scope of the engagement. Answer (C) is incorrect. The preliminary survey must be completed and the engagement objectives set before the engagement scope can be established. Answer (D) is incorrect. The engagement work program is the last of the four steps listed.

4. Which of the following statements is an engagement objective?

- A. Observe the deposit of the day's cash receipts.
- B. Analyze the pattern of any cash shortages.
- C. Evaluate whether cash receipts are adequately safeguarded.
- D. Recompute each month's bank reconciliation.

Answer (C) is correct.
REQUIRED: The engagement objective.
DISCUSSION: Engagement objectives are broad statements developed by internal auditors that define intended engagement accomplishments (The IIA Glossary). Procedures are the means to reach conclusions related to the objectives. Evaluating whether cash receipts are adequately safeguarded is an objective because it states what the engagement is to accomplish.
Answer (A) is incorrect. Observation is a procedure. Answer (B) is incorrect. Analysis is a procedure. Answer (D) is incorrect. Recomputation is a procedure.

4.2 Planning and Risk Assessment

5. An external consultant is developing methods for the management of a city's capital facilities. An appropriate scope of an engagement to evaluate the consultant's product is to

- A. Review the consultant's contract to determine its propriety.
- B. Establish the parameters of the value of the items being managed and controlled.
- C. Determine the adequacy of the risk management and control systems for the management of capital facilities.
- D. Review the handling of idle equipment.

Answer (C) is correct.
REQUIRED: The appropriate scope of an engagement to evaluate a consultant's product.
DISCUSSION: "In planning the engagement, internal auditors must consider:

- The objectives of the activity being reviewed and the means by which the activity controls its performance;
- The significant risks to the activity, its objectives, resources, and operations and the means by which the potential impact of risk is kept to an acceptable level;
- The adequacy and effectiveness of the activity's governance, risk management, and control processes compared to a relevant framework or model; and
- The opportunities for making significant improvements to the activity's governance, risk management, and control processes" (Perf. Std. 2201).

Answer (A) is incorrect. The review of the consultant's contract to determine its propriety is related to the procurement decision. Answer (B) is incorrect. The establishment of parameters for values of items being managed and controlled is a management responsibility. Answer (D) is incorrect. Management must determine policies regarding idle equipment. Some equipment may be retained for emergency use.

6. Which of the following is **least** likely to be placed on the agenda for discussion at a pre-engagement meeting?

- A. Objectives and scope of the engagement.
- B. Client personnel needed.
- C. Sampling plan and key criteria.
- D. Expected starting and completion dates.

Answer (C) is correct.
REQUIRED: The item least likely to be discussed at a pre-engagement meeting.
DISCUSSION: Possible objectives and scope for the engagement, the client personnel to whom the auditors need access, and the expected start and completion dates for the engagement are all appropriate matters for discussion at a pre-engagement meeting. The sampling plan cannot be drafted until risk is assessed and the engagement objectives are set.

7. As part of planning an engagement, the internal auditor in charge does all of the following **except**

A. Determine the period covered.

B. Conduct meetings with management responsible for the activity under review.

C. Distribute reports from meetings with management.

D. Determine to whom engagement results will be communicated.

Answer (D) is correct.

REQUIRED: The part of planning an engagement not performed by the internal auditor.

DISCUSSION: The CAE determines how, when, and to whom engagement results will be communicated (PA 2200-1, para. 5).

Answer (A) is incorrect. The internal auditor determines engagement requirements not determined by the CAE. The internal auditor's determinations include the period covered, estimated completion dates, and the final engagement communication format. Answer (B) is incorrect. The internal auditor informs those in management who need to know about the engagement and conducts meetings with management responsible for the activity under review. Answer (C) is incorrect. The internal auditor conducts meetings with management responsible for the activity under review, summarizes and distributes the discussions and any conclusions reached from the meetings, and retains the documentation in the engagement working papers.

8. Internal auditors must make a preliminary assessment of risks when conducting an assurance engagement. This assessment may involve quantitative (objective) and subjective factors. The **least** subjective factor is

A. The organization's recognized losses on derivatives.

B. The auditor's assessment of management responses.

C. Changes in the auditee's business forecast.

D. The evaluation of internal control.

Answer (A) is correct.

REQUIRED: The least subjective risk factor.

DISCUSSION: In planning the engagement, internal auditors must consider the significant risks and the means by which the potential impact of risk is kept to an acceptable level (Perf. Std. 2201). Risk factors have differing degrees of objectivity. The most objective (least subjective) factors are facts. The organization's losses on derivatives are facts and therefore objective to the extent measurable. Objective information is such that it can be supported by facts or numbers. Subjective information is a judgment and may be interpreted differently by different people.

Answer (B) is incorrect. The auditor's assessment of management responses is a professional judgment. Answer (C) is incorrect. The business forecast is not a fact. Answer (D) is incorrect. The evaluation of internal control is based on professional judgment. Information based on judgment is subjective.

9. During a preliminary survey of the accounts receivable function, an internal auditor discovered a potentially major control deficiency while preparing a flowchart. What immediate action should the internal auditor take regarding the weakness?

A. Perform sufficient testing to determine its cause and effect.

B. Report it to the level of management responsible for corrective action.

C. Schedule a separate engagement to evaluate that segment of the accounts receivable function.

D. Highlight the weakness to ensure that procedures to test it are included in the engagement work program.

Answer (D) is correct.

REQUIRED: The immediate action to be taken given a discovery of a potentially major control deficiency.

DISCUSSION: One purpose of the risk assessment is to highlight areas that should be addressed during the engagement. A potentially major control deficiency is a significant area warranting special emphasis and should be noted to ensure the needed coverage in the engagement work program.

Answer (A) is incorrect. Testing of the control will be performed during the field work phase of the engagement. Answer (B) is incorrect. There is no need to report the potential defect. Testing is needed before reporting the defect to management. Answer (C) is incorrect. A separate engagement is not needed.

10. Data-gathering activities such as interviewing operating personnel, identifying standards to be used to evaluate performance, and assessing risks inherent in a department's operations are typically performed in which phase of an audit engagement?

A. Field work.

B. Preliminary survey.

C. Engagement program development.

D. Examination and evaluation of evidence.

Answer (B) is correct.
REQUIRED: The phase of an audit engagement in which data gathering occurs.
DISCUSSION: Engagement planning should include performing, as appropriate, a survey to (1) become familiar with the activities, risks, and controls to identify areas for engagement emphasis and (2) invite client comments and suggestions from engagement clients (PA 2210.A1-1, para. 3). Among other things, the survey should include discussions with the engagement client (e.g., interviews with operating personnel) and documenting key control activities (including identifying performance standards).

11. Which of the following activities represents the greatest risk to a post-merger manufacturing organization and is therefore most likely to be the subject of an internal audit engagement?

A. Combining imprest funds.

B. Combining purchasing functions.

C. Combining legal functions.

D. Combining marketing functions.

Answer (B) is correct.
REQUIRED: The activity representing the greatest risk.
DISCUSSION: The financial exposure in the purchasing function is ordinarily greater than in, for example, the legal and marketing functions. Also, purchasing functions ordinarily represent the greatest exposure to loss of the items listed and are therefore most likely to be evaluated. After a merger, risk is heightened because of the difficulty of combining the systems of the two organizations. Thus, the likelihood of an engagement is increased.
Answer (A) is incorrect. Imprest funds are typically immaterial in amount. Answer (C) is incorrect. Legal functions do not typically represent a risk of loss as great as the purchasing functions. Answer (D) is incorrect. Marketing functions do not typically represent a risk of loss as great as the purchasing functions.

4.3 Risk-Based Audit Plan

12. The term "risk" is best defined as the possibility that

A. An internal auditor will fail to detect a material misstatement that causes financial statements or internal reports to be misstated or misleading.

B. An event could occur affecting the achievement of objectives.

C. Management will, either knowingly or unknowingly, make decisions that increase the potential liability of the organization.

D. Financial statements or internal records will contain material misstatements.

Answer (B) is correct.
REQUIRED: The best definition of risk according to the *Standards*.
DISCUSSION: According to The IIA Glossary, risk is "the possibility of an event occurring that will have an impact on the achievement of objectives. Risk is measured in terms of impact and likelihood."
Answer (A) is incorrect. Detection risk is a component of audit risk. Answer (C) is incorrect. The risk of increasing the organization's liability could be termed management decision-making risk. Answer (D) is incorrect. Risk is not limited to misstated financial statements.

13. A chief audit executive may use risk analysis in preparing work schedules. Which of the following is **not** considered in performing a risk analysis?

A. Issues relating to organizational governance.

B. Skills available on the internal audit staff.

C. Results of prior engagements.

D. Major operating changes.

Answer (B) is correct.
REQUIRED: The item not considered in performing a risk analysis.
DISCUSSION: The skills of the internal audit staff do not affect the risk associated with potential engagement clients.
Answer (A) is incorrect. Issues relating to organizational governance are factors that should be considered. Answer (C) is incorrect. Results of prior engagements should be considered. Answer (D) is incorrect. Major operating changes should be considered.

14. Risk modeling or risk analysis is often used in conjunction with development of long-range engagement work schedules. The key input in the evaluation of risk is

A. Previous engagement results.

B. Management concerns and preferences.

C. Specific requirements of professional standards.

D. Judgment of the internal auditors.

Answer (D) is correct.
    REQUIRED: The key input in the evaluation of risk.
    DISCUSSION: Assessing the risk of an activity entails analysis of numerous factors, estimation of probabilities and amounts of potential losses, and an appraisal of the costs and benefits of risk reduction. Consequently, in assessing the magnitude of risk associated with any factor in a risk model, informed judgment by the internal auditor is required.
    Answer (A) is incorrect. The informed judgment of the internal auditor is still required to assess the magnitude of risk indicated by previous engagement results. Answer (B) is incorrect. To assess the risk posed by management concerns, informed judgment of the internal auditor is required. Answer (C) is incorrect. Professional standards do not specify the basic inputs for a risk analysis.

15. Risk assessment is a systematic process for assessing and integrating professional judgments about probable adverse conditions or events. Which of the following statements reflects the appropriate action for the chief audit executive to take?

A. The CAE should generally assign engagement priorities to activities with higher risks.

B. The CAE should restrict the number of sources of information used in the risk assessment process.

C. Work schedule priorities should be established to lead the CAE in the risk assessment process.

D. The risk assessment process should be conducted at least every 3 to 5 years.

Answer (A) is correct.
    REQUIRED: The appropriate action for the chief audit executive to take regarding risk assessment.
    DISCUSSION: Audit work schedules are based on, among other things, an assessment of risk and exposures. Prioritizing is needed to make decisions for applying resources. A variety of risk models exist to assist the CAE. Most risk models use risk factors, such as impact, likelihood, materiality, asset liquidity, management competence, quality of and adherence to internal controls, degree of change or stability, timing and results of last audit engagement, complexity, and employee and government relations (PA 2010-1, para. 5).
    Answer (B) is incorrect. Internal auditors are expected to identify and evaluate significant risk exposures In the normal course of their duties. Thus, they not only use risk analysis to plan engagements but also to assist management and the board by examining, evaluating, reporting, and recommending improvements on the adequacy and effectiveness of the management's risk processes. For these purposes, the CAE should incorporate information from a variety of sources into the risk assessment process. The *Standards* place no limit on such sources. Answer (C) is incorrect. The risk assessment process should be used to determine work schedule priorities. Answer (D) is incorrect. The risk assessment should be undertaken at least every year.

16. The chief audit executive of a manufacturer is updating the long-range engagement work schedule. There are several possible assignments that can fill a given time spot. Information on potential monetary exposure and key internal controls has been gathered. Based on perceived risk, select the assignment of greatest merit.

A. Precious metals inventory -- carrying amount, US $1,000,000; separately stored, but access not restricted.

B. Branch office petty cash -- ledger amount, US $50,000; 10 branch offices, equal amounts; replenishment of accounts requires three separate approvals.

C. Sales force travel expenses -- budget, US $1,000,000; 50 sales people; all expenditures over US $25 must be receipted.

D. Expendable tools inventory -- carrying amount, US $500,000; issued by tool crib attendant upon receipt of authorization form.

Answer (A) is correct.
    REQUIRED: The item of greatest concern based on perceived audit risk.
    DISCUSSION: Among the many considerations in judging an item's risk are the ease with which it can be converted to cash, its accessibility, and its monetary value. The precious metals inventory should receive special emphasis because of its high inherent risk. The inventory can be easily converted to cash, access is not restricted, and its monetary value is relatively high.
    Answer (B) is incorrect. The monetary exposure of petty cash is much smaller than for the other proposed engagements, and the related controls are very stringent. Answer (C) is incorrect. Although the monetary value of the sales force travel expense is identical to that of the precious metal inventory, the exposure is divided among 50 people, and the receipting requirement provides substantial safety against false claims. Answer (D) is incorrect. The expendable tools inventory is subject to adequate control.

4.4 Internal Audit Resource Requirements

17. Which of the following is the best source of a chief audit executive's information for planning staffing requirements?

A. Discussions of internal audit needs with senior management and the board.

B. Review of internal audit staff education and training records.

C. Review internal audit staff size and composition of similarly sized organizations in the same industry.

D. Interviews with existing internal audit staff.

Answer (A) is correct.
REQUIRED: The best source of a CAE's information for planning staffing requirements.
DISCUSSION: Ensuring the sufficiency of internal audit resources is ultimately a responsibility of the organization's senior management and board. The CAE should assist them in discharging this responsibility (PA 2030-1, para. 1).
Answer (B) is incorrect. The scheduled work is the first consideration in determining the number and qualifications of the staff required. Review of staff education and training records is a subsequent step. Answer (C) is incorrect. The staffing plan must consider the unique needs of a particular organization. The review of staff size and composition of similarly sized organizations in the same industry may not satisfy the engagement objectives for a particular organization. Answer (D) is incorrect. The scheduled work is the first consideration in determining the number and qualifications of the staff required. Interviews with existing staff occur later.

18. The capabilities of individual staff members are key features in the effectiveness of an internal audit activity. What is the primary consideration used when staffing an internal audit activity?

A. Background checks.

B. Job descriptions.

C. Continuing education.

D. Organizational orientation.

Answer (B) is correct.
REQUIRED: The primary consideration used when staffing an internal audit activity.
DISCUSSION: The skills, capabilities, and technical knowledge of the internal audit staff are to be appropriate for the planned activities (PA 2030-1, para. 2). Properly formulated job descriptions provide a basis for identifying job qualifications (including training and experience). Hence, they facilitate recruiting human resources with the necessary attributes.
Answer (A) is incorrect. Background checks help ensure that statements made by prospective employees are accurate. However, they are not the primary requisite. Answer (C) is incorrect. Continuing education occurs after the proper people are hired. Answer (D) is incorrect. A thorough orientation helps the new employee become productive more rapidly. However, it will not compensate for hiring the wrong person.

19. By comparing job descriptions with the qualifications and duties of the individuals currently holding those jobs, a manager can

A. Complete the human resource planning cycle.

B. Determine whether the organization is appropriately staffed.

C. Forecast future personnel needs.

D. Determine which employees should be promoted.

Answer (B) is correct.
REQUIRED: The purpose of comparing job descriptions with the qualifications and duties of the individuals holding the jobs.
DISCUSSION: A job description summarizes the duties and qualifications required for a job. It is prepared based on a job analysis, which is a systematic procedure for observing work and determining what tasks should be accomplished to achieve organizational goals. By comparing the job description with the actual employees and their qualifications, a manager can determine whether the organization has placed appropriate individuals in jobs best suited to their abilities.
Answer (A) is incorrect. The human resource planning cycle refers to the entire process. Examining job descriptions is merely a part of the job analysis process. Answer (C) is incorrect. A forecast of future needs requires knowledge of future plans and a projection of resource and staff requirements. Answer (D) is incorrect. To determine which employees should be promoted, a manager needs performance data.

20. When determining the number and experience level of an internal audit staff to be assigned to an engagement, the chief audit executive should consider all of the following **except** the

A. Complexity of the engagement.

B. Available internal audit activity resources.

C. Training needs of internal auditors.

D. Lapsed time since the last engagement.

Answer (D) is correct.
REQUIRED: The least appropriate criterion for assigning a staff auditor to a specific audit.
DISCUSSION: Lapsed time since the last engagement is a factor affecting engagement scheduling, not staffing.
Answer (A) is incorrect. The complexity of the engagement determines the experience and skills required of the assigned staff. Answer (B) is incorrect. Available resources are a factor in a staffing decision. Answer (C) is incorrect. The training needs of individual auditors are a factor in a staffing decision.

21. In most organizations, the rapidly expanding scope of internal auditing responsibilities requires continual training. What is the main purpose of such a training program?

A. To comply with continuing education requirements of professional organizations.

B. To use slack periods in engagement scheduling.

C. To help individuals to achieve personal career goals.

D. To achieve both individual and organizational goals.

Answer (D) is correct.

REQUIRED: The main purpose of a training program.

DISCUSSION: By being informed and up to date, internal auditors are better prepared to reach their personal goals. In addition, internal audit responsibilities are more readily discharged by auditors having the required knowledge, skills, and other competencies.

Answer (A) is incorrect. The CAE should establish a program for selecting and developing human resources, but compliance with continuing education requirements of professional organizations is not the primary purpose. Answer (B) is incorrect. Training can be conducted during slack periods, but this is not the primary objective. Answer (C) is incorrect. Both personal and internal audit goals should be achieved.

22. Although all the current members of an internal audit activity have good records of performance, the manager is not sure if any of the members are ready to assume a management role. Which of the following is an advantage of bringing in an outsider rather than promoting from within?

A. Management training costs are reduced when a qualified outsider is hired.

B. The manager can be sure that the new position will be filled by a competent employee.

C. Bringing in an outsider is a less expensive alternative than promoting from within.

D. The "modeling" effect is strengthened by bringing in a new role model.

Answer (A) is correct.

REQUIRED: The advantage of hiring managers from outside the firm.

DISCUSSION: Hiring an experienced manager reduces management training costs because the person has already been trained.

Answer (B) is incorrect. The manager is relying on outside information to evaluate the candidate and cannot be certain the employee is competent until (s)he begins work. Answer (C) is incorrect. Hiring an outsider is usually more expensive than promoting from within. Answer (D) is incorrect. The "modeling" effect occurs when employees see that deserving coworkers are promoted to better paying, higher-status jobs.

4.5 Staff and Resources

23. As a means of controlling projects and avoiding time-budget overruns, decisions to revise time budgets for an engagement should normally be made

A. Immediately after the survey.

B. When a significant risk exposure has been substantiated.

C. When inexperienced staff are assigned to an engagement.

D. Immediately after expanding tests to establish reliability of observations.

Answer (A) is correct.

REQUIRED: The timing of decisions to revise time budgets for an audit.

DISCUSSION: If appropriate, a survey should be conducted to (1) become familiar with the activities, risks, and controls to identify areas for engagement emphasis and (2) invite comments and suggestions from engagement clients (PA 2210.A1-1, para. 3). This survey may lead to a determination that activities other than or in addition to those contemplated by the long-range engagement work schedule are necessary. Consequently, revision of the time budget may then be indicated.

Answer (B) is incorrect. When a risk exposure has been substantiated, no further engagement work is required. Answer (C) is incorrect. The assignment of inexperienced staff should have no effect on the decision to revise the time budget. Answer (D) is incorrect. Expanded tests should have no effect on the time budget; the budget would have already been expanded as necessary.

24. The internal auditor-in-charge has just been informed of the next engagement, and the engagement team has been assigned. Select the appropriate phase for finalizing the engagement budget.

A. During formulation of the long-range plan.

B. After the preliminary survey.

C. During the initial planning meeting.

D. After the completion of all field work.

Answer (B) is correct.

REQUIRED: The proper phase in which to finalize the audit budget.

DISCUSSION: A survey permits an informed approach to planning and carrying out engagement work and is an effective tool for allocating the internal audit activity's resources where they can be used most effectively. Among other things, the results of the survey should include preliminary estimates of time and resource requirements. Thus, after the preliminary survey has been completed, the final engagement budget can be prepared.

Answer (A) is incorrect. An initial budget is determined during the formulation of the long-range plan, but revisions based on the preliminary survey may be required. Answer (C) is incorrect. At the initial planning meeting stage, the project is not sufficiently defined to complete the final budget. Answer (D) is incorrect. After the completion of field work, the budget is no longer useful as a control and evaluation tool.

25. As a particular engagement is being planned in a high-risk area, the chief audit executive determines that the available staff does not have the requisite skills to perform the assignment. The best course of action consistent with engagement planning principles is to

A. Not perform the engagement because the requisite skills are not available.

B. Use the engagement as a training opportunity and let the internal auditors learn as the engagement is performed.

C. Consider using external resources to supplement the needed knowledge, skills, and other competencies and complete the assignment.

D. Perform the engagement but limit the scope in light of the skill deficiency.

Answer (C) is correct.

REQUIRED: The course of action when the internal audit staff does not have adequate skills to perform the engagement.

DISCUSSION: In determining the resources needed to perform the engagement, the CAE must consider the knowledge, skills, and other competencies of the internal audit staff when selecting internal auditors for the engagement (PA 2230-1, para. 1). The CAE considers the use of external resources when additional knowledge and competencies are required.

Answer (A) is incorrect. Not performing the engagement is unacceptable, especially for a high-risk area. Answer (B) is incorrect. Engagements must be properly supervised. The internal audit activity has no one to provide this supervision. Answer (D) is incorrect. Limiting the scope of the engagement is done only when the requisite skills are not available even from external resources. If the scope is limited, management must be informed of the constraint in an interim report.

Practice even more exam-emulating questions in **Gleim CIA Test Prep**!

STUDY UNIT FIVE
ENGAGEMENT PROCEDURES AND SUPERVISION

(9 pages of outline)

This study unit is the first of two covering **Section II: Managing Individual Engagements** from The IIA's CIA Exam Syllabus. This section makes up 40% to 50% of Part 2 of the CIA exam and is tested at the **proficiency level**. The relevant portion of the syllabus is highlighted below. (The complete syllabus is in Appendix B.)

II. **MANAGING INDIVIDUAL ENGAGEMENTS (40%–50%)**

A. **Plan Engagements**
    4. Determine engagement procedures and prepare engagement work program
B. **Supervise Engagement**
    1. Direct / supervise individual engagements
    2. Nurture instrumental relations, build bonds, and work with others toward shared goals
    3. Coordinate work assignments among audit team members when serving as the auditor-in-charge of a project
    4. Review work papers
    5. Conduct exit conference
    6. Complete performance appraisals of engagement staff

C. **Communicate Engagement Results**
D. **Monitor Engagement Outcomes**

5.1 PROCEDURES AND WORK PROGRAM

Performance Standard 2240
Engagement Work Program

Internal auditors must develop and document work programs that achieve the engagement objectives.

---

1. **Engagement Procedures**

    a. Many questions on the CIA exam require the selection of engagement procedures. Few such questions are answerable based on memorization of lists. Moreover, no text can feasibly present comprehensive lists of all possible procedures. Thus, a candidate must be able to apply knowledge of auditing concepts to unfamiliar situations when choosing procedures.

    b. Procedures are performed to obtain sufficient, reliable, relevant, and useful information to achieve the engagement objectives.

        1) An auditor's **physical examination** provides the most persuasive form of evidence.

        2) Direct **observation** by the auditor, e.g., of performance of work by client personnel, is the next most persuasive.

        3) Information originating from a **third party** is less persuasive than information gathered directly by the auditor but more persuasive than information originating from the client.

        4) Information originating with the **client** can be somewhat persuasive in documentary form, especially if it is subject to effective internal control. But client oral testimony is the least persuasive of all.

        5) Original documents are more persuasive than copies, which can be altered.

2. **Selection of Engagement Procedures**

    a. A crucial problem-solving skill on Part 2 of the CIA exam is the ability to determine which of the many possible audit engagement procedures is appropriate in a given situation.

b. The chart below describes some of the possible engagement procedures and the information provided by these procedures.

Information Provided by Procedure	Procedures
Sales and Receivables were all accounted for.	Trace shipping documents with sales invoices and journal entries. Account for the numerical sequence of sales orders, shipping documents, invoices, etc.
Sales occurred.	Vouch sample of recorded sales to customer orders and shipping documents.
Accounts receivable are valid assets.	Confirm accounts receivables.
Accounts receivable are measured appropriately.	Classify receivables by age, and compare collection rates within classifications with those of prior years (also called aging the accounts receivable). Trace cash receipts to specific accounts. Review delinquent customers' credit ratings.
Cash transactions occurred.	Vouch a sample of recorded cash receipts to accounts receivable and customer orders. Vouch a sample of recorded cash disbursements to approved vouchers.
Cash reported actually exists.	Count cash on hand. Send bank confirmations. Prepare bank reconciliations.
Inventory transactions occurred.	Vouch a sample of recorded purchases to documentation. Vouch a sample of recorded cost of sales to documentation.
Inventory actually exists.	Observe inventory and make test counts.
Inventory amounts are measured appropriately.	Determine whether some inventory is obsolete. Ensure manufactured goods are tested for reasonableness.
Inventory balance contains all inventory owned at year end.	Analytical Procedures should be used. A commonly used ratio is the inventory turnover ratio.
Purchases occurred.	Vouch a sample of recorded payables to documentation, e.g., requisitions, purchase orders, receiving reports, and approved invoices.
Accounts Payable are all accounted for.	Analytical Procedures should be used to form expectations with which to compare management's representations. Trace subsequent payments to recorded payables. Collect supporting documentation and search for unmatched documents to determine whether relevant documents have been lost, misplaced, or misfiled.
Transactions affecting property, plant, and equipment are accounted for.	Analytical Procedures should be used. Typical ratios include rate of return on plant assets and plant assets to total assets.
Transactions were recorded in the proper period.	Cutoff test. Documents are traced to the accounting records for several days prior to and after year end to determine proper recognition in the appropriate period.
Transactions and events were recorded appropriately.	Obtain management representation letter that includes assertions that transactions and events were recorded appropriately.
Amounts are appropriately described and disclosures are fairly and clearly expressed.	Inspect financial statements. Evaluate note disclosures. Inspect any other relevant documentation.

c.   **Basic Procedures**

1)   Three basic procedures performed by internal auditors to gather information are (a) observing conditions, (b) interviewing people, and (c) examining records.

2)   **Observation** is effective for verifying whether (a) particular assets, such as inventory or equipment, exist or (b) a certain process or procedure is being performed appropriately at a moment in time.

a)   However, observation provides less persuasive information about the assertions of completeness, rights, valuation, and presentation and disclosure. For example, merely observing inventory does not determine whether the engagement client has rights in it.

3)   **Interviewing** (inquiring) is especially helpful in obtaining an understanding of client operations because of the opportunity to ask questions to clarify preceding answers or to pursue additional information.

a)   A supplement to interviewing is the use of an **internal control questionnaire**. It consists of a series of questions about the controls designed to prevent or detect errors or fraud.

i)   Answers to the questions help the internal auditor to identify specific policies and procedures relevant to specific assertions. They also help in the design of tests of controls to evaluate their effectiveness.

ii)   The questionnaire provides a means for ensuring that specific concerns are not overlooked, but it is not sufficient for an understanding of the entire system. Thus, the evidence obtained is indirect and requires corroboration by means of observation, interviews, flowcharting, examination of documents, etc.

b)   Evidence obtained by interviews should be corroborated by gathering objective data.

4)   **Examining** (inspecting) records is used in many audit activities. The methods predominantly used are discussed below.

a)   Verification is a broad term for the process of determining the validity of information.

d.   Other specific procedures that are variations of the basic procedure of examining records include the following:

1)   **Confirmations** are letters to third parties asking them to verify the existence and valuation of a relevant monetary amount in the client's records, such as an amount held in trust by a brokerage house.

a)   Confirmations are commonly used to verify the amounts of accounts receivable, goods on consignment, and liabilities.

b)   **Positive** confirmations are used when the amounts being confirmed are material. The recipient is asked to sign and return the letter with a positive assertion that the amount is either correct or incorrect.

i)   Because the amounts involved are material, unanswered positive confirmations require follow-up. They are thus more time-consuming than negative confirmations.

c)   **Negative** confirmations are used when the amounts being confirmed are immaterial or when controls are deemed to be functioning extremely well.

i)   The use of negative confirmations assumes that the recipients will complain only if they have a dispute with the amount. Thus, if a negative confirmation is unanswered, the auditor concludes that the amount has been confirmed.

1) **Tracing and Vouching**

    a) **Tracing** follows a transaction forward from the triggering event to a resulting event, ensuring that the transaction was accounted for properly.

        i) Tracing is used to gain assurance regarding the completeness assertion, for example, that a liability was properly accrued for all goods received.

    b) **Vouching** tracks a result backwards to the originating event, ensuring that a recorded amount is properly supported.

        i) Vouching is used to gain assurance regarding the existence assertion, for example, that a receivable claimed on the statement of financial position is supported by a sale to a customer.

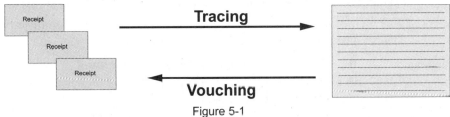

Figure 5-1

The terms "tracing" and "vouching" are defined above using classic auditing definitions. However, the CIA exam may use the word "tracing" to mean either process. Be extremely careful when encountering questions on this topic and focus on which process is relevant, not which term is used.

2) **Reperformance** (Recalculation)

    a) Reperformance consists of duplicating the client's work and comparing the results. This is most useful for checking arithmetic accuracy and the correct posting of amounts from source documents to journals to ledgers.

3) **Analytical Procedures**

    a) Analytical procedures are evaluations of financial information made by an analysis of relationships among financial and nonfinancial data. The basic premise is that plausible relationships among data may reasonably be expected to exist and continue in the absence of known conditions to the contrary.

    b) During the planning phase, analytical procedures are used by the internal auditor to determine the nature, extent, and timing of auditing procedures. The objective is to identify such things as the existence of unusual transactions and events and amounts, ratios, and trends that might indicate matters which require further investigation.

    c) Common analytical procedures performed by the internal auditor include (1) analysis of common-size financial statements, (2) ratio analysis, (3) trend analysis, (4) analysis of future-oriented information, and (5) internal and external benchmarking.

    d) **Scanning** is a use of professional judgment to review accounting data to identify significant or unusual items to test.

3.   **Engagement Work Program**

Implementation Standard 2240.A1

Work programs must include the procedures for identifying, analyzing, evaluating, and documenting information during the engagement. The work program must be approved prior to its implementation, and any adjustments approved promptly.

---

a.   The internal auditor plans and performs the engagement, with supervisory review and approval. A primary result of engagement planning is the preparation of the work program. The work program is a "document that lists the procedures to be followed during the engagement, designed to achieve the engagement plan" (The IIA Glossary).

1)   The most important elements of the engagement work program are listed in Practice Advisory 2200-1, *Engagement Planning*:

a)   Prior to the start of the engagement, the internal auditor prepares a program that

i)   States the objectives of the engagement.

ii)   Identifies technical requirements, objectives, risks, processes, and transactions to be examined.

iii) States the nature and extent of testing.

iv)   Documents the procedures for collecting, analyzing, interpreting, and documenting information.

v)   Is modified during the engagement with the approval of the CAE.

2)   Other features of the work program are described in Practice Advisory 2240-1, *Engagement Work Program:*

a)   Internal auditors develop and obtain documented approval of work programs before starting the engagement. The work program includes methods to be used, such as technology-based audit and sampling techniques.

b)   Collecting, analyzing, interpreting, and documenting information are supervised to provide reasonable assurance that objectives are met and the auditor's objectivity is maintained.

b.   **Use of a Pro Forma Work Program**

1)   A pro forma (standard) work program is used for repeated engagements related to similar operations. It is ordinarily modified over a period of years in response to problems encountered.

a)   The pro forma work program ensures at least minimum coverage; provides comparability; and saves resources when operations at different locations have similar activities, risks, and controls.

b)   However, a pro forma work program is not appropriate for a complex or changing operating environment. The engagement objectives and related procedures may no longer be relevant.

Stop and review! You have completed the outline for this subunit. Study multiple-choice questions 1 through 14 beginning on page 128.

5.2 SUPERVISION

1. **Supervision at the Engagement Level**

Performance Standard 2340
Engagement Supervision

Engagements must be properly supervised to ensure objectives are achieved, quality is assured, and staff is developed.

---

a. Supervision is needed at all levels of the internal audit activity from planning to performance to reporting results. The CAE may delegate the task of supervision on individual engagements.

Interpretation of Standard 2340

The extent of supervision required will depend on the proficiency and experience of internal auditors and the complexity of the engagement. The chief audit executive has overall responsibility for supervising the engagement, whether performed by or for the internal audit activity, but may designate appropriately experienced members of the internal audit activity to perform the review. Appropriate evidence of supervision is documented and retained.

---

b. The following are specific requirements in Practice Advisory 2340-1, *Engagement Supervision*:

1) Supervision by the CAE (or designee) is relevant to all phases of the engagement. The process includes

   a) Ensuring auditors collectively possess the required knowledge, skills, and other competencies.

   b) Providing instructions during planning and approving the engagement program.

   c) Ensuring the program is completed (unless changes are justified and authorized) and objectives are met.

   d) Determining working papers support observations, conclusions, and recommendations.

   e) Ensuring communications are accurate, objective, clear, concise, constructive, and timely.

   f) Developing internal auditors' proficiency.

2) The CAE is responsible for all internal audit engagements and significant professional judgments. The CAE adopts suitable means to

   a) Minimize the risk of inconsistent professional judgments or other actions inconsistent with those of the CAE and

   b) Resolve differences in professional judgment between the CAE and staff members.

      i) The means of conflict resolution may include

      - Discussion of facts,
      - Inquiries or research,
      - Working-paper documentation of differences, and,
      - For an ethical issue, referral to an individual responsible for such matters.

2. **Relationships**

    a.   To ensure complete cooperation, senior management is responsible for notifying other departments of the existence of the internal audit activity.

        1) Partnering with management at all levels is one of the best ways for internal auditors to obtain information.

        2) Employees are another source of information.

    b.   Internal auditors need effective interpersonal skills to promote the internal audit activity throughout the organization. According to The IIA Competency Framework, internal auditors nurture relationships when they

        1) Cultivate and maintain extensive informal networks.

        2) Create opportunities and events to help people build relationships with each other.

        3) Compliment and affirm others.

        4) Build relationships by sharing personal experiences and perspectives.

        5) Keep others in the loop.

        6) Seek opportunities for contact that build relationships.

        7) Initiate and participate in conversations that enhance approachability.

        8) Are recognized as an approachable and resourceful individual.

        9) Use diplomacy and tact.

    c.   Internal auditors rely on collaboration and cooperation among departments and other groups to work toward shared goals. During an engagement, internal auditors have a unique opportunity to build credibility and to promote the goals of adding value and improving the organization's operations.

3. **Coordination during the Engagement**

    a.   The auditor-in-charge should coordinate work assignments among audit team members during the engagement.

    b.   Coordination during the engagement ensures that engagement objectives will be met efficiently and effectively.

Stop and review! You have completed the outline for this subunit. Study multiple-choice questions 15 through 19 beginning on page 132.

5.3 WORK PAPERS, EXIT MEETINGS, AND STAFF EVALUATIONS

1. **Purpose of Working Papers**

    a.   Working papers facilitate supervision of the engagement. They serve as a means of communication between internal auditors and the auditor in charge.

    b.   The importance of working paper review within the internal audit activity is stated in Practice Advisory 2340-1, *Engagement Supervision*:

        1) All working papers are reviewed to ensure that (a) they support engagement communications and (b) all necessary procedures are performed.

            a) The reviewer initials and dates each working paper to provide evidence of review. Other methods include

                i)   Completing a review checklist,

                ii) Preparing a memorandum on the review, or

                iii) Evaluating and accepting reviews within the working paper software.

  2) Written review notes record questions arising from the review. When clearing review notes, the auditor ensures that the working papers provide adequate evidence that questions raised have been resolved. The reviewer may

    a) Retain the notes as a record of questions raised, steps taken, and results.

    b) Discard the notes after questions are resolved and working papers are amended to provide requested information.

2. Exit Meetings

  a. Exit meetings are an important part of the communication process. Practice Advisory 2440-1, *Disseminating Results*, explains this part of the process:

    1) Internal auditors discuss conclusions and recommendations with appropriate management before the CAE issues the final communications. The discussion usually occurs during the engagement or at post-engagement (exit) meetings.

  b. The primary purpose of an exit meeting is to ensure the accuracy of the information used by an internal auditor.

    1) A secondary purpose is to improve relations with engagement clients. The discussions during the exit meeting not only provide a quality control review but also are a courtesy that enhances the auditor-client relationship.

    2) In addition, the exit meeting is an important element of the participative approach to internal auditing. It involves the client in the engagement process as well as in any recommended changes arising from the engagement.

      a) People are more likely to accept changes if they have participated in the decisions and in the methods used to implement changes.

    3) Discussions at the exit meeting should be documented in case a dispute arises.

  c. Supervisors should attend exit meetings to maintain good client relationships and reinforce audit observations.

NOTE: This section also is relevant to Study Unit 6.

3. Staff Performance Appraisals

  a. The CAE is responsible for ensuring that the internal audit activity has sufficient resources, including employees with the knowledge, skills, and other competencies appropriate for planned activities.

    1) Thus, as part of the resource management process, a written appraisal of each internal auditor's performance is required at least annually.

    2) Furthermore, at the conclusion of any major audit engagement, supervisory personnel should complete performance appraisals for all audit staff who worked on the engagement.

      a) Such appraisals help (1) the CAE to assess future training needs and current staff abilities and (2) staff to identify areas of personal strength and weakness.

Stop and review! You have completed the outline for this subunit. Study multiple-choice questions 20 through 25 beginning on page 113.

QUESTIONS

5.1 Procedures and Work Program

1. The purpose of including a time budget in an engagement work program is to

    A. Provide an objective means of evaluating the internal auditor's competence.

    B. Ensure timely completion of the engagement.

    C. Provide a means of controlling and evaluating the progress of the engagement.

    D. Restrict the scope of the engagement.

Answer (C) is correct.
    REQUIRED: The purpose of a time budget in an engagement work program.
    DISCUSSION: Supervision includes, among other things, ensuring the approved engagement program is completed unless changes are justified and authorized (PA 2340-1, para. 1). For this purpose, a time budget is necessary to evaluate and control the progress of the engagement. It permits comparison of the actual time spent on a procedure with its allotted time.
    Answer (A) is incorrect. Whether an internal auditor remains within the time budget is affected by many factors other than professional competence. Answer (B) is incorrect. The establishment of a budget cannot ensure that work will be completed on a timely basis. Answer (D) is incorrect. A time budget is not intended to limit the scope of the engagement.

2. One of the primary roles of an engagement work program is to

    A. Serve as a tool for planning and conducting engagement work.

    B. Document an internal auditor's evaluations of controls.

    C. Provide for a standardized approach to the engagement.

    D. Assess the risks associated with the activity under review.

Answer (A) is correct.
    REQUIRED: The item that states one of the primary roles of an engagement work program.
    DISCUSSION: Among other things, work programs state the objectives of the engagement, identify technical requirements, and state the nature and extent of testing required (PA 2200-1, para. 1).
    Answer (B) is incorrect. Engagement working papers include results of control evaluations. Answer (C) is incorrect. The work program may not be consistent from year to year given the changing conditions to which the engagement client must adapt. Since the work program must reflect the current year's situation, standardization may not be appropriate. Answer (D) is incorrect. The risk assessment in the planning phase helps to identify objectives, a step that must be taken before the work program can be developed.

3. Engagement work programs testing controls ordinarily must

    A. Be specifically designed for each operation evaluated.

    B. Be generalized to fit all situations without regard to departmental lines.

    C. Be generalized so as to be usable at all locations of a particular department.

    D. Reduce costly duplication of effort by ensuring that every aspect of an operation is examined.

Answer (A) is correct.
    REQUIRED: The true statement about work programs.
    DISCUSSION: A work program must be adapted to the specific needs of the engagement after the internal auditor establishes the engagement objectives and scope and determines the resources required. A pro forma (standard) work program is not appropriate for a complex or changing environment. Its stated objectives and procedures may no longer be relevant.
    Answer (B) is incorrect. A work program must allow for variations resulting from changing circumstances and varied conditions. Answer (C) is incorrect. A generalized program cannot consider variations in circumstances and conditions. Answer (D) is incorrect. Every aspect of an operation need not be examined. Only those likely to conceal problems and difficulties must be considered.

4. An internal auditor has just completed a survey to become familiar with the organization's payroll operations as part of an unplanned engagement. Which of the following most likely is performed next?

    A. Assign internal audit personnel.

    B. Establish initial engagement objectives.

    C. Write the engagement work program.

    D. Conduct field work.

Answer (C) is correct.
    REQUIRED: The step most likely following the survey.
    DISCUSSION: The survey allows the internal auditor to become familiar with the engagement client and therefore provides input to the work program.
    Answer (A) is incorrect. Internal audit personnel are usually assigned before the survey. Answer (B) is incorrect. Initial objectives for an unplanned engagement address the issues that prompted the engagement. Accordingly, objectives are specified before the survey. Answer (D) is incorrect. Field work can be performed only after the work program has been written and approved. Thus, field work cannot immediately follow the survey.

5. Writing an engagement work program most likely occurs at which stage of the engagement?

A. During the planning stage.

B. Subsequent to evaluating risk management and control systems.

C. As the engagement is performed.

D. At the end of each engagement when the standard work program should be revised for the next engagement to ensure coverage of noted problem areas.

Answer (A) is correct.
REQUIRED: The stage of the engagement during which the work program most likely is written.
DISCUSSION: The engagement work program is the culmination of the planning stage.
Answer (B) is incorrect. The work program states the procedures to be followed during the engagement (The IIA Glossary). It normally is the culmination of the planning stage. Answer (C) is incorrect. The work program normally is written during the planning stage, not as the engagement is performed. However, the work program may be modified during the engagement. Answer (D) is incorrect. Although revising the work program at the end of one engagement for the next engagement is allowed, it should still be written during the planning phase.

6. A work program for a comprehensive assurance engagement to evaluate a purchasing function should include

A. Procedures arranged by relative priority based upon perceived risk.

B. A statement of the engagement objectives for the operation under review with agreement by the engagement client.

C. Procedures to accomplish engagement objectives.

D. A focus on risks affecting the financial statements as opposed to controls.

Answer (C) is correct.
REQUIRED: The content of a work program for a comprehensive engagement to evaluate a purchasing function.
DISCUSSION: Work programs are a necessary part of engagement planning. They include the procedures for collecting, analyzing, interpreting, and documenting information during the engagement (PA 2240-1, para. 2).
Answer (A) is incorrect. Engagement procedures normally are arranged in an order that will most efficiently complete the work program. Answer (B) is incorrect. Engagement objectives are stated, but they do not need to be agreed to by the engagement client. Answer (D) is incorrect. The engagement should not be narrowly focused on the reliability and integrity of financial information.

7. Which result of an analytical procedure suggests the existence of obsolete merchandise?

A. Decrease in the inventory turnover rate.

B. Decrease in the ratio of gross profit to sales.

C. Decrease in the ratio of inventory to accounts payable.

D. Decrease in the ratio of inventory to accounts receivable.

Answer (A) is correct.
REQUIRED: The analytical procedure that might uncover obsolete merchandise.
DISCUSSION: Inventory turnover is equal to cost of sales divided by average inventory. If inventory is increasing at a faster rate than sales, the turnover rate decreases and suggests a buildup of unsalable inventory. The ratios of gross profit to sales, inventory to accounts payable, and inventory to accounts receivable do not necessarily change when obsolete merchandise is on hand.

8. Which of the following engagement objectives will be accomplished by tracing a sample of accounts receivable debit entries to customer invoices and related shipping documents?

A. Sales are properly recorded.

B. Sales are billed at the correct prices.

C. Accounts receivable represent valid sales.

D. Customer credit is approved.

Answer (C) is correct.
REQUIRED: The audit objective accomplished by tracing a sample of accounts receivable debit entries to customer invoices and related shipping documents.
DISCUSSION: The process described is vouching. It begins with amounts recorded in the ledger and tracks backwards to the source documents. The purpose is to detect fictitious sales and ensure that each claimed sale is properly supported.
Answer (A) is incorrect. The objective of determining whether sales are properly recorded is accomplished by tracing a sample of sales invoices to accounts receivable. Answer (B) is incorrect. The objective of determining whether sales are billed at the correct prices is accomplished by tracing invoice prices to the organization's approved price list. Answer (D) is incorrect. The objective of determining whether customer credit is approved is accomplished by examining sales documents for proper approvals by credit personnel.

9. Vouching entails verifying recorded amounts by examining the underlying documents from the _____ documents to the _____ documents.

    A. Final; original.

    B. Final; previous.

    C. Original; final.

    D. Original; subsequent.

Answer (A) is correct.
    REQUIRED: The definition of the term vouching.
    DISCUSSION: Vouching entails verifying recorded amounts by examining the underlying documents from the final documents to the original documents. The engagement objective of working backward is to provide information that recorded amounts reflect valid transactions. Vouching supports the existence or occurrence assertion. Vouching is irrelevant to the completeness assertion, because the existence of records of some transactions does not prove that all transactions were recorded.
    Answer (B) is incorrect. Vouching entails the examination of final documents to original documents. Answer (C) is incorrect. Vouching is designed to support the engagement objective of working backward to provide information that recorded amounts reflect valid transactions. Answer (D) is incorrect. It implies the comparison of the original to the next copy. Vouching entails examination from the final document to the original.

10. A production manager ordered excessive raw materials for delivery to a separate company owned by the manager. The manager falsified receiving documents and approved the invoices for payment. Which of the following audit procedures would most likely detect this fraud?

    A. Select a sample of cash disbursements and compare purchase orders, receiving reports, invoices, and check copies.

    B. Select a sample of cash disbursements and confirm the amount purchased, purchase price, and date of shipment with the vendors.

    C. Observe the receiving dock and count materials received; compare the counts to receiving reports completed by receiving personnel.

    D. Perform analytical tests, comparing production, materials purchased, and raw materials inventory levels; investigate differences.

Answer (D) is correct.
    REQUIRED: The engagement procedure most likely to detect a purchasing fraud.
    DISCUSSION: Analytical auditing procedures provide internal auditors with an efficient and effective means of assessing and evaluating information collected in an engagement. The assessment results from comparing information with expectations identified or developed by the internal auditor. Analytical auditing procedures are useful in identifying, among other things, differences that are not expected; the absence of differences when they are expected; potential errors, potential fraud or illegal acts; or other unusual or nonrecurring transactions or events. Hence, the analytical procedures should identify an unexplained increase in materials used.
    Answer (A) is incorrect. Given that documents have been falsified, supporting documents exist for each cash disbursement. Answer (B) is incorrect. The vendors will confirm all transactions. Answer (C) is incorrect. Given that the improper orders are shipped to another location, observing receiving dock counts will not detect the fraud.

11. An internal auditor has set an engagement objective of determining whether mail room staff is fully used. Which of the following engagement techniques will best meet this objective?

    A. Inspection of documents.

    B. Observation.

    C. Inquiry.

    D. Analytical review.

Answer (B) is correct.
    REQUIRED: The engagement technique to meet the engagement objective of determining whether mail room staff is fully used.
    DISCUSSION: By observing mail room operations at various times on various days of the week, the internal auditor can note whether incoming or outgoing mail backlogs exist and whether mail room staff are busy on mail room activities, idle, or working on other projects.
    Answers (A), (C), and (D) are incorrect. Observation is the best technique to determine if the staff is fully used.

12. Which of the substantive field work procedures presented below provides the best information about completeness of recorded revenues?

A. Reconciling the sales journal to the general ledger control account.

B. Vouching charges made to the accounts receivable subsidiary ledger to supporting shipping records.

C. Vouching shipping records to the customer order file.

D. Reconciling shipping records to recorded sales.

Answer (D) is correct.
REQUIRED: The procedure that provides the best information about completeness of recorded revenues.
DISCUSSION: The completeness assertion relates to whether all transactions that should be presented are included. To test this assertion with regard to revenues from sales of goods shipped, the internal auditor might trace shipping documents to sales data to determine whether items shipped have been recorded as revenues.
Answer (A) is incorrect. Reconciling the sales journal to the general ledger control account would fail to detect unrecorded sales, which would result in no entries to the sales journal or accounts receivable. Answer (B) is incorrect. Vouching charges made to the accounts receivable subsidiary ledger to supporting shipping records would fail to detect unrecorded sales, which would result in no entries to the sales journal or accounts receivable. Answer (C) is incorrect. Vouching shipping records to the customer order file merely establishes that goods shipped were ordered, not that they were recorded as sales.

13. Which of the following procedures provides the most relevant information to determine the adequacy of the allowance for doubtful accounts receivable?

A. Confirm the receivables.

B. Analyze the following month's payments on the accounts receivable balances outstanding.

C. Test the controls over the write-off of accounts receivable to ensure that management approves all write-offs.

D. Analyze the allowance through an aging of receivables and an analysis of current economic data.

Answer (D) is correct.
REQUIRED: The procedure to determine the adequacy of the allowance for doubtful accounts receivable.
DISCUSSION: The purpose of an allowance for doubtful accounts is to state accounts receivable at net realizable value. Consequently, an appropriate method of estimating collectibility of the receivables should be applied. Because the probability of collection is inversely proportional to the age of the receivables, aging the receivables provides information that is highly relevant. Current economic conditions are also relevant because collectibility varies with changes in the economic cycle.
Answer (A) is incorrect. Accounts receivable confirmations are more likely to be effective for the existence assertion than for the valuation and completeness assertions. Answer (B) is incorrect. Although subsequent collections provide the best information about collectibility, they do not indicate the value of uncollected receivables. Answer (C) is incorrect. Testing the controls over write-offs provides no information about valuation.

5.2 Supervision

14. Which of the following activities does **not** constitute engagement supervision?

A. Preparing a preliminary engagement work program.

B. Providing appropriate instructions to the internal auditors.

C. Reviewing engagement working papers.

D. Ensuring that engagement communications meet appropriate criteria.

Answer (A) is correct.
    REQUIRED: The activity not constituting supervision.
    DISCUSSION: Preparing a preliminary engagement work program is part of engagement planning, not an aspect of engagement supervision.
    Answer (B) is incorrect. Providing appropriate instructions to the internal auditors is an aspect of engagement supervision. Answer (C) is incorrect. Reviewing engagement working papers is an aspect of engagement supervision. Answer (D) is incorrect. Ensuring that engagement objectives are achieved is an aspect of engagement supervision.

15. Supervision of an internal audit engagement should include

A. Determining that engagement working papers adequately support the engagement observations.

B. Assigning staff members to the particular engagement.

C. Determining the scope of the engagement.

D. Appraising each internal auditor's performance on at least an annual basis.

Answer (A) is correct.
    REQUIRED: The extent of supervision of an engagement.
    DISCUSSION: Among other things, supervision includes ensuring that (1) the approved engagement work program is completed unless changes are justified and authorized, and (2) working papers adequately support engagement observations, conclusions, and recommendations (PA 2340-1).
    Answer (B) is incorrect. Engagement resource allocation is a planning function, not a supervisory function. Answer (C) is incorrect. Determining the engagement scope is a planning function, not a supervisory function. Answer (D) is incorrect. Appraising performance on an annual basis is not a supervisory function of a specific engagement but is part of the management of the human resources of the internal audit activity.

16. Determining that engagement objectives have been met is part of the overall supervision of an engagement and is the ultimate responsibility of the

A. Staff internal auditor.

B. Board.

C. Engagement supervisor.

D. Chief audit executive.

Answer (D) is correct.
    REQUIRED: The person(s) with ultimate responsibility for determining that engagement objectives have been met.
    DISCUSSION: The CAE has overall responsibility for supervising the engagement (Inter. Std. 2340).
    Answer (A) is incorrect. The chief audit executive, not a staff internal auditor, has the responsibility to determine that engagement objectives have been met. Answer (B) is incorrect. The chief audit executive, not the audit committee, has the responsibility to determine that engagement objectives have been met. Answer (C) is incorrect. The chief audit executive, not the engagement supervisor, has the responsibility to determine that engagement objectives have been met.

17. Which of the following best describes engagement supervision?

A. The manager of each engagement has the ultimate responsibility for supervision.

B. Supervision is primarily exercised at the final review stage of an engagement to ensure the accuracy of the engagement communications.

C. Supervision is most important in the planning phase of the engagement to ensure appropriate coverage.

D. Supervision is a continuing process beginning with planning and ending with the conclusion of the engagement.

Answer (D) is correct.
    REQUIRED: The best description of engagement supervision.
    DISCUSSION: The CAE (or designee) provides appropriate engagement supervision. Supervision is a process that begins with planning and continues throughout the engagement (PA 2340-1, para. 1).
    Answer (A) is incorrect. The CAE has the ultimate responsibility for supervision. Answer (B) is incorrect. Supervision begins with planning and continues throughout the engagement. Answer (C) is incorrect. Supervision is equally important in all phases of the engagement.

18. The engagement team leader is **least** likely to have a primary role in

    A. Allocating budgeted engagement hours among assigned staff.

    B. Updating the permanent files.

    C. Reviewing the working papers.

    D. Preparing the critique sheet for the engagement.

Answer (B) is correct.
    REQUIRED: The least likely primary role for an audit team leader.
    DISCUSSION: The engagement team leader (sometimes called a senior) is responsible for planning the engagement, coordinating the staff, and supervising the work. Updating the permanent files is a task most likely performed by the staff.
    Answer (A) is incorrect. Allocating budgeted engagement hours among assigned staff is a planning task. Answer (C) is incorrect. Reviewing the working papers is a supervisory activity. Answer (D) is incorrect. Preparing the critique sheet for the engagement is also a supervisory activity performed by the engagement team leader.

5.3 Work Papers, Exit Meetings, and Staff Evaluations

19. During the working-paper review, an internal auditing supervisor finds that the internal auditor's observations are not adequately cross-referenced to supporting documentation. The supervisor will most likely instruct the internal auditor to

    A. Prepare a working paper to indicate that the full scope of the engagement was carried out.

    B. Familiarize himself or herself with the sequence of working papers so that (s)he will be able to answer questions about the conclusions stated in the final engagement communication.

    C. Eliminate any cross-references to other working papers because the system is unclear.

    D. Provide a cross-referencing system that shows the relationship among observations, conclusions, recommendations, and the related facts.

Answer (D) is correct.
    REQUIRED: The instruction to an internal auditor who has not adequately cross-referenced to supporting documentation.
    DISCUSSION: Cross-referencing is important because it simplifies review either during the engagement or subsequently by creating a trail of related items through the working papers. It thus facilitates preparation of the final engagement communication and later engagements for the same engagement client.
    Answer (A) is incorrect. A full set of properly indexed and cross-referenced working papers, not a separate analysis, is necessary. Answer (B) is incorrect. Proper cross-referencing avoids the need to memorize the locations of supporting information. Answer (C) is incorrect. Cross-references should be added, not deleted.

20. Engagement working papers are reviewed to ensure that

    A. They are properly cross-referenced to the engagement communications.

    B. No issues are open at the conclusion of the field work.

    C. They meet or exceed the work standards of the organization's external auditors.

    D. They are properly referenced for easy follow-up within the next year.

Answer (B) is correct.
    REQUIRED: The purpose of reviewing engagement working papers.
    DISCUSSION: All engagement working papers are reviewed to ensure they support engagement communications and necessary audit procedures are performed (PA 2340-1, para. 3).

21. When conducting a performance appraisal of an internal auditor who has been a below-average performer, an inappropriate procedure is to

    A. Notify the internal auditor of the upcoming appraisal several days in advance.

    B. Use objective, impartial language.

    C. Use generalizations.

    D. Document the appraisal.

Answer (C) is correct.
    REQUIRED: The inappropriate method for conducting a performance appraisal of an internal auditor.
    DISCUSSION: In a performance appraisal of a below-average performer, it is appropriate and advisable to notify the employee of the upcoming appraisal, use objective language, and document the appraisal. It is not appropriate to use generalizations when making a performance appraisal of a below-average performer. Rather, the evaluator must cite specific information and be prepared to support assertions with evidence.

22. One purpose of the exit meeting is for the internal auditor to

    A. Require corrective action.

    B. Review and verify the appropriateness of the engagement communication based upon client input.

    C. Review the performance of internal auditors assigned to the engagement.

    D. Present the final engagement communication to management.

Answer (B) is correct.

    REQUIRED: The purpose of the exit meeting.

    DISCUSSION: Internal auditors discuss conclusions and recommendations with appropriate levels of management before the CAE issues the final engagement communications. This is usually accomplished during the course of the engagement or at post-engagement meetings (PA 2440-1, para. 1). Another technique is the review of draft engagement conclusions, observations, and recommendations by management of the activity reviewed. These discussions and reviews help ensure that there have been no misunderstandings or misinterpretations of fact by providing the opportunity for the engagement client to clarify specific items and to express views of the observations, conclusions, and recommendations (para. 2).

    Answer (A) is incorrect. Only management can require corrective action. Answer (C) is incorrect. Internal auditor performance is reviewed in private with the individual employee, not at the exit meeting. Answer (D) is incorrect. The exit meeting is normally based on draft communications. The final engagement communication is subject to modification based on the results of the exit meeting.

23. The effectiveness of an internal auditing engagement is related to the results and the action taken on those results. Which of the following activities contributes to engagement effectiveness?

    A. Conducting an exit meeting with engagement clients.

    B. Adhering to a time budget.

    C. Preparing weekly time reports.

    D. Having budget revisions approved by the project supervisor.

Answer (A) is correct.

    REQUIRED: The activity that contributes to audit assignment effectiveness.

    DISCUSSION: An exit meeting (post-engagement meeting) is an opportunity for discussion of engagement results, i.e., observations, conclusions, and recommendations. The effectiveness of an engagement is enhanced by the exit meeting because it provides the engagement client an opportunity to clarify specific items and to express views of the observations, conclusions, and recommendations.

    Answer (B) is incorrect. Adhering to a time budget contributes to efficiency, not effectiveness. Answer (C) is incorrect. Preparing weekly time reports contributes to efficiency, not effectiveness. Answer (D) is incorrect. Having budget revisions approved by the project supervisor contributes to efficiency, not effectiveness.

24. An internal auditing manager is reviewing the engagement working papers prepared by the staff. Which of the following review comments is true?

    A. Each working paper should include the actual and the budgeted times related to such engagement work.

    B. Including copies of all the forms and directives of the engagement client constitutes over-documentation.

    C. Conclusions need not be documented in the working papers when the engagement objectives are achieved.

    D. Each working paper should include a statement regarding the engagement client's cooperation.

Answer (B) is correct.

    REQUIRED: The review comment that is true.

    DISCUSSION: All engagement working papers are reviewed to ensure they support engagement communications and necessary audit procedures are performed (PA 2340-1, para. 3). However, adequate support includes only those forms and directives that are relevant to the engagement or to the observations, conclusions, and recommendations. Thus, including copies of all the forms and directives of the client constitutes over-documentation.

    Answer (A) is incorrect. Actual and budgeted times are documented in the budget section of the working papers and not on each working paper. Answer (C) is incorrect. Conclusions should be documented in the working papers whether or not the engagement objectives are achieved. Answer (D) is incorrect. Only noncooperation is likely to be documented.

Practice even more exam-emulating questions in **Gleim CIA Test Prep!**

STUDY UNIT SIX
COMMUNICATE RESULTS AND MONITOR OUTCOMES

(20 pages of outline)

This study unit is the second of two covering **Section II: Managing Individual Engagements** from The IIA's CIA Exam Syllabus. This section makes up 40% to 50% of Part 2 of the CIA exam and is tested at the **proficiency level**. The relevant portion of the syllabus is highlighted below. (The complete syllabus is in Appendix B.)

II. **MANAGING INDIVIDUAL ENGAGEMENTS (40%–50%)**

   A. **Plan Engagements**

   B. **Supervise Engagement**

   C. **Communicate Engagement Results**

      1. Initiate preliminary communication with engagement clients

      2. Communicate interim progress

      3. Develop recommendations when appropriate

      4. Prepare report or other communication

      5. Approve engagement report

      6. Determine distribution of the report

      7. Obtain management response to the report

      8. Report outcomes to appropriate parties

   D. **Monitor Engagement Outcomes**

      1. Identify appropriate method to monitor engagement outcomes

      2. Monitor engagement outcomes and conduct appropriate follow-up by the internal audit activity

      3. Conduct follow-up and report on management's response to internal audit recommendations

      4. Report significant audit issues to senior management and the board periodically

---

6.1 COMMUNICATION WITH CLIENTS

  1. **Engagement Communications**

     a. Engagement communications are intended to inform, persuade, and obtain results. They (1) explain the internal auditors' observations, conclusions, and recommendations; (2) attempt to convince the recipients of the communication of their value and validity; and (3) promote beneficial change.

        1) Auditors must be skilled in dealing with people so as to maintain satisfactory relationships with clients.

        2) Because communication is needed for relationship building, auditors also must be skilled in oral and written communications that effectively convey engagement objectives, evaluations, conclusions, and recommendations.

2.   **Preliminary Communication**

    a.   The CAE generally notifies client management about the timing of the audit, the reasons for it, the preliminary scope, and the estimated client resources needed.

        1)   For an assurance service, the person or group directly involved with the entity, operation, function, system, or other subject matter is the process owner.

        2)   For a consulting service, the person or group seeking advice is the engagement client (Introduction to the *Standards*).

        3)   For the sake of convenience, The IIA and this text use the term **engagement client** for both assurance and consulting services.

    b.   Before this communication, the internal audit activity gathers basic information about the client, for example, about its industry, principal personnel, processes, major inputs and outputs, and control environment.

        1)   Some information may be acquired by sending a questionnaire to the client early in the audit process. The answers are then discussed at the preliminary meeting.

        2)   This preliminary notice is omitted when the engagement involves such activities as a surprise cash count or procedures related to suspected fraud.

3.   **Interim Communication**

    a.   Interim (progress) communications provide a prompt means of documenting a situation requiring immediate action.

        1)   They are preliminary and should indicate that

            a)   Only current information, that is, an incomplete study, is the basis for such communications.

            b)   The final engagement communication will follow up on the topics covered.

        2)   Progress communications prepared by the internal audit staff should be reviewed by the chief audit executive or other supervisory personnel.

        3)   Progress communications about deficiency observations should have the same structure as communications on observations. Deficiencies are described in records of engagement observations and are communicated to management in the form of a single-page executive summary.

        4)   Progress communications also may be used to report the status of long, sensitive, or otherwise special engagements to the clients and senior management.

    b.   Guidance for interim reporting is provided in Practice Advisory 2410-1, *Communication Criteria*:

        1)   **Interim reports** (oral or written) transmitted formally or informally communicate

            a)   Information needing immediate attention,
            b)   A change in the scope of the engagement, or
            c)   The progress of a long-duration engagement.

        2)   The use of interim reports does not reduce or eliminate the need for a final report.

Stop and review! You have completed the outline for this subunit. Study multiple-choice questions 1 through 3 on page 155.

6.2 REPORTING TO SENIOR MANAGEMENT AND THE BOARD

Performance Standard 2060
Reporting to Senior Management and the Board

The chief audit executive must report periodically to senior management and the board on the internal audit activity's purpose, authority, responsibility, and performance relative to its plan. Reporting must also include significant risk exposures and control issues, including fraud risks, governance issues, and other matters needed or requested by senior management and the board.

---

1. **The CAE's Duty to Report**

    a. According to Practice Advisory 2060-1, *Reporting to Senior Management and the Board*, reporting provides assurance to senior management and the board about governance, risk management, and control. The CAE must communicate and interact directly with the board.

        1) The CAE should agree with the board about (a) the frequency and nature of reporting, (b) the internal audit activity's charter, and (c) performance.

            a) Performance reporting should relate to the most recently approved plan to report (1) significant deviations from the approved audit plan, staffing plans, and financial budgets; (2) reasons for the deviations; and (3) action needed or taken.

            b) The CAE also must communicate the results of the quality assurance and improvement program.

        2) Significant risk exposures and control issues may result in unacceptable exposure to internal and external risks, including control weaknesses, fraud, illegal acts, errors, inefficiency, waste, ineffectiveness, conflicts of interest, and financial viability.

        3) Senior management and the board determine the responses to significant issues.

            a) They may assume the risk of not correcting the reported condition because of cost or other considerations.

            b) Senior management should inform the board of decisions about all significant issues raised by internal auditing.

        4) When the CAE believes that senior management has accepted an unacceptable risk, the CAE must discuss the matter with senior management. The CAE should

            a) Understand management's basis for the decision,
            b) Identify the cause of any disagreement,
            c) Determine whether management has the authority to accept the risk, and
            d) Preferably resolve the disagreement.

        5) If the CAE and senior management cannot agree, the CAE must inform the board.

            a) If possible, the CAE and management should jointly present their positions.

            b) CAEs should consider timely discussion of financial reporting issues with the external auditors.

    b. The CAE may share and discuss the contents of the report with senior management before presenting it to the board.

Interpretation of Standard 2060

The frequency and content of reporting are determined in discussion with senior management and the board and depend on the importance of the information to be communicated and the urgency of the related actions to be taken by senior management or the board.

---

2.   **Communication and Approval**

Performance Standard 2020
<u>Communication and Approval</u>

The chief audit executive must communicate the internal audit activity's plans and resource requirements, including significant interim changes, to senior management and the board for review and approval. The chief audit executive must also communicate the impact of resource limitations.

---

    a.   Detailed guidance is provided in Practice Advisory 2020-1, *Communication and Approval*:

        1)   The CAE annually submits a summary of the (a) internal audit plan, (b) work schedule, (c) staffing plan, and (d) financial budget.

            a)   The CAE also submits all significant interim changes.
            b)   The scope of work and any limitations on it should be disclosed.

        2)   These communications should suffice to allow senior management and the board to determine whether internal audit's objectives and plans are consistent with (a) those of the organization and (b) the internal audit charter.

Stop and review! You have completed the outline for this subunit. Study multiple-choice questions 4 through 6 on page 156.

6.3 RECOMMENDATIONS

1.   **Develop Recommendations**

    a.   After identifying, analyzing, evaluating, and documenting engagement information, the internal auditor makes observations and forms conclusions about the engagement objectives based on the information.

        1)   Recommendations are based on observations and conclusions and may be general or specific. They call for action to correct existing conditions or improve operations and may suggest approaches to correcting or enhancing performance as a guide for management in achieving desired results.

2.   **Four Attributes of Observations and Recommendations**

    a.   Observations and recommendations result from comparing criteria (the correct state) with condition (the current state). When conditions meet the criteria, communication of satisfactory performance may be appropriate. Observations and recommendations are based on the following attributes defined in Practice Advisory 2410-1, *Communication Criteria*:

        1)   **Criteria** are the standards, measures, or expectations used in making an evaluation or verification (the correct state).

        2)   The **condition** is the factual evidence that the internal auditor found in the examination (the current state).

        3)   The **cause** is the reason for the difference between expected and actual conditions.

        4)   The **effect** is the risk or exposure the organization or others encounter because the condition is not consistent with the criteria (the impact of the difference).

            a)   In determining the risk or exposure, internal auditors consider the effect their observations and recommendations may have on the organization's operations and financial statements.

    b.   Observations and recommendations also may include client accomplishments, related issues, and supportive information.

NOTE: The word "findings" is often used as a synonym for "observations" on the CIA exam.

3.   Examples of criteria for evaluating operations include

    a.   Organizational policies and procedures delegating authority and assigning responsibilities,

    b.   Textbook illustrations of generally accepted practices, and

    c.   Codification of best practices in similar organizations.

4.   **Favorable observations** should be short and simple. For example, "Production schedules, levels, and quality were at or ahead of budgeted levels in every case."

5.   **Unfavorable observations** need further explanation to justify recommended changes. The following are examples:

    a.   **Summary**

       1)   Because of inaccurate inventory records, the supply department bought unneeded supplies costing US $75,000.

    b.   **Criteria**

       1)   Established procedures provide that excess materials returned by the production department shall be entered on the records of the supply department to show the levels of inventory currently on hand and available for issuance.

    c.   **Condition (facts)**

       1)   Our tests disclosed that, for a period of 6 months, supplies returned from production had not been entered on the supply department's records.

    d.   **Cause**

       1)   We found that the employees responsible for the posting of returned supplies had not been instructed in their duties. In addition, supervisors had not been monitoring the process.

    e.   **Effect**

       1)   As a result of the inaccurate inventory records, the organization bought unneeded supplies costing about US $75,000.

    f.   **Recommendation**

       1)   We reviewed the conditions with the manager of the supply department, and he agreed to bring the inventory records up to date, issue job instructions to the workers spelling out the need to record returned supplies, and instruct supervisors to monitor the process in the future and to submit written reports on their periodic reviews.

    g.   **Corrective action taken**

       1)   Before we concluded our examination, the manager took all three steps. Our subsequent spot checks showed that the action was effective. We therefore consider this observation closed.

6.   Practice Advisory 2410-1, *Communication Criteria*, provides guidance for communicating recommendations:

   a.   The internal auditor may communicate recommendations, acknowledgments of satisfactory performance, and corrective actions.

      1)   Recommendations are based on observations and conclusions. They may suggest approaches to correcting or enhancing performance and be general or specific.

         a)   For example, the internal auditor may (1) recommend a general course of action and specific suggestions for implementation or (2) suggest further investigation or study.

Stop and review! You have completed the outline for this subunit. Study multiple-choice questions 7 through 10 beginning on page 156.

6.4 PREPARE REPORT OR OTHER COMMUNICATION

1.   **Final Engagement Communication**

   a.   Internal auditors are expected to make known the results of their work.

Performance Standard 2400
Communicating Results

Internal auditors must communicate the results of engagements.

---

   b.   The CAE has overall responsibility for the internal audit activity. However, the auditor-in-charge organizes and drafts the final communication for a specific engagement.

   c.   The IIA provides specific criteria to be included with the results of engagements.

Performance Standard 2410
Criteria for Communicating

Communications must include the engagement's objectives and scope as well as applicable conclusions, recommendations, and action plans.

Implementation Standard 2410.A1

Final communication of engagement results must, where appropriate, contain the internal auditors' opinion and/or conclusions. When issued, an opinion or conclusion must take account of the expectations of senior management, the board, and other stakeholders and must be supported by sufficient, reliable, relevant, and useful information.

---

   d.   Practice Advisory 2410-1, *Communication Criteria*, provides guidance for performing the communication functions stated in Performance Standard 2410.

      1)   A final communication may vary by organization or type of engagement. However, it contains at least the purpose, scope, and results of the engagement.

      2)   A final communication may include background information, such as activities reviewed and the status of observations, conclusions, recommendations from prior reports, and summaries of the communication's content.

      3)   **Purpose** statements describe the objectives and may explain why the engagement was conducted and what it was expected to achieve.

4) **Scope** statements identify the audited activities and may include the time period reviewed and related activities not reviewed to define the engagement. They also may describe the nature and extent of engagement work.

5) **Results** include observations, conclusions, opinions, recommendations, and action plans.

6) **Observations** (findings) are relevant statements of fact. A final communication contains those observations necessary for understanding the conclusions and recommendations. Less significant matters may be communicated informally.

7) **Conclusions and opinions** are evaluations of the effects of the observations and recommendations. They are clearly identified. Conclusions may address the entire engagement scope or specific aspects. They may cover (but are not limited to) whether

   a) Operating or program objectives conform with the organization's,
   b) Those objectives are being met, and
   c) The activity under review is functioning as intended.

8) An opinion may include an overall assessment of controls or be limited to specific controls or aspects of the engagement.

9) Client accomplishments included in the final communication may be necessary to present fairly the existing conditions and provide perspective and balance.

   a) Client's views about conclusions, opinions, or recommendations also may be included.

10) The internal auditor reaches agreement with the client about results and any necessary plan of corrective action. Disagreements are fully disclosed, including both positions and the reasons.

   a) The client's written comments may be presented in the report, an appendix, or a cover letter.

11) Certain information is excluded from a general-use report because it is privileged, proprietary, or related to improper acts. It is disclosed in a separate report.

   a) If senior management is involved, report distribution is to the board.

12) A signed report is issued at the end of the engagement.

   a) Summary reports are appropriate for levels above the client. They may be issued separately from, or with, the final communication.
   b) The auditor authorized to sign is designated by the CAE.
   c) If reports are distributed electronically, the internal audit activity keeps a signed report on file.

      i) The term "signed" means a manual or electronic signature in the report or on a cover letter.

Implementation Standard 2410.A2

Internal auditors are encouraged to acknowledge satisfactory performance in engagement communications.

---

e. Internal auditors should provide positive feedback to engagement clients when appropriate. This practice helps to develop good relations with clients and may improve their receptiveness to the audit findings.

2. **Purposes of Internal Audit Communications**

    a. According to Practice Advisory 1210-1, internal auditors should be skilled in oral and written communications to clearly and effectively convey such matters as engagement objectives, evaluations, conclusions, and recommendations.

    b. The following are purposes of internal audit communications:

        1) Inform (tell what was found),

        2) Persuade (convince management of the worth and validity of the audit findings), and

        3) Get results (move management toward change and improvement).

    c. Providing useful and timely information and promoting improvements in operations are goals of internal auditors.

        1) To accomplish these goals, engagement communications should meet the expectations, perceptions, and needs of operating and senior management.

        2) For the benefit of senior management, the communication should provide appropriately generalized information regarding matters of significance to the organization as a whole. For the benefit of operating management, the communication should emphasize details of operations.

3. **Definitions of the Qualities of Communications**

Performance Standard 2420
Quality of Communications

Communications must be accurate, objective, clear, concise, constructive, complete, and timely.

---

    a. The IIA issued an Interpretation of the Performance Standard above to define each quality.

Interpretation of Standard 2420

- Accurate communications are free from errors and distortions and are faithful to the underlying facts.

- Objective communications are fair, impartial, and unbiased and are the result of a fair-minded and balanced assessment of all relevant facts and circumstances.

- Clear communications are easily understood and logical, avoiding unnecessary technical language and providing all significant and relevant information.

- Concise communications are to the point and avoid unnecessary elaboration, superfluous detail, redundancy, and wordiness.

- Constructive communications are helpful to the engagement client and the organization and lead to improvements where needed.

- Complete communications lack nothing that is essential to the target audience and include all significant and relevant information and observations to support recommendations and conclusions.

- Timely communications are opportune and expedient, depending on the significance of the issue, allowing management to take appropriate corrective action.

---

    b. Further guidance is provided in Practice Advisory 2420-1, *Quality of Communications*:

        1) Data and evidence are processed with care and precision.

        2) Observations, conclusions, and recommendations are unbiased.

        3) Unnecessary technical language is avoided, and context for all significant and relevant information is provided.

4)   Communications are meaningful but concise.

5)   The content and tone are useful and positive, and objectives are focused.

6)   Communications are consistent with the entity's style and culture.

7)   Results are not unduly delayed.

4.   **Other Characteristics of Effective Communications**

a.   The presentation should be **coherent**, that is, logically ordered and integrated.

b.   Sentences should be short and use simple but appropriate vocabulary.

c.   Good writing is **consistent**. Inconsistent style, sentence structure, format, and vocabulary are confusing.

d.   Active-voice verbs are generally (not always) preferable to passive-voice verbs. The active voice is more concise, vivid, and interesting.

e.   The Seven Seas (7 Cs) is a useful memory aid. Good writing is

1)   Clear.
2)   Correct (accurate and objective).
3)   Concise.
4)   Consistent.
5)   Constructive.
6)   Coherent
7)   Complete and timely.

f.   Emphasis

1)   Successful communication between the internal auditor and the engagement client partially depends on achieving appropriate emphasis. Both parties should be aware of the most important points in their discussion.

2)   Graphic illustrations (e.g., pictures, charts, or graphs), oral and written repetition (e.g., summaries) and itemized lists (bulleted or numbered) are good ways of emphasizing information.

3)   Using audiovisual aids to support a discussion of major points results in the most retention of information. One study concluded that 85% of the information presented in this way will be remembered after 3 hours, and 65% after 3 days.

g.   Word selection (diction) can affect the recipient of an engagement communication in either written or oral form.

1)   In general, language should be fact-based and neutral. But if the internal auditor's objective is to persuade an individual to accept recommendations, words with strong or emotional connotations should be used.

a)   However, words that are connotation-rich have strong but unpredictable effects. A common example is using the word "fraud" rather than the more neutral "irregularity."

2)   Using too strong a word or a word inappropriate for the particular recipient may induce an unwanted response. Thus, high-connotation language should be chosen carefully to appeal to the specific recipient.

5.   **Errors and Omissions**

Performance Standard 2421
Errors and Omissions

If a final communication contains a significant error or omission, the chief audit executive must communicate corrected information to all parties who received the original communication.

---

a.   The correction of an error or omission in an internal audit communication need not be in written form.

6.   **The Conformance Phrase**

Performance Standard 2430
Use of "Conducted in Conformance with the *International Standards for the Professional Practice of Internal Auditing*"

Internal auditors may report that their engagements are "conducted in conformance with the *International Standards for the Professional Practice of Internal Auditing*" only if the results of the quality assurance and improvement program support the statement.

---

7.   **Nonconformance**

Performance Standard 2431
Engagement Disclosure of Nonconformance

When nonconformance with the Definition of Internal Auditing, the Code of Ethics, or the *Standards* impacts a specific engagement, communication of the results must disclose the:

- Principle or rule of conduct of the Code of Ethics or *Standard(s)* with which full conformance was not achieved;
- Reason(s) for nonconformance; and
- Impact of nonconformance on the engagement and the communicated engagement results.

---

8.   **Overall Opinions**

Performance Standard 2450
Overall Opinions

When an overall opinion is issued, it must take into account the expectations of senior management, the board, and other stakeholders and must be supported by sufficient, reliable, relevant, and useful information.

Interpretation of Standard 2450

The communication will identify:

- The scope, including the time period to which the opinion pertains;
- Scope limitations;
- Consideration of all related projects including the reliance on other assurance providers;
- The risk or control framework or other criteria used as a basis for the overall opinion; and
- The overall opinion, judgment, or conclusion reached.

The reasons for an unfavorable overall opinion must be stated.

---

a.   The outline in this section is based on Practice Guide, *Formulating and Expressing Internal Audit Opinions*.

b.   Internal auditors may be asked by stakeholders to express macro opinions or micro opinions, depending on the scope of the engagement.

1)   The assurance for the organization as a whole is a **macro opinion**. It is usually based on multiple audit projects. For example, a macro opinion may be expressed on

a)   The overall system of internal control over financial reporting

b)   Controls over compliance with laws and regulations, such as health and safety, when they are performed in multiple countries or subsidiaries

        c) Controls, such as budgeting and performance management, when they are performed in multiple subsidiaries and coverage extends to the majority of assets, revenues, etc.

  2) The assurance for a component of operations is a **micro opinion**. It is usually based on one or a few audit projects. For example, a micro opinion may be expressed on

        a) An individual business process or activity in one organization, department, or location.

        b) Internal control at a reporting unit when all work is performed in one audit.

        c) Compliance with policies, laws, and regulations regarding data privacy when the work is performed in one or a few business units.

  3) The need for audit opinions and the ability to express them depends on, among other things,

        a) The needs of stakeholders;
        b) The scope, nature, timing, and extent of audit work;
        c) The sufficiency of resources to complete the work; and
        d) Assessing the results.

 c. **Stakeholder requirements** for opinions should be clarified by the CAE with senior management and the board. Thus, the nature of the service to be performed should be determined prior to the engagement.

  1) Discussions with stakeholders about an opinion may include

        a) Why it is being requested.
        b) The timing for issuance and type of opinion.
        c) The form of opinion (e.g., written or verbal).
        d) The level of assurance.
        e) The period covered.
        f) The scope (e.g., whether it is limited to operational controls).

           i) The scope definition commonly extends to (a) the parts of the entity covered, (b) controls addressed, and (c) the time period or moment in time for which the opinion is expressed.

        g) Suitable criteria to be used, i.e., a framework of factors relevant to the auditee against which outcomes may be measured.

           i) The internal audit activity determines whether the entity has identified appropriate governance, risk management, and control practices. Thus, the auditee should provide a statement of risk tolerance or risk appetite and materiality thresholds. Without these principles, an opinion should not be expressed.

        h) Potential users.

 d. The CAE considers the organizational effect if the report is distributed to **outside users**.

  1) Consultation with legal counsel is appropriate.

 e. The following are **planning** factors:

  1) The characteristics of macro and micro opinions.
  2) Whether positive or negative assurance will be expressed.
  3) The purpose and use of any special requests.
  4) The audit evidence to support the opinion and the time required for the work.
  5) Agreement with stakeholders on the criteria used.

6) The need to develop an approach to provide sufficient, relevant evidence. This approach may combine the results of previous audits or identify areas of significance and risk.

    a) If multiple projects are required, they should be identified.

7) The consideration of related projects (including reliance on the work of others or self-assessments) and allowing time for the final assessment.

8) Whether resources and skills are adequate. If not, the auditor may (a) decline to express the opinion or (b) qualify the opinion (by excluding certain areas or risks from the scope).

    a) Discussions with management and communication of the plan, including its timing and scope and the criteria to be used.

f. Macro opinions are generally in writing and in the form of **positive assurance**.

1) The CAE provides macro opinions because (s)he has an overview of micro audit results.

2) Positive assurance (reasonable assurance) is the highest level and requires the highest level of evidence.

    a) The assertion may be binary, for example, that controls are (are not) effective, or risks are (are not) effectively managed.

3) Variations in positive assurance may include the use of commonly understood grades of the effectiveness of control or risk management.

    a) Examples include color coding (red-yellow-green) or a grading scale (1 to 4).

4) A **qualified opinion** indicates an exception to the general opinion, for example, that controls were satisfactory with the exception of accounts payable controls.

g. **Evaluating results** may involve rating individual audit findings and their significance relative to a project, risk category, or the organization as a whole.

1) The auditor considers the magnitude or significance (materiality) of a key business objective that is fundamental to the opinion, including the residual risk that it will not be achieved.

2) The implications of audit issues or findings (impact) are considered and understood in the context of the opinion to be given (micro or macro).

3) Another factor to be considered in a macro opinion is rating the risks that the controls in place will not permit management's objectives to be achieved.

h. The **use of grades** requires careful wording, particularly terms such as "adequate" or "inadequate" and "satisfactory" or "unsatisfactory." Wording should be clear and well defined.

1) General terms may not sufficiently define the meaning. For example, the term "effective" usually refers to effectiveness in design and operation. The opinion needs to indicate whether both meanings are included.

2) Clarity is improved if the organization has adopted a broadly understood definition of internal controls, such as the COSO model.

3) Use of a grading scale generally requires a well-defined evaluation structure. For example, an opinion may state how much better or worse controls are than a defined benchmark.

4) Increased precision in the information provided in an opinion normally increases the amount of evidence needed to support the opinion.

    i.   **Negative assurance**, sometimes referred to as limited assurance, is a statement that nothing came to the auditor's attention about an objective, such as the effectiveness of internal control or adequacy of a risk management process.

        1) The internal auditor takes no responsibility for the sufficiency of the audit scope and procedures.

        2) Occasionally, internal auditing may be asked for an informal opinion (oral opinion) on the adequacy of governance, risk management, or control policies and processes, either at the macro or micro level.

            a) If possible, the expression of such an opinion should be based on objective evidence.

            b) The same factors are considered as in expressing a written opinion.

            c) In some instances, internal auditing should decline to issue an oral opinion, especially given a lack of sufficient evidence or work to support the opinion.

    j.   If the CAE intends to rely on the **work of others**, appropriate steps should be taken, including assessing the competency, independence, and objectivity of the other assurance providers.

        1) Such reliance should be included in discussions with key stakeholders and, if significant, the board.

    k.   The use of opinions has **legal** significance because of the increased reliance on internal audit reports. However, reliance might result in legal liability if a control failure is discussed after issuance of the report. Moreover, the CAE's certification credentials may have legal implications if noncompliance issues arise.

        1) Thus, the CAE should use appropriate language in the report and provide a disclaimer that notifies the reader of any limitations on the assurance given.

            a) The CAE should state that it is not possible to provide absolute assurance and should encourage readers to consider all legal Implications.

Stop and review! You have completed the outline for this subunit. Study multiple-choice questions 11 through 15 beginning on page 158.

6.5 APPROVE AND DISTRIBUTE REPORTS

Performance Standard 2440
<u>Disseminating Results</u>

The chief audit executive must communicate results to the appropriate parties.

Interpretation of Standard 2440

The chief audit executive is responsible for reviewing and approving the final engagement communication before issuance and for deciding to whom and how it will be disseminated. When the chief audit executive delegates these duties, he or she retains overall responsibility.

---

1. **Engagement Report Approval and Distribution**

    a.   Practice Advisory 2440-1, *Disseminating Results*, provides guidance on this topic.

        1) Prior to issuing the final communication, internal auditors discuss conclusions and recommendations with appropriate management. The discussion is usually during the engagement or at an exit meeting.

            a) Another technique is client review of a draft.

       b)   The discussions and reviews provide the client with an opportunity for clarification and an expression of views.

    2)   Participants in discussions and reviews usually have knowledge of detailed operations and can authorize corrective action.

2.   **Disseminating Results**

    a.   Final communications are distributed to all those having a direct interest in the engagement. They include persons able to ensure due consideration of engagement results, that is, those who can take corrective action or ensure that it is taken. Higher-level persons, such as the board of directors, may receive a summary, and communications may be distributed to other interested or affected parties.

       1)   Each communication should contain a distribution sheet listing the distributees and indicating with whom it has been reviewed in draft. Distributees include the following:

          a)   The executive to whom the internal audit activity reports

          b)   The person or persons to whom replies will be addressed

          c)   Persons responsible for the activity or activities reviewed, e.g., auditee management

          d)   Persons required to take corrective action

3.   **Legal Considerations**

    a.   Internal auditors must consider the sensitivity of the information contained in their engagement communications and the possible effects on the organization if it is misused or misinterpreted by unauthorized persons.

    b.   Practice Advisory 2400-1, *Legal Considerations in Communicating Results*, begins with a cautionary note by The IIA:

CAUTION: Internal auditors are encouraged to consult legal counsel in matters involving legal issues. This guidance is based primarily on the legal systems (e.g., in the USA) that protect information and work performed for, or communicated to, an engaged attorney (attorney-client privilege).

       1)   The internal auditors need to be careful when drafting communications about legal issues, including noncompliance with laws and regulations. Policies and procedures should guide the handling of such matters.

          a)   A close relationship with legal counsel and compliance officials also is encouraged.

       2)   Preparation of engagement records may conflict with legal counsel's desire not to create evidence discoverable in legal proceedings that could harm the organization.

          a)   Accordingly, the relationship of legal counsel with the auditors needs to be governed by proper planning and policy making. For example, roles need to be defined, and methods of communication need to be established.

          b)   Moreover, both parties need to promote an ethical and preventive perspective throughout the organization by educating management about the established policies.

       3)   An attorney-client privilege arises when communication about legal assistance for the client is made between privileged persons in confidence.

          a)   This privilege also may apply to communications with third parties working with the attorney.

4) A privilege of critical self-analysis, for example, in auditors' work products, may be available in some courts.

    a) This privilege is based on the belief that the confidentiality of the self-analysis outweighs the public interest.

    b) Documents protected usually need to be (1) a work product (e.g., a memo or computer program), (2) prepared in anticipation of a lawsuit, and (3) completed by someone working at the direction of an attorney.

5) Documents delivered to the attorney before the attorney-client relationship is formed generally are not protected by the privilege.

Stop and review! You have completed the outline for this subunit. Study multiple-choice questions 16 through 18 beginning on page 159.

6.6 OBTAIN MANAGEMENT'S RESPONSE

1. **Responses to the Report**

    a. Reviews of drafts of communications with engagement clients (management or others) are a courtesy to them and a form of insurance for the engagement.

    b. Clients may have discussed all such matters during the engagement. They should be given the opportunity to read what will be sent to their superiors. Moreover, seeing the draft report may cause clients to view the results differently.

        1) Thus, an exit meeting (discussed further in Study Unit 5, Subunit 3) improves relations with clients. It involves them in the engagement process (a participative or consultative approach) and ensures that misunderstandings or misinterpretations are avoided. Moreover, the exit meeting may increase client support for appropriate action.

    c. Reviewing results in draft form with the client may detect omissions or inaccuracies before the final communication is issued.

        1) Documenting these discussions and reviews can be valuable in preventing or resolving disputes.

    d. The auditor carefully considers the following before the review:

        1) The person(s) with whom the draft should be reviewed.

        2) The feasibility of performing some reviews on a group basis.

        3) The timing and order of the reviews.

        4) Sending the draft to the client before the meeting.

        5) The need for face-to-face discussions. Sending copies of the draft to interested parties and receiving their written comments may be sufficient.

    e. The auditor should be in charge of the post-engagement meeting.

    f. The auditor should be prepared for conflicts and questions.

        1) When the auditor has previously experienced difficulty with an individual, that individual's superior may be invited to attend.

        2) To be able to answer questions promptly, the auditor may wish to prepare notes.

        3) The auditor should be flexible on matters not affecting the substance of the matters communicated.

            a) However, the auditor should never negotiate the opinion.

    g. Disagreements are explained in the engagement communications.

    h. When the reviews result in significant changes, the other people with whom the draft was reviewed should have an opportunity to see, or be told of, the revisions.

    i. The auditor maintains careful records of the post-engagement meeting, of any objections, and of the manner in which conflicts were resolved.

j.   When copies of the draft are sent to concerned parties for review, the auditor

1)   Asks for the timely return of the draft with any appropriate comments.
2)   Sets a specific due date for the return of the draft.
3)   Offers to meet with those who wish to discuss the draft further.

k.   Responses by clients about internal auditors' actions should go to both management and the internal auditors to ensure the accountability of the internal audit activity. This process is a way of

1)   Judging the internal auditors' performance,
2)   Improving future engagements by identifying areas of weak performance,
3)   Bettering internal auditor-client relations through a greater sense of participation,
4)   Minimizing conflicts, and
5)   Helping clients to understand the difficulties faced by the internal auditors.

Stop and review! You have completed the outline for this subunit. Study multiple-choice question 19 on page 160.

6.7 REPORT OUTCOMES

1.   **Report Outcomes to Appropriate Parties**

a.   The final step in communicating engagement results is reporting outcomes to appropriate parties. Internal auditors must consider the treatment of sensitive information and communications outside the organization.

2.   **Sensitive Information**

a.   Practice Advisory 2440-2, *Communicating Sensitive Information Within and Outside the Chain of Command*, provides the internal auditor with guidance on dealing with sensitive information:

1)   The auditors may possess critically sensitive and substantial information with significant potential adverse consequences. If the new information is substantial and credible, the auditors normally communicate it on a timely basis to senior management and the board.

a)   The communication is typically through the internal audit activity's usual chain of command, i.e., from staff to supervisor to chief audit executive.

2)   If the CAE then concludes that senior management is exposing the organization to unacceptable risk and is not taking appropriate action, (s)he presents the information and differences of opinion to the board.

3)   Laws, regulations, or common practices may require immediate reporting of sensitive occurrences, e.g., fraudulent financial reporting or illegal acts, to the board.

4)   Auditors may need to consider communicating outside the chain of command or the organization (internal or external whistleblowing, respectively).

a)   Most whistleblowers act internally. However, those who act outside the organization typically mistrust its response, fear retaliation, or have health or safety concerns.

i)   If an internal auditor elects internal whistleblowing, (s)he must cautiously evaluate the evidence, the reasonableness of the conclusions, and the merits of possible actions. Such action may be appropriate if it results in responsible action by senior management or the board.

5) Public servants may be required to report illegal or unethical acts, and some laws protect citizen whistleblowers. Thus, auditors need to be aware of applicable laws and must obtain legal advice if uncertain of legal requirements or consequences.

    a) Members of The IIA and CIAs also follow the provisions of The IIA's Code of Ethics.

    b) An auditor's professional duty and ethical responsibility is to evaluate the evidence and the reasonableness of his or her conclusions. The auditor then decides whether further actions may be needed to protect

        i) The organization,
        ii) Its stakeholders,
        iii) The outside community, or
        iv) The institutions of society.

    c) The auditor also needs to consider the duty of confidentiality. The advice of legal counsel and other experts may be needed.

6) The auditor must make a professional decision about his or her obligation to the employer.

    a) The decision to communicate outside the chain of command should be based on a well-informed opinion that the wrongdoing is supported by the evidence and that a legal, professional, or ethical obligation requires action.

b. Information that is privileged, proprietary, or related to improper or illegal acts is disclosed in a separate communication and distributed to the board.

3. **Communications Outside the Organization**

Implementation Standard 2440.A2

If not otherwise mandated by legal, statutory, or regulatory requirements, prior to releasing results to parties outside the organization the chief audit executive must:

- Assess the potential risk to the organization;
- Consult with senior management and/or legal counsel as appropriate; and
- Control dissemination by restricting the use of the results.

---

a. Further guidance is provided in Practice Advisory 2440.A2-1, *Communications Outside the Organization*:

1) Auditors review guidance for disseminating information outside the organization. If guidance does not exist, auditors facilitate adoption of policies. These policies address

    a) Authorization requirements,
    b) The approval process,
    c) Guidelines for types of information that may be reported,
    d) Authorized recipients and what they may receive,
    e) Legal considerations, and
    f) Other information includible in outside communications (e.g., nature of assurance, opinions, guidance, advice, or recommendations).

2) Requests for existing information are reviewed to determine its suitability for disclosure. A request for information that must be created or determined results in a new internal audit engagement.

    a) It may be possible to create a special-purpose report based on existing information that is suitable for outside disclosure.

3) Outside dissemination considers

a) The need for a written agreement;
b) Identifying persons related to the report or information;
c) Identification of objectives, scope, and procedures;
d) Nature of the report or other communication; and
e) Copyright issues.

4) The internal auditor may discover information reportable to senior management or the board during an engagement that requires outside disclosure. As a result, the CAE needs to communicate suitably to the board.

b. Engagements to generate internal audit reports or communications outside the organization need to be conducted in accordance with applicable standards. The report or other communication should refer to such standards.

EXAMPLE

An internal auditor discovered fraud committed by members of management and is unsure of whom to disclose this information.

In most cases of whistleblowing, whistleblowers will disclose sensitive information internally, even if not within the normal chain of command. If they trust the policies and mechanisms of the organization to investigate the problem, information can be shared with the appropriate internal parties. However, if the whistleblower doubts the problem will be properly investigated by the corporation, (s)he may consider disclosing the problem to an outside party.

Stop and review! You have completed the outline for this subunit. Study multiple-choice questions 20 and 21 on page 161.

6.8 MONITOR ENGAGEMENT OUTCOMES

Performance Standard 2500
Monitoring Progress

The chief audit executive must establish and maintain a system to monitor the disposition of results communicated to management.

---

1. **Monitor Outcomes**

a. An engagement does not end once outcomes are reported to appropriate parties. The final steps involve monitoring engagement outcomes and following up. Practice Advisory 2500-1, *Monitoring Progress*, provides guidance.

1) The CAE establishes procedures to monitor the disposition of reported results. They include a(n)

a) Time frame for management's response,
b) Evaluation and verification of the response (if appropriate),
c) Follow-up (if appropriate), and
d) Communications process that reports unsatisfactory responses (including assumption of risk) to the appropriate senior management or the board.

2) Observations and recommendations needing immediate action are monitored until correction or implementation, respectively.

3) Observations and recommendations are addressed to managers responsible for corrective action.

4) Management responses and action plans are received and evaluated during the engagement or within a reasonable time afterward. Responses need to be sufficient for the CAE to evaluate the adequacy and timeliness of proposed actions.

5) The internal audit activity receives periodic updates from management to evaluate the status of its efforts to correct observations or implement recommendations.

6) Information from other units involved in follow-up or correction is received and evaluated.

7) The status of responses is reported to senior management or the board.

2. **Follow-Up Process**

Implementation Standard 2500.A1

The chief audit executive must establish a follow-up process to monitor and ensure that management actions have been effectively implemented or that senior management has accepted the risk of not taking action.

---

   a. Follow-up is the element of monitoring that evaluates the adequacy, effectiveness, and timeliness of actions on reported observations and recommendations, including those by other auditors. Practice Advisory 2500.A1-1, *Follow-up Process*, provides guidance.

     1) The internal audit activity charter defines the responsibility for follow-up. The CAE defines its nature, timing, and extent after considering the

       a) Significance of what is reported,
       b) Effort and cost of correction,
       c) Effect of failure of correction,
       d) Complexity of correction, and
       e) Time period involved.

     2) The CAE includes follow-up as part of the work schedule. Scheduling depends on the risk involved and the difficulty and timing of corrective action.

     3) If action already taken suffices, follow-up may be part of the next engagement.

     4) Auditors verify that actions remedy underlying conditions.

     5) Follow-up should be documented.

     6) Follow-up also includes determining whether senior management or the board has assumed the risk of not taking corrective action on reported observations.

   b. The following is a more detailed description of the follow-up process:

     1) The internal auditor should

       a) Receive all replies by the engagement client to the engagement communications

       b) Evaluate the adequacy of those replies

       c) Be convinced that the action taken will cure the the defects

     2) The internal auditor is in the best position to carry out this responsibility. (S)he is

       a) Better acquainted with the facts than senior management or other control centers in the organization

       b) More objective than the operating manager who must take the corrective action

     3) The responsibility for determining whether corrective action is adequate should be coupled with the authority to evaluate the adequacy of replies to engagement communications. The internal auditor should

       a) Report to management when corrective actions are not timely or effective.

       b) Submit periodic reports to management on open engagement observations and recommendations.

4) The adequacy of a response depends on the circumstances in each case. In general, a satisfactory response

a) Addresses itself to the complete problem, not just to specific items included in the internal auditor's sample.

b) Shows that action also has been taken to prevent a recurrence of the deficient condition.

5) In evaluating the reply, the internal auditor should be satisfied that the action promised is actually taken. The auditor should

a) Obtain copies of revised procedures issued to correct conditions.

b) Make any field tests needed to provide assurance that the condition has been corrected.

6) A formal system should be designed to keep engagements open until adequate corrective action is assured. For example,

a) Provisions should be made for the formal opening and closing of engagements.

b) The internal auditors should issue a formal statement of closure, supported by copies of replies to engagement communications and explanations of the action taken to ensure the adequacy and effectiveness of corrective measures.

i) Closure reports are directed to the chief audit executive.

c) Engagements should not be removed from the internal audit activity's open engagements listing until all required corrective actions have been taken and evaluated.

3. **Acceptance of Excessive Risk**

Performance Standard 2600
Communicating the Acceptance of Risks

When the chief audit executive concludes that management has accepted a level of risk that may be unacceptable to the organization, the chief audit executive must discuss the matter with senior management. If the chief audit executive determines that the matter has not been resolved, the chief audit executive must communicate the matter to the board.

---

a. Management decides the action taken in response to engagement results. The CAE assesses this action for timely resolution. The extent of follow-up also is a function of follow-up work done by others.

b. Senior management may assume the risk of noncorrection. The decisions on all significant engagement observations and recommendations are reported to the board.

Stop and review! You have completed the outline for this subunit. Study multiple-choice questions 22 through 25 beginning on page 161.

QUESTIONS

6.1 Communication with Clients

1. During an engagement involving the receiving section of the purchasing division, the internal auditor discovers that a receiving problem might be the result of procedures followed in the procurement section. The internal audit activity's management agrees that the internal auditor should extend the engagement, on a limited scale, into the procurement section. According to the *Standards*, which device should be used to communicate the change in engagement scope to the engagement client?

A. An informal notification of the involved supervisor.

B. A formal written communication to the involved supervisor.

C. A written interim communication to the involved supervisor and the same distribution as the original correspondence scheduling the engagement.

D. No communication is necessary if the internal audit activity's charter specifies the unrestricted scope of its work.

Answer (C) is correct.
    REQUIRED: The device used to communicate a change in audit scope to the auditee.
    DISCUSSION: Interim reports are written or oral and may be transmitted formally or informally. Interim reports are used to communicate information that requires immediate attention, to communicate a change in engagement scope for the activity under review, or to keep management informed of engagement progress when engagements extend over a long period (PA 2410-1, para. 14).

2. You are conducting an engagement to evaluate the organization's marketing effort. You agreed to keep the marketing vice president informed of your progress on a regular basis. What method should be used for those progress reports?

A. Oral or written interim reports.

B. Written reports signed by the chief audit executive.

C. Copies of working paper summaries.

D. Briefing by the appropriate marketing first-line supervisor.

Answer (A) is correct.
    REQUIRED: The method of progress reporting.
    DISCUSSION: Interim reports are written or oral and may be transmitted formally or informally. Interim reports are used to communicate information that requires immediate attention, to communicate a change in engagement scope for the activity under review, or to keep management informed of engagement progress when engagements extend over a long period (PA 2410-1, para. 14).
    Answer (B) is incorrect. An oral report is acceptable.
Answer (C) is incorrect. Engagement communications, not working papers, should be submitted to engagement clients.
Answer (D) is incorrect. The internal auditors, not a marketing supervisor, should submit engagement communications.

3. Which of the following is **false** with respect to the use of interim engagement communications? Interim engagement communications

A. Are used to communicate information that requires immediate attention.

B. Are used to communicate a change in engagement scope for the activity under review.

C. Keep management informed of engagement progress when engagements extend over a long period of time.

D. Eliminate the need for issuing final engagement communications.

Answer (D) is correct.
    REQUIRED: The false statement about interim engagement communications.
    DISCUSSION: Interim reports are written or oral and may be transmitted formally or informally. They are used to communicate information that requires immediate attention, to communicate a change in engagement scope for the activity under review, or to keep management informed of engagement progress when engagements extend over a long period. The use of interim reports does not diminish or eliminate the need for a final report (PA 2410-1, para. 14).

6.2 Reporting to Senior Management and the Board

4. Who reviews and approves a summary of the internal audit plan?

- A. Senior management and the board.
- B. The audit committee and the board.
- C. Senior management only.
- D. The chief audit executive (CAE) only.

Answer (A) is correct.
REQUIRED: The person(s) responsible for approvals of the internal audit plan.
DISCUSSION: The CAE will annually submit a summary of the internal audit plan, work schedule, staffing plan, and financial budget to senior management and the board for review and approval (PA 2020-1, para. 1).
Answer (B) is incorrect. The CAE also submits the internal audit plan to senior management. Answer (C) is incorrect. The CAE also submits the internal audit plan to the board. Answer (D) is incorrect. The audit plan is submitted to senior management and the board.

5. As the chief audit executive, you have determined that the acquisition of some expensive, state-of-the-art software for paperless working paper files will be useful. Identify the preferred method for presenting your request to senior management.

- A. The effect of not obtaining the software.
- B. Statement of need.
- C. Comparison with other internal audit activities.
- D. Evaluation of the software's technical specifications.

Answer (A) is correct.
REQUIRED: The preferred method for presenting a request for resources needed by internal auditing.
DISCUSSION: The CAE must communicate the internal audit activity's plans and resource requirements to senior management and the board for review and approval. The CAE also must communicate the effect of resource limitations (Perf. Std. 2020).
Answer (B) is incorrect. The need must be weighed against the cost. Answer (C) is incorrect. Other internal audit activities may have different cost-benefit relationships. Answer (D) is incorrect. Specialists, not senior management, will perform this evaluation.

6. Bobby Fitz, CAE, believes that the internal controls over cash disbursements need major revisions. Mr. Fitz discussed this matter with senior management and was very alarmed at their acceptance of this serious risk. What action should Mr. Fitz take next?

- A. Report the matter to the board immediately.
- B. Understand management's basis for accepting the risk.
- C. Determine whether management has the authority to accept the risk.
- D. Further attempt to resolve the disagreement.

Answer (B) is correct.
REQUIRED: The action in a situation when the CAE disagrees with senior management.
DISCUSSION: The first thing the CAE should do is understand management's basis for the decision. It is possible that management has knowledge about the risk that the CAE does not. This knowledge may prove it suitable to accept the risk.
Answer (A) is incorrect. While this is an action the CAE could take, the CAE should first understand and try to further resolve the disagreement before reporting it to the board. Answer (C) is incorrect. While this is an action the CAE should take, the CAE should first understand management's basis for accepting the risk. Answer (D) is incorrect. While this is an action the CAE should take, the CAE should first understand management's basis for accepting the risk. This is the last step the CAE should attempt before informing the board.

6.3 Recommendations

7. Recommendations should be included in audit reports to

- A. Provide management with options for addressing audit findings.
- B. Ensure that problems are resolved in the manner suggested by the auditor.
- C. Minimize the amount of time required to correct audit findings.
- D. Guarantee that audit findings are addressed, regardless of cost.

Answer (A) is correct.
REQUIRED: The reason to include recommendations in an engagement communication.
DISCUSSION: Recommendations are based on the internal auditor's observations and conclusions. They call for action to correct existing conditions or improve operations and may suggest approaches to correcting or enhancing performance as a guide for management in achieving desired results (PA 2410-1, para. 9).
Answer (B) is incorrect. Problems must be resolved in the manner deemed appropriate by management, not the auditor. However, the auditor is responsible for monitoring the disposition of results communicated to management. Answer (C) is incorrect. Providing recommendations may or may not enable management to reduce the costs/time of addressing audit findings. Answer (D) is incorrect. Management may assume the risk of not taking corrective action on reported observations, for example, because of cost.

8. An engagement communication relating to an engagement performed at a bank categorizes observations as "deficiencies" for major problems and "other areas for improvement" for less serious problems. Which of the following excerpts is properly included under "other areas for improvement?"

A. Many secured loans did not contain hazard insurance coverage for tangible property collateral.

B. Loan officers also prepare the cashier's checks for disbursement of the loan proceeds.

C. The bank is incurring unnecessary postage cost by not combining certain special mailings to checking account customers with the monthly mailing of their statements.

D. At one branch a large amount of cash was placed on a portable table behind the teller lines.

Answer (C) is correct.
   REQUIRED: The excerpt properly included under "other areas for improvement" in an engagement communication.
   DISCUSSION: The attributes of engagement observations include effect, the risk or exposure, because the condition is inconsistent with the criteria. Moreover, the internal auditor must determine the degree of the risk or exposure. That the bank incurs unnecessary postage expense by not combining mailings warrants mentioning but does not constitute a serious risk or exposure.
   Answer (A) is incorrect. A lack of hazard insurance coverage for collateral is a serious risk or exposure for the bank that could have a material effect on its financial statements. Answer (B) is incorrect. Loan officers should not be permitted to prepare disbursement checks and grant loans to bank customers. These are duties that must be segregated to prevent possible employee defalcations. Answer (D) is incorrect. Failure to limit access to cash violates internal control policies assigning cash to specific individuals for accountability purposes.

9. While performing an operational engagement involving the firm's production cycle, an internal auditor discovers that, in the absence of specific guidelines, some engineers and buyers routinely accept vacation trips paid by certain of the firm's vendors. Other engineers and buyers will not accept even a working lunch paid for by a vendor. Which of the following actions should the internal auditor take?

A. None. The engineers and buyers are professionals. An internal auditor should not inappropriately interfere in what is essentially a personal decision.

B. Informally counsel the engineers and buyers who accept the vacation trips. This helps prevent the possibility of kickbacks, while preserving good internal auditor-engagement client relations.

C. Formally recommend that the organization establish a code of ethics. Guidelines of acceptable conduct, within which individual decisions may be made, should be provided.

D. Issue a formal engagement communication naming the personnel who accept vacations but make no recommendations. Corrective action is the responsibility of management.

Answer (C) is correct.
   REQUIRED: The internal auditor's action upon discovering an absence of guidelines regarding employee-vendor relations.
   DISCUSSION: The internal auditor may communicate recommendations for improvements, acknowledgments of satisfactory performance, and corrective actions. Recommendations are based on the internal auditor's observations and conclusions. They call for action to correct existing conditions or improve operations and may suggest approaches to correcting or enhancing performance as a guide for management in achieving desired results. Recommendations can be general or specific (PA 2410-1, para. 9). Accordingly, the internal auditor's responsibility in these circumstances is to recommend adoption of a code of ethics.
   Answer (A) is incorrect. Internal auditors are charged with the responsibility of evaluating what they examine and of making recommendations, if appropriate. Answer (B) is incorrect. Management is charged with the responsibility of making any corrections necessary within its department. Answer (D) is incorrect. Internal auditors should make recommendations if appropriate.

10. A recommendation in a final engagement communication should address what attribute?

A. Cause.

B. Statement of condition.

C. Criteria.

D. Effect.

Answer (A) is correct.
   REQUIRED: The attribute of a recommendation.
   DISCUSSION: A recommendation must address the cause attribute in order to describe the necessary corrective action.
   Answer (B) is incorrect. The condition attribute simply describes "what is" to serve as a basis for comparison with given criteria. Answer (C) is incorrect. Criteria describe "what should be" and are compared with the statement of condition. Answer (D) is incorrect. The effect attribute addresses the importance of an observation.

6.4 Prepare Report or Other Communication

11. Which of the following is the most appropriate method of reporting disagreement between the internal auditor and the engagement client concerning engagement observations and recommendations?

A. State the internal auditor's position because the report is designed to provide the internal auditor's independent view.

B. State the engagement client's position because management is ultimately responsible for the activities reported.

C. State both positions and identify the reasons for the disagreement.

D. State neither position. If the disagreement is ultimately resolved, there will be no reason to report the previous disagreement. If the disagreement is never resolved, the disagreement should not be reported because there is no mechanism to resolve it.

Answer (C) is correct.
REQUIRED: The most appropriate method of reporting disagreement between the auditor and the auditee about audit findings and recommendations.
DISCUSSION: As part of the internal auditor's discussions with the engagement client, the internal auditor obtains agreement on the results of the engagement and on any necessary plan of action to improve operations. If the internal auditor and engagement client disagree about the engagement results, the engagement communications state both positions and the reasons for the disagreement. The engagement client's written comments may be included as an appendix to the engagement report in the body of the report or in a cover letter (PA 2410-1, para. 12).

12. During the exit conference, the manager of the engagement client objected to a valid observation about a major control deficiency because the manager felt the observation was based upon a "biased sample and immaterial risk." What step should the internal auditor take?

A. Let some neutral group coordinate the follow-up effort after the final engagement communication is issued.

B. Include the engagement client's comments in the report but recommend corrective action.

C. Review the condition during the next annual engagement to determine whether the deficiency is major or minor.

D. Research a compromise by modifying the wording of the conclusion.

Answer (B) is correct.
REQUIRED: The appropriate action when an auditee manager disagrees with findings.
DISCUSSION: As part of the internal auditor's discussions with the engagement client, the internal auditor obtains agreement on the results of the engagement and on any necessary plan of action to improve operations. If the internal auditor and engagement client disagree about the engagement results, the engagement communications state both positions and the reasons for the disagreement. The engagement client's written comments may be included as an appendix to the engagement report in the body of the report or in a cover letter (PA 2410-1, para. 12).
Answer (A) is incorrect. The internal audit activity's responsibility does not end with the issuance of a final engagement communication. Follow-up is required. Answer (C) is incorrect. Waiting a year is too long if a major deficiency is involved. Answer (D) is incorrect. The conclusion (opinion) may not be compromised.

13. An internal auditor has uncovered illegal acts committed by a member of senior management. Such information

A. Should be excluded from the internal auditor's engagement communication and discussed orally with the senior manager.

B. Must be immediately reported to the appropriate government authorities.

C. May be disclosed in a separate communication and distributed to all senior management.

D. May be disclosed in a separate communication and distributed to the board.

Answer (D) is correct.
REQUIRED: The appropriate action when an internal auditor discovers illegal acts committed by a member of senior management.
DISCUSSION: Certain information is not appropriate for disclosure to all report recipients because it is privileged, proprietary, or related to improper or illegal acts. Disclose such information in a separate report. Distribute the report to the board if the conditions being reported involve senior management (PA 2410-1, para. 13).
Answer (A) is incorrect. Although improper or illegal acts may be disclosed in a separate communication, the internal auditor should not discuss such information with individuals who have committed such acts. Answer (B) is incorrect. In general, internal auditors are responsible to their organization's management rather than outside agencies. In the case of fraud, statutory filings with regulatory agencies may be required. Answer (C) is incorrect. Such information should be communicated to individuals to whom senior managers report.

14. An internal audit activity's evaluation of sales contracts revealed that a bribe had been paid to secure a major contract. The strong possibility existed that a senior executive had authorized the bribe. Which of the following best describes the proper distribution of the completed final engagement communication?

   A. The report should be distributed to the chief executive officer and the appropriate regulatory agency.

   B. The report should be distributed to the board, the chief executive officer, and the independent external auditor.

   C. The chief audit executive should provide the board a copy of the report and decide whether further distribution is appropriate.

   D. The report should be distributed to the board, the appropriate law enforcement agency, and the appropriate regulatory agency.

Answer (C) is correct.
   REQUIRED: The proper distribution of the completed audit report if a senior executive may have authorized a bribe.
   DISCUSSION: Certain information is not appropriate for disclosure to all report recipients because it is privileged, proprietary, or related to improper or illegal acts. Disclose such information in a separate report. Distribute the report to the board if the conditions being reported involve senior management (PA 2410-1, para. 13).

15. Which of the following is most appropriate for inclusion in the summary of a final engagement communication?

   A. Engagement client responses to recommendations.

   B. A concise statement of engagement observations.

   C. Reference to areas not covered by the engagement.

   D. Discussion of recommendations given in prior years' engagement communications.

Answer (B) is correct.
   REQUIRED: The most appropriate inclusion in the management summary of a formal audit report.
   DISCUSSION: A signed report is issued after the engagement's completion. Summary reports highlighting engagement results are appropriate for levels of management above the engagement client (PA 2410-1, para. 15).
   Answer (A) is incorrect. Engagement client responses to recommendations are appropriately included in the body of the communication rather than in the summary. Answer (C) is incorrect. A reference to areas not covered by the engagement communications is appropriately included in the body of the communication rather than in the summary. Answer (D) is incorrect. A discussion of recommendations given in prior years' engagement communications is appropriately included in the body of the communication rather than in the summary.

6.5 Approve and Distribute Reports

16. An engagement performed at an organization's payroll department has revealed various control weaknesses. These weaknesses, along with recommendations for corrective actions, were addressed in the final engagement communication. This communication should be most useful to the organization's

   A. Treasurer.

   B. Audit committee of the board of directors.

   C. Payroll manager.

   D. President.

Answer (C) is correct.
   REQUIRED: The person most likely to benefit from the receipt of a payroll department engagement communication.
   DISCUSSION: The CAE distributes the final engagement communication to the management of the audited activity and to those members of the organization who can ensure engagement results are given due consideration and take corrective action or ensure that corrective action is taken (PA 2440-1, para. 4). A communication on control weaknesses in the payroll function should be most useful to the payroll manager because (s)he is in a position to take corrective action.
   Answer (A) is incorrect. The treasurer is not responsible for the payroll department. Answer (B) is incorrect. The audit committee is not in operational control of the department. Answer (D) is incorrect. The president is not in operational control of the department.

17. Which of the following combinations of participants is most appropriate to attend an exit meeting?

A. The responsible internal auditor and representatives from management who are knowledgeable about detailed operations and who can authorize implementation of corrective action.

B. The chief audit executive and the executive in charge of the activity or function reviewed.

C. Staff internal auditors who conducted the field work and operating personnel in charge of the daily performance of the activity or function reviewed.

D. Staff auditors who conducted the field work and the executive in charge of the activity or function reviewed.

Answer (A) is correct.
REQUIRED: The combination of participants most appropriate to attend an exit meeting.
DISCUSSION: The level of participants in the discussions and reviews may vary by organization and nature of the report; they generally include those individuals who are knowledgeable of detailed operations and who can authorize the implementation of corrective action (PA 2440-1, para. 3).
Answer (B) is incorrect. The CAE and the executive in charge of the activity reviewed might not be knowledgeable about the details. Answer (C) is incorrect. Staff auditors and operating personnel might not have the necessary perspectives or authority. Answer (D) is incorrect. The staff auditors might lack the proper perspective and authority.

18. The chief audit executive (CAE) or a designee is required to decide to whom the final engagement communication will be distributed. Observations concerning significant internal control weakness are included in an engagement communication on the accounts payable system of an organization whose securities are publicly traded. Which of the following is the most likely reason that the CAE has chosen to send copies of this engagement communication to the board and the external auditor?

A. The board and external auditor are normally sent copies of all internal audit engagement communications as a courtesy.

B. The board and external auditor will need to take corrective action based on the observations.

C. The activities of the board and external auditor may be affected because of the potential for misstated financial statements.

D. A regulatory agency's guidelines require such distribution.

Answer (C) is correct.
REQUIRED: The most likely reason for distributing copies of an engagement communication containing observations about significant control weaknesses in the accounts payable system.
DISCUSSION: The CAE distributes the final engagement communication to the management of the audited activity and to those members of the organization who can ensure engagement results are given due consideration and take corrective action or ensure that corrective action is taken (PA 2440-1, para. 4). The potential for misstated financial statements created by the internal control weaknesses should be of interest to the board and the external auditor.
Answer (A) is incorrect. Normal distribution is to management of the activity under review and others in a position to take corrective action or ensure that corrective action is taken. Answer (B) is incorrect. Operating management is responsible for taking corrective action. Answer (D) is incorrect. Such a requirement is unlikely.

6.6 Obtain Management's Response

19. Which of the following is a possible disadvantage when the draft engagement communication is provided to local management for review and comment?

A. The engagement client may take corrective action before the final communication is issued.

B. The engagement client will have an opportunity to rebut observations and recommendations.

C. Genuine consideration for the engagement client will be demonstrated.

D. Discussion of the report might center unduly on words rather than on the substantive issues.

Answer (D) is correct.
REQUIRED: The possible disadvantage when the draft report is provided to local management.
DISCUSSION: The internal auditor should be prepared for conflicts and questions and possibly time-consuming disagreement over semantic matters. While showing flexibility on matters not affecting the report's substance, the internal auditor's response to these conflicts should never be to negotiate the engagement conclusions.

6.7 Report Outcomes

20. Which of the following should **not** be one of the primary reasons why an internal auditor may communicate sensitive information outside the normal chain of command?

   A. The desire to stop the wrongful, harmful, or improper activity.

   B. Legal advice indicates that the internal auditor should disclose the sensitive information to an outside party.

   C. A professional obligation requires disclosure of the activity to an outside party.

   D. The internal auditor does not agree with how the board or directors or management may correct the problem.

Answer (D) is correct.
   REQUIRED: The item not a primary reason that an internal auditor should disclose sensitive information to an outside party.
   DISCUSSION: An internal auditor who communicates sensitive information outside the chain of command should be motivated by the desire to stop the wrongful, harmful, or improper activity; legal advice; or a professional obligation. A personal disagreement is the least satisfactory reason.
   Answer (A) is incorrect. The primary motive of outside disclosure to get management or the board of directors to stop the activity they are engaged in. Answer (B) is incorrect. The internal auditor will often consult legal counsel before deciding what course of action to take with regard to the activity. Answer (C) is incorrect. A professional obligation often forces the internal auditor to disclose to outside parties. The IIA's Code of Ethics requires IIA members and certified internal auditors to adhere to the disclosure requirements of illegal or unethical acts.

21. An internal auditor has a professional duty to do each of the following with regard to sensitive information **except**

   A. Consider the duty of confidentiality.

   B. Disclose sensitive information that the internal auditor has a legal obligation to disclose.

   C. Consider whether further action is needed to protect the interests of the organization, the community, or the institutions of society.

   D. Seek the advice of legal counsel or other experts.

Answer (D) is correct.
   REQUIRED: The action the internal auditor does not have a professional duty to do.
   DISCUSSION: Although the advice of legal counsel or other experts is recommended, the internal auditor does not have a professional duty to seek such advice. Discussing the information with lawyers or experts may help provide a different perspective on the circumstances as well as offer opinions about various actions.
   Answer (A) is incorrect. The internal auditor is supposed to respect the value and ownership of information and avoid disclosing it without appropriate authority. Answer (B) is incorrect. An internal auditor must disclose information that (s)he is legally or professionally required to disclose. Answer (C) is incorrect. The internal auditor has a professional duty and an ethical responsibility to evaluate the sensitive evidence and decide whether further action is needed to protect the interests of parties that may be adversely affected.

6.8 Monitor Engagement Outcomes

22. After an engagement report with adverse observations has been communicated to appropriate engagement client personnel, internal auditing's proper action is to

   A. Schedule a follow-up engagement.

   B. Implement corrective action indicated by the observations.

   C. Examine further the data supporting the observations.

   D. Assemble new data to support the observations.

Answer (A) is correct.
   REQUIRED: The proper action after an audit report with adverse findings has been communicated to appropriate auditee personnel.
   DISCUSSION: The CAE must establish and maintain a system to monitor the disposition of results communicated to management (Perf. Std. 2500).
   Answer (B) is incorrect. The internal audit activity ordinarily has no responsibility to implement corrective action. Answer (C) is incorrect. Data have already been examined. Answer (D) is incorrect. Data have already been examined.

23. An audit committee is concerned that management is not addressing all internal audit observations and recommendations. What should the audit committee do to address this situation?

A. Require managers to provide detailed action plans with specific dates for addressing audit observations and recommendations.

B. Require all managers to confirm when they have taken action.

C. Require the chief executive officer to report why action has not been taken.

D. Require the chief audit executive to establish procedures to monitor progress.

Answer (D) is correct.

REQUIRED: The audit committee's action when management is not addressing all internal audit observations and recommendations.

DISCUSSION: The CAE must establish and maintain a system to monitor the disposition of results communicated to management (Perf. Std. 2500).

Answer (A) is incorrect. Management is responsible for ensuring action on all internal audit observations and recommendations, but some actions may take time to complete. It is not feasible to expect that all will be resolved when an audit committee meets. Answer (B) is incorrect. The internal audit activity must monitor progress. Waiting for management confirmation may lead to harmful delays. Answer (C) is incorrect. Management should report reasons for inaction.

24. An internal auditor found that employees in the maintenance department were not signing their time cards. This situation also existed during the last engagement. The internal auditor should

A. Include this observation in the current engagement communication.

B. Ask the manager of the maintenance department to assume the resulting risk.

C. Withhold conclusions about payroll internal control in the maintenance department.

D. Instruct the employees to sign their time cards.

Answer (A) is correct.

REQUIRED: The proper auditor action when the internal auditor discovers that employees do not sign their time cards.

DISCUSSION: The internal auditor determines whether the desired results were achieved or if senior management or the board has assumed the risk of not taking action or implementing the recommendation (PA 2500.A1-1, para. 1).

Answer (B) is incorrect. Asking the manager of the maintenance department to assume the resulting risk is not within the internal auditor's authority, and it would not remedy the situation. However, the internal auditor should ascertain whether senior management has decided to assume the risk. Answer (C) is incorrect. The final engagement communication must contain conclusions about internal control of payroll in the maintenance department. Answer (D) is incorrect. The internal auditor should not supervise maintenance department employees.

25. Management is beginning to take corrective action on personnel department deficiencies reported during the last engagement performed by the internal audit activity. The internal auditor should

A. Oversee the corrective action.

B. Postpone the next engagement of the personnel department until the corrective action is completed.

C. Refrain from judging whether the corrective action will remedy the deficiencies.

D. Follow up to see that the corrective action satisfies the engagement recommendations.

Answer (D) is correct.

REQUIRED: The internal auditor's action regarding corrective action on personnel department deficiencies reported during the last internal audit.

DISCUSSION: The CAE must establish a follow-up process to monitor and ensure that management actions have been effectively implemented or that senior management has accepted the risk of not taking action (Impl. Std. 2500.A1).

Answer (A) is incorrect. Internal auditors should not perform operating functions. Answer (B) is incorrect. A follow-up engagement should be considered if engagement observations were especially significant. Moreover, no reason is given for postponing the next regular engagement. Answer (C) is incorrect. Internal auditors must determine that management actions have been effectively implemented or that senior management has accepted the risk of not taking action.

Practice even more exam-emulating questions in **Gleim CIA Test Prep!**

STUDY UNIT SEVEN
FRAUD RISKS AND CONTROLS

(9 pages of outline)

This study unit covers **Section III: Fraud Risks and Controls** from The IIA's CIA Exam Syllabus. This section makes up 5% to 15% of Part 2 of the CIA exam and is tested at the **proficiency level** (unless otherwise indicated below). The relevant portion of the syllabus is highlighted below. (The complete syllabus is in Appendix B.)

III. FRAUD RISKS AND CONTROLS (5%–15%)

A. Consider the potential for fraud risks and identify common types of fraud associated with the engagement area during the engagement planning process

B. Determine if fraud risks require special consideration when conducting an engagement

C. Determine if any suspected fraud merits investigation

D. Complete a process review to improve controls to prevent fraud and recommend changes

E. Employ audit tests to detect fraud

F. Support a culture of fraud awareness, and encourage the reporting of improprieties

G. Interrogation/investigative techniques – *Awareness Level (A)*

H. Forensic auditing – *Awareness Level (A)*

The prevention or detection of fraud is one of the most important issues in auditing. Practice Advisory 2120-2, *Managing the Risk of the Internal Audit Activity*, states, "Every organization will experience control breakdowns. Often times when controls fail or frauds occur, someone will ask: 'Where were the internal auditors?'" Thus, the expectations of stakeholders regarding the ability of internal auditors to detect fraud are emphasized in this study unit.

7.1 FRAUD -- RISKS AND TYPES

1. **Definition from The IIA Glossary**

    a. Fraud is "any illegal act characterized by deceit, concealment, or violation of trust. These acts are not dependent upon the threat of violence or physical force. Frauds are perpetrated by parties and organizations to obtain money, property, or services; to avoid payment or loss of services; or to secure personal or business advantage."

2. **Overview**

    a. The internal auditor should consider the potential for fraud risks in the assessment of control design and the determination of audit procedures to perform.

    1) Internal auditors should obtain reasonable assurance that objectives for the process under review are achieved and material control deficiencies are detected.

    2) The consideration of fraud risks and their relation to specific audit work are documented.

b.   Internal auditors should have sufficient knowledge of fraud to identify red flags indicating fraud may have been committed.

1)   This knowledge includes the characteristics of fraud, the methods used to commit fraud, and the various fraud schemes associated with the activities reviewed.

c.   Internal auditors should be alert to opportunities that could allow fraud, such as control deficiencies.

1)   If significant control deficiencies are detected, additional procedures may be performed to determine whether fraud has occurred.

d.   Internal auditors should evaluate the indicators of fraud and decide whether any further action is necessary or whether an investigation should be recommended.

e.   Internal auditors should evaluate whether

1)   Management is actively overseeing the fraud risk management programs,

2)   Timely and sufficient corrective measures have been taken with respect to any noted control deficiencies, and

3)   The plan for monitoring the program is adequate.

f.   If appropriate, internal auditors should recommend an investigation.

3.   **Characteristics of Fraud**

a.   Pressure or incentive is the need a person tries to satisfy by committing the fraud.

1)   **Situational pressure** can be personal (e.g., financial difficulties in an employee's personal life) or organizational (e.g., the desire to release positive news to the financial media).

b.   Opportunity is the ability to commit the fraud.

1)   **Opportunity to commit** is especially a factor in low-level employee fraud. Poor controls over cash, merchandise, and other organizational property, as well as a lack of compensating accounting controls, are enabling factors.

2)   This characteristic is the one that the organization can most influence, e.g., by means of controls.

c.   **Rationalization** occurs when a person attributes his or her actions to rational and creditable motives without analysis of the true and, especially, unconscious motives.

1)   Feeling underpaid is a common rationalization for low-level fraud.

4.   **Effects of Fraud**

a.   Monetary losses from fraud are significant, but its full cost is immeasurable in terms of time, productivity, and reputation, including customer relationships.

b.   Thus, an organization should have a fraud program that includes awareness, prevention, and detection programs. It also should have a fraud risk assessment process to identify fraud risks.

5.   **Types of Fraud**

a.   **Asset misappropriation** is stealing cash or other assets (supplies, inventory, equipment, and information). The theft may be concealed, e.g., by adjusting records. An example is embezzlement, the intentional appropriation of property entrusted to one's care.

b.   **Skimming** is theft of cash before it is recorded, for example, accepting payment from a customer but not recording the sale.

c.   **Disbursement fraud** involves payment for fictitious goods or services, overstatement of invoices, or use of invoices for personal reasons.

d.   **Expense reimbursement fraud** is payment for fictitious or inflated expenses, for example, an expense report for personal travel, nonexistent meals, or extra mileage.

e.   **Payroll fraud** is a false claim for compensation, for example, overtime for hours not worked or payments to fictitious employees.

f.   **Financial statement misrepresentation** often overstates assets or revenue or understates liabilities and expenses. Management may benefit by selling stock, receiving bonuses, or concealing another fraud.

g.   **Information misrepresentation** provides false information, usually to outsiders in the form of fraudulent financial statements.

h.   **Corruption** is an improper use of power, e.g., bribery. It often leaves little accounting evidence. These crimes usually are uncovered through tips or complaints from third parties. Corruption often involves the purchasing function.

i.   **Bribery** is offering, giving, receiving, or soliciting anything of value to influence an outcome. Bribes may be offered to key employees such as purchasing agents. Those paying bribes tend to be intermediaries for outside vendors.

j.   A **conflict of interest** is an undisclosed personal economic interest in a transaction that adversely affects the organization or its shareholders.

k.   A **diversion** redirects to an employee or outsider a transaction that would normally benefit the organization.

l.   **Wrongful use** of confidential or proprietary information is fraudulent.

m.   A **related-party fraud** is receipt of a benefit not obtainable in an arm's-length transaction.

n.   **Tax evasion** is intentionally falsifying a tax return.

6.   **Low-Level Fraud vs. Executive Fraud**

a.   Fraud committed by staff or line employees most often consists of theft of property or embezzlement of cash. The incentive might be relief of economic hardship, the desire for material gain, or a drug or gambling habit. This type of fraud is intended to benefit individuals.

1)   Stealing petty cash or merchandise, lapping accounts receivable, and creating nonexistent vendors are common forms of low-level fraud.

b.   Fraud at the executive level is very different. The incentive is usually either maintaining or increasing the stock price, receiving a large bonus, or both. This type of fraud is intended to benefit the organization.

1)   Executive level fraud consists most often of materially misstating financial statements.

7.   **Symptoms of Fraud**

a.   A **document symptom** is any tampering with the accounting records to conceal a fraud. Keeping two sets of books or forcing the books to reconcile are examples.

b.   A **lifestyle symptom** is an unexplained rise in an employee's social status or level of material consumption.

c.   A **behavioral symptom** (i.e., a drastic change in an employee's behavior) may indicate the presence of fraud. Guilt and other forms of stress associated with perpetrating and concealing the fraud may cause noticeable changes in behavior.

8.   **Some Indicators of Possible Fraud**

a.   Frauds and their indicators (red flags) have different forms. The following list includes potential motives, opportunities, and rationalization:

1)   Lack of employee rotation in sensitive positions, such as cash handling
2)   Inappropriate combination of job duties
3)   Unclear lines of responsibility and accountability
4)   Unrealistic sales or production goals
5)   An employee who refuses to take vacations or refuses promotion
6)   Established controls not applied consistently

7) High reported profits when competitors are suffering from an economic downturn
8) High turnover among supervisory positions in finance and accounting areas
9) Excessive or unjustifiable use of sole-source procurement
10) An increase in sales far out of proportion to the increase in cost of goods sold

9. **Types of Fraudulent Processes**

   a. Lapping Receivables

     1) In this fraud, a person (or persons) with access to both customer payments and accounts receivable records steals a customer's payment. The shortage in that customer's account is then covered with a subsequent payment from another customer.

     2) The process continues until (a) a customer complains about his or her payment not being posted, (b) an absence by the perpetrator allows another employee to discover the fraud, or (c) the perpetrator covers the amount stolen.

   b. Check Kiting

     1) Kiting exploits the delay between (a) depositing a check in one bank account and (b) clearing the check through the bank on which it was drawn. This practice is only possible when manual checks are used. The widespread use of electronic funds transfer and other networked computer safeguards make electronic kiting difficult.

     2) A check is kited when (a) a person (the kiter) writes an insufficient funds check on an account in one bank and (b) deposits the check in another bank.

     3) The second bank immediately credits the account for some or all of the amount of the check, enabling the kiter to write other checks on that (nonexistent) balance. The kiter then covers the insufficiency in the first bank with another source of funds. The process can proceed in a circle of accounts at any number of banks.

10. **Responsibility for Detection**

   a. Internal auditors are not responsible for the detection of all fraud, but they always must be alert to the possibility of fraud.

> **Implementation Standard 1210.A2**
>
> Internal auditors must have sufficient knowledge to evaluate the risk of fraud and the manner in which it is managed by the organization, but are not expected to have the expertise of a person whose primary responsibility is detecting and investigating fraud.

     1) According to Implementation Standard 1220.A1, internal auditors must exercise due professional care by, among other things, considering the "probability of significant errors, fraud, or noncompliance."

     2) Thus, internal auditors must consider the probability of fraud when developing engagement objectives (Implementation Standard 2210.A2).

> **Implementation Standard 2120.A2**
>
> The internal audit activity must evaluate the potential for the occurrence of fraud and how the organization manages fraud risk.

   b. An internal auditor's responsibilities for detecting fraud include evaluating fraud indicators and deciding whether any additional action is necessary or whether an investigation should be recommended.

Stop and review! You have completed the outline for this subunit. Study multiple-choice questions 1 through 8 beginning on page 172.

7.2 FRAUD -- INVESTIGATION

1. **Fraud Investigation**

   a. An investigation gathers sufficient information to determine (1) whether fraud has occurred, (2) the loss exposures, (3) who was involved, and (4) how fraud occurred. It should discover the full nature and extent of the fraud.

   b. Internal auditors, lawyers, and other specialists usually conduct fraud investigations.

   c. The investigation and resolution activities must be in accordance with local law, and the auditors should work effectively with legal counsel and become familiar with relevant laws.

   d. Management implements controls over the investigation. They include (1) developing policies and procedures, (2) preserving evidence, (3) responding to the results, (4) reporting, and (5) communications.

      1) Such standards often are documented in a **fraud policy**, and the internal audit activity may assist in the evaluation of the policy.

      2) Policies and procedures address (a) the rights of individuals; (b) the qualifications of investigators; (c) the relevant laws; and (d) the disciplining of employees, suppliers, or customers, including legal measures.

      3) The authority and responsibilities of those involved in the investigation, especially the investigator and legal counsel, should be clear.

      4) Internal communications about an ongoing investigation should be minimized.

      5) A policy needs to specify the investigator's role in determining whether a fraud has been committed. Either the investigator or management decides whether fraud has occurred, and management decides whether to notify outside authorities.

   e. The **role of the internal audit activity** in investigations needs to be defined in its charter as well as in fraud policies and procedures.

      1) For example, internal auditing may

         a) Have the primary responsibility for fraud investigations,

         b) Act as a resource for investigations, or

         c) Avoid involvement because it is responsible for assessing investigations or lacks resources.

      2) Any role is acceptable if its effect on independence is recognized and managed appropriately.

      3) Internal auditors typically not only assess investigations but also advise management about the process, including control improvements.

      4) To maintain proficiency, fraud investigation teams must obtain sufficient knowledge of (a) fraudulent schemes, (b) investigation techniques, and (c) applicable laws.

      5) If the internal audit activity is responsible for the investigation, it may use in-house staff, outsourcing, or a combination.

   f. An **investigation plan** is developed for each investigation.

      1) The lead investigator determines the knowledge, skills, and other competencies needed.

      2) The process includes obtaining assurance that no potential conflict of interest exists with those investigated or any employees of the organization.

3) Planning should consider the following:

    a) Gathering evidence using surveillance, interviews, or written statements

    b) Documenting and preserving evidence, the legal rules of evidence, and the business uses of the evidence

    c) Determining the extent of the fraud

    d) Determining the methods used to perpetrate the fraud

    e) Evaluating the cause of the fraud

    f) Identifying the perpetrators

4) The investigation should be coordinated with management, legal counsel, and other specialists.

5) Investigators need to be prudent, consistent, and knowledgeable of the rights of persons within the scope of the investigation and the reputation of the organization itself.

6) The level and extent of complicity in the fraud throughout the organization needs to be assessed. This assessment can be critical to avoid (a) destroying or tainting crucial evidence and (b) obtaining misleading information from persons who may be involved.

7) The investigation needs to secure evidence collected and follow chain-of-custody procedures.

2. **Interrogation of Employees**

    a. A fraud-related interrogation differs significantly from a normal interview.

        1) The purpose of a typical interview is to gather facts. In an interrogation, the internal auditor has already gathered pertinent facts and is seeking confirmation.

        2) At no time should the internal auditor accuse the employee of committing a crime. If the accusation is unprovable, the organization could have legal liability.

    b. The IIA's Practice Guide, *Internal Auditing and Fraud*, provides the following guidance:

        1) "Typically, the accused individual is interviewed after most applicable evidence has been obtained. Many investigators prefer to approach the accused with sufficient evidence that will support the goal to secure a confession."

        2) "Generally the accused is interviewed by two people: (1) an experienced investigator and (2) another individual who takes notes during the interview and later functions as a witness if needed."

        3) "In addition, it is essential that all information obtained from the interview is rendered correctly."

    c. The internal auditor should guide the conversation from the general to the specific.

        1) Open questions are generally used early in the interrogation, and closed questions are used later as the auditor comes closer to obtaining a confession.

            a) Open questions are of the type, "Describe your role in the vendor approval process."

            b) Closed questions are of the type, "Do you personally verify the existence of every vendor who seeks approval?"

        2) Normal interviewing methods regarding nonthreatening tone and close observation of body language apply.

    d. The employee should not be allowed to return to his or her normal work area upon completion of the interrogation.

        1) Because the employee is now alert to the fraud investigation, (s)he might be tempted to destroy valuable evidence.

Stop and review! You have completed the outline for this subunit. Study multiple-choice questions 9 through 11 on page 174.

7.3 FRAUD -- CONTROLS

1. **Responsibility for Controls**

   a. Control is the principal means of preventing fraud.

   b. Management is primarily responsible for establishing and maintaining control.

   c. Internal auditors are primarily responsible for preventing fraud by examining and evaluating the adequacy and effectiveness of control.

      1) They are not responsible for designing and implementing fraud prevention controls.

      2) However, internal auditors acting in a consulting role can help management identify and assess risk and determine the adequacy of the control environment.

         a) Internal auditors also are in a unique position within the organization to recommend changes to improve the control environment.

2. **Controls**

   a. No text can feasibly present lists of all possible controls. Part 1 of CIA Review contains extensive guidance on control concepts, terminology, and methods. They apply to the design and implementation of controls that are relevant to, among many other things, the prevention and detection of fraud.

Stop and review! You have completed the outline for this subunit. Study multiple-choice questions 12 through 15 beginning on page 175.

7.4 FRAUD -- PROCEDURES

1. **Engagement Procedures**

   a. The nature and extent of the specific procedures performed to detect and investigate fraud depend on many circumstances. They include (1) the features of the specific engagement, (2) the unique characteristics of the organization, and (3) the internal auditor's risk assessment.

      1) Accordingly, no text can feasibly present lists of all procedures relative to fraud. However, analytical procedures are routinely performed in many engagements. They may provide an early indication of fraud.

   b. Internal auditors should have an awareness of the circumstances in which their own procedures and expertise may be insufficient. Thus, they may need to make use of specialists.

      1) For example, forensic experts may supply special knowledge regarding

         a) Authenticity of documents and signatures,
         b) Mechanical sources of documents (printers, typewriters, computers, etc.),
         c) Paper and ink chemistry, and
         d) Fingerprint analysis.

   c. **Forensic auditing** is the use of accounting and auditing knowledge and skills in matters having civil or criminal legal implications. Engagements involving fraud, litigation support, and expert witness testimony are examples.

      NOTE: Study Unit 5, Subunit 1, has a full treatment of engagement procedures and the evidence they provide.

Stop and review! You have completed the outline for this subunit. Study multiple-choice questions 16 through 23 beginning on page 176.

7.5 FRAUD -- AWARENESS

1. **Fraud Prevention System**

   a. Fraud prevention involves actions to discourage fraud and limit the exposure when it occurs. A strong ethical culture and setting the correct tone at the top are essential to prevention.

   b. Overlapping control elements of a fraud prevention program are presented below. They are based on the following components of the COSO control framework:

      1) The control environment includes such elements as a code of conduct, ethics policy, or fraud policy.

      2) A fraud risk assessment generally includes the following:

         a) Identifying and prioritizing fraud risk factors and fraud schemes
         b) Mapping existing controls to potential fraud schemes and identifying gaps
         c) Testing operating effectiveness of fraud prevention and detection controls
         d) Documenting and reporting the fraud risk assessment

      3) Control activities are policies and procedures for business processes that include authority limits and segregation of duties.

      4) Fraud-related information and communication practices promote the fraud risk management program and the organization's position on risk. The means used include fraud awareness training and confirming that employees comply with the organization's policies.

         a) A fraud hotline is a convenient way for employees to report suspected improprieties.

      5) Monitoring evaluates antifraud controls through independent evaluations of the fraud risk management program and use of it.

2. **Fraud Reporting**

   a. The chief audit executive is responsible for fraud reporting. It consists of the various oral or written, interim, or final communications to management or the board regarding the status and results of fraud investigations.

      1) A formal communication may be issued at the conclusion of the investigation that includes time frames, observations, conclusions, resolution, and corrective action to improve controls.

      2) It may need to be written in a manner that provides confidentiality for some of the people involved.

      3) The needs of the board and management, legal requirements, and policies and procedures should be considered.

   b. A draft of the proposed final communication should be submitted to legal counsel for review. To be covered by the attorney-client privilege, the report must be addressed to counsel.

   c. Any incident of significant fraud, or incident that leads the internal auditors to question the level of trust placed in one or more individuals, must be timely reported to senior management and the board.

   d. If previously issued financial statements for 1 or more years may have been adversely affected, senior management and the board also should be informed.

3. **Resolution of Fraud Incidents**

   a. Resolution consists of determining actions to be taken after the investigation is complete.

      1) Management and the board are responsible for resolving fraud incidents.

   b. Resolution may include the following:

      1) Providing closure to persons who were found innocent or reported a problem
      2) Disciplining an employee
      3) Requesting voluntary financial restitution
      4) Terminating contracts with suppliers
      5) Reporting the incident to law enforcement or regulatory bodies, encouraging them to prosecute, and cooperating with them
      6) Filing a civil suit to recover the amount taken
      7) Filing an insurance claim
      8) Complaining to the perpetrator's professional association
      9) Recommending control improvements

4. **Communication of Fraud Incidents**

   a. Management or the board determines whether to inform parties outside the organization after consultation with such individuals as legal counsel, human resources personnel, and the CAE.

      1) The organization may need to notify government agencies of certain types of fraudulent acts. It also may need to notify its insurers, bankers, and external auditors of instances of fraud.

   b. Internal communications are a strategic tool used by management to reinforce its position relating to integrity and to show why internal controls are important.

5. **Opinion on Fraud-Related Controls**

   a. The internal auditor may be asked by management or the board to express an opinion on internal controls related to fraud. The following provide relevant guidance:

      1) Standards and Practice Advisories related to communication of results (Performance Standard 2400, etc.)
      2) Practice Guide, *Formulating and Expressing Internal Audit Opinions*

   b. While an opinion on fraud-related controls is acceptable, it would be inappropriate for an internal auditor to give an opinion on the culpability of a fraud suspect.

Stop and review! You have completed the outline for this subunit. Study multiple-choice questions 24 and 25 on page 180.

QUESTIONS

7.1 Fraud -- Risks and Types

1. One factor that distinguishes fraud from other employee crimes is that fraud involves

    A. Intentional deception.

    B. Personal gain for the perpetrator.

    C. Collusion with a party outside the organization.

    D. Malicious motives.

Answer (A) is correct.
    REQUIRED: The factor that distinguishes fraud from other employee crimes.
    DISCUSSION: Fraud is defined in The IIA Glossary as "any illegal act characterized by deceit, concealment, or violation of trust. These acts are not dependent upon the threat of violence or physical force. Frauds are perpetrated by parties and organizations to obtain money, property, or services; to avoid payment or loss of services; or to secure personal or business advantage."

2. In the course of their work, internal auditors must be alert for fraud and other forms of white-collar crime. The important characteristic that distinguishes fraud from other varieties of white-collar crime is that

    A. Fraud is characterized by deceit, concealment, or violation of trust.

    B. Unlike other white-collar crimes, fraud is always perpetrated against an outside party.

    C. White-collar crime is usually perpetrated for the benefit of an organization, but fraud benefits an individual.

    D. White-collar crime is usually perpetrated by outsiders to the detriment of an organization, but fraud is perpetrated by insiders to benefit the organization.

Answer (A) is correct.
    REQUIRED: The trait distinguishing fraud from other white-collar crimes.
    DISCUSSION: Fraud is defined in The IIA Glossary as "any illegal act characterized by deceit, concealment, or violation of trust. These acts are not dependent upon the threat of violence or physical force."
    Answer (B) is incorrect. Fraud may be perpetrated internally. Answer (C) is incorrect. Fraud may be perpetrated for the organization's benefit or for otherwise unselfish reasons. Answer (D) is incorrect. Fraud may be perpetrated by insiders and outsiders, and it may be either beneficial or detrimental to an organization.

3. Which of the following wrongful acts committed by an employee constitutes fraud?

    A. Libel.

    B. Embezzlement.

    C. Assault.

    D. Harassment.

Answer (B) is correct.
    REQUIRED: The employee act constituting fraud.
    DISCUSSION: Fraud is defined in The IIA Glossary as "any illegal act characterized by deceit, concealment, or violation of trust. These acts are not dependent upon the threat of violence or physical force. Frauds are perpetrated by parties and organizations to obtain money, property, or services; to avoid payment or loss of services; or to secure personal or business advantage." Embezzlement is the intentional appropriation of property entrusted to one's care. The embezzler converts property to his or her own use and conceals the theft.
    Answer (A) is incorrect. Libel is defamation published in a relatively permanent form (newspaper, letter, film, etc.). Answer (C) is incorrect. The tort of assault entails placing another in reasonable fear of a harmful or offensive bodily contact. Answer (D) is incorrect. Harassment is the act of persistently annoying another.

4. A key feature that distinguishes fraud from other types of crime or impropriety is that fraud always involves the

    A. Violent or forceful taking of property.

    B. Deceitful wrongdoing of management-level personnel.

    C. Unlawful conversion of property that is lawfully in the custody of the perpetrator.

    D. False representation or concealment of a material fact.

Answer (D) is correct.
    REQUIRED: The key distinguishing feature of fraud.
    DISCUSSION: Fraud is defined in The IIA Glossary as "any illegal act characterized by deceit, concealment, or violation of trust. These acts are not dependent upon the threat of violence or physical force."
    Answer (A) is incorrect. Fraud usually does not involve force or violence. Answer (B) is incorrect. Employees at any level in an organization can commit fraud. Answer (C) is incorrect. Embezzlement is the unlawful conversion of property that is lawfully in the custody of the perpetrator.

5. In an organization with a separate division that is primarily responsible for the prevention of fraud, the internal audit activity is responsible for

- A. Examining and evaluating the adequacy and effectiveness of that division's actions taken to prevent fraud.
- B. Establishing and maintaining that division's system of internal control.
- C. Planning that division's fraud prevention activities.
- D. Controlling that division's fraud prevention activities.

Answer (A) is correct.
REQUIRED: The responsibility of the internal audit activity in an organization with a separate fraud prevention division.
DISCUSSION: Control is the principal means of preventing fraud. Management is primarily responsible for the establishment and maintenance of control. Internal auditors are primarily responsible for preventing fraud by examining and evaluating the adequacy and effectiveness of control.
Answer (B) is incorrect. Establishing and maintaining control is a responsibility of management. Answer (C) is incorrect. Planning fraud prevention activities is a responsibility of management. Answer (D) is incorrect. Controlling fraud prevention activities is a responsibility of management.

6. A significant employee fraud took place shortly after an internal auditing engagement. The internal auditor may not have properly fulfilled the responsibility for the prevention of fraud by failing to note and report that

- A. Policies, practices, and procedures to monitor activities and safeguard assets were less extensive in low-risk areas than in high-risk areas.
- B. A system of control that depended upon separation of duties could be circumvented by collusion among three employees.
- C. There were no written policies describing prohibited activities and the action required whenever violations are discovered.
- D. Divisional employees had not been properly trained to distinguish between bona fide signatures and cleverly forged ones on authorization forms.

Answer (C) is correct.
REQUIRED: The way in which the internal auditor may not have properly fulfilled the responsibility for the prevention of fraud.
DISCUSSION: Management is responsible for establishing and maintaining internal control. Thus, management also is responsible for the fraud prevention program. The control environment element of this program includes a code of conduct, ethics policy, or fraud policy to set the appropriate tone at the top. Moreover, organizations should establish effective fraud-related information and communication practices, for example, documentation and dissemination of policies, guidelines, and results.
Answer (A) is incorrect. For cost-benefit reasons, controls should be more extensive in high-risk areas. Answer (B) is incorrect. Even the best system of control can often be circumvented by collusion. Answer (D) is incorrect. Forgery, like collusion, can circumvent even an effective control.

7. Internal auditors have a responsibility for helping to deter fraud. Which of the following best describes how this responsibility is usually met?

- A. By coordinating with security personnel and law enforcement agencies in the investigation of possible frauds.
- B. By testing for fraud in every engagement and following up as appropriate.
- C. By assisting in the design of control systems to prevent fraud.
- D. By evaluating the adequacy and effectiveness of controls in light of the potential exposure or risk.

Answer (D) is correct.
REQUIRED: The responsibility of internal auditing to deter fraud.
DISCUSSION: Control is the principal means of preventing fraud. Management is primarily responsible for the establishment and maintenance of control. Internal auditors are primarily responsible for preventing fraud by examining and evaluating the adequacy and effectiveness of control.
Answer (A) is incorrect. Investigating possible frauds involves detection, not deterrence. Answer (B) is incorrect. Testing for fraud in every engagement is not required. Answer (C) is incorrect. Designing control systems impairs an internal auditor's objectivity.

8. The internal audit activity's responsibility for preventing fraud is to

- A. Establish internal control.
- B. Maintain internal control.
- C. Evaluate the system of internal control.
- D. Exercise operating authority over fraud prevention activities.

Answer (C) is correct.
REQUIRED: The internal audit activity's responsibility for preventing fraud.
DISCUSSION: Control is the principal means of preventing fraud. Management, in turn, is primarily responsible for the establishment and maintenance of control. Internal auditors are primarily responsible for preventing fraud by examining and evaluating the adequacy and effectiveness of control.
Answer (A) is incorrect. Establishing internal control is management's responsibility. Answer (B) is incorrect. Maintaining internal control is management's responsibility. Answer (D) is incorrect. Operating authority is a management function.

7.2 Fraud -- Investigation

9. Which of the following gives the internal auditor the authority to investigate fraud?

    A. The Standards.

    B. Common law.

    C. Management.

    D. The IIA's Code of Ethics.

Answer (C) is correct.
    REQUIRED: The source of an internal auditor's authority to investigate fraud.
    DISCUSSION: Any fraud investigation undertaken by internal auditors must be authorized by management.
    Answer (A) is incorrect. The internal auditor has authority only to recommend an investigation. Answer (B) is incorrect. An internal auditor has no authority under common law. Answer (D) is incorrect. The IIA's Code of Ethics does not mention fraud investigation.

10. When conducting fraud investigations, internal auditors should

    A. Clearly indicate the extent of the internal auditors' knowledge of the fraud when questioning suspects.

    B. Assign personnel to the investigation in accordance with the engagement schedule established at the beginning of the fiscal year.

    C. Perform its investigation independently of lawyers, security personnel, and specialists from outside the organization who are involved in the investigation.

    D. Assess the probable level of, and the extent of complicity in, the fraud within the organization.

Answer (D) is correct.
    REQUIRED: The role of the internal auditors in fraud investigations.
    DISCUSSION: When conducting fraud investigations, internal auditors or others should assess the level of, and the extent of complicity in, the fraud within the organization. This assessment can be critical to ensuring that (1) crucial evidence is not tainted or destroyed and (2) misleading information is not obtained from persons who may be involved.
    Answer (A) is incorrect. By always giving the impression that additional evidence is in reserve, the internal auditors are more apt to obtain complete and truthful answers. Answer (B) is incorrect. Fraud investigations usually occur unexpectedly and cannot be scheduled in advance. Also, the fraud investigation must be conducted by individuals having the appropriate expertise, even if another engagement must be delayed. Answer (C) is incorrect. The internal auditors should coordinate their activities with management, legal counsel, and other specialists.

11. Questions used to interrogate individuals suspected of fraud should

    A. Adhere to a predetermined order.

    B. Cover more than one subject or topic.

    C. Move from the general to the specific.

    D. Direct the individual to a desired answer.

Answer (C) is correct.
    REQUIRED: The method of asking questions used to interrogate individuals suspected of fraud.
    DISCUSSION: Internal auditors should be skilled in dealing with people and in communicating effectively. One important communications skill is the ability to conduct an effective interview. For example, initial questions in a fraud interview should be broad. In contrast with a directive approach emphasizing narrowly focused questions, this nondirective approach is more likely to elicit clarifications and unexpected observations from employees who are under suspicion.
    Answer (A) is incorrect. The interviewee's answer may suggest a follow-up question that should be asked before asking the next planned question. Answer (B) is incorrect. This interviewing technique may be confusing for the respondent. Answer (D) is incorrect. The interrogator should avoid leading questions, that is, questions that suggest an answer.

7.3 Fraud -- Controls

12. A purchasing agent received expensive gifts from a vendor in return for directing a significant amount of business to that vendor. Which of the following organizational policies most effectively prevents such an occurrence?

A. All purchases exceeding specified monetary amounts should be approved by an official who determines compliance with budgetary requirements.

B. Important high-volume materials should regularly be purchased from at least two different sources in order to afford supply protection.

C. The purchasing function should be decentralized so each department manager or supervisor does his or her own purchasing.

D. Competitive bids should be solicited on purchases to the maximum extent that is practicable.

Answer (D) is correct.
REQUIRED: The policy that most effectively prevents or detects bribery by a vendor.
DISCUSSION: In the absence of special circumstances, competitive bidding is a legitimate and effective means of obtaining the lowest price consistent with quality. It is a practice that exploits competition in the market place. Competitive bidding also serves as a control over fraud by restricting the ability of a purchasing agent to reward a favored vendor.
Answer (A) is incorrect. The problem is vendor selection, not authorization of purchases. Answer (B) is incorrect. A purchasing agent could still display favoritism to one of the vendors. Answer (C) is incorrect. Decentralization creates more opportunities for buyer fraud.

13. Which of the following controls is the **least** effective in preventing a fraud conducted by sending purchase orders to bogus vendors?

A. Require that all purchases be made from an authorized vendor list maintained independently of the individual placing the purchase order.

B. Require that only approved vendors be paid for purchases, based on actual production.

C. Require contracts with all major vendors from whom production components are purchased.

D. Require that total purchases for a month not exceed the total budgeted purchases for that month.

Answer (D) is correct.
REQUIRED: The control least effective in preventing a fraud involving bogus vendors.
DISCUSSION: Requiring that total purchases for a month not exceed the total budgeted purchases for that month controls the total amount of expenditures, not whether a purchase has been requested and authorized, with whom the purchase orders are placed, or whether goods purchased are received.

14. A potential problem for a manufacturer is that purchasing agents may take kickbacks or receive gifts from vendors in exchange for favorable contracts. Which of the following is the **least** effective in preventing this problem?

A. A specific organizational policy prohibiting the acceptance of anything of value from a vendor.

B. An organizational code of ethics that prohibits such activity.

C. A requirement for the purchasing agent to develop a profile of all vendors before the vendors are added to the authorized vendor list.

D. The establishment of long-term contracts with major vendors, with the contract terms approved by senior management.

Answer (C) is correct.
REQUIRED: The least effective control to prevent purchasing agents from taking kickbacks or gifts from vendors.
DISCUSSION: A requirement for the purchasing agent to develop a profile of all vendors is the least effective approach because it concerns only the authorization of vendors, a function that should be performed independently of the purchasing agent. It does not address the purchasing agent's relationships with approved vendors.
Answer (A) is incorrect. A policy prohibiting kickbacks and gifts from vendors provides guidance and influences behavior. Answer (B) is incorrect. A code of ethics gives direction to the purchasing agents and is helpful in influencing behavior. Answer (D) is incorrect. Approval of long-term vendor contracts by senior management is an effective procedure that is increasingly being used by many organizations.

15. A programmer's accumulation of roundoff errors into one account, which is later accessed by the programmer, is a type of computer fraud. The best way to prevent this type of fraud is to

A. Build in judgment with reasonableness tests.

B. Independently test programs during development and limit access to the programs.

C. Segregate duties of systems development and programming.

D. Use control totals and check the results of the computer.

Answer (B) is correct.
    REQUIRED: The best way to prevent computer fraud.
    DISCUSSION: Programmers should not have access to programs used in processing. The accumulation of roundoff errors into one person's account is a procedure written into the program. Independent testing of a program will lead to discovery of this programmed fraud.
    Answer (A) is incorrect. Reasonableness tests will not detect this irregularity. In this particular type of fraud, all of the amounts will balance. Answer (C) is incorrect. Segregation of duties between systems development and programming would not prevent this type of error. The skills required to construct the program are possessed by programmers. Answer (D) is incorrect. This particular fraud will result in balanced entries. Thus, control totals would not detect the fraud.

7.4 Fraud -- Procedures

16. A production manager for a moderate-sized manufacturer began ordering excessive raw materials and had them delivered to a wholesale business that the manager was running on the side. The manager falsified receiving documents and approved the invoices for payment. Which of the following procedures is most likely to detect this fraud?

A. Take a sample of cash disbursements; compare purchase orders, receiving reports, invoices, and check copies.

B. Take a sample of cash disbursements; confirm the amount purchased, purchase price, and date of shipment with the vendors.

C. Observe the receiving dock and count materials received; compare the counts with receiving reports completed by receiving personnel.

D. Perform analytical tests, comparing production, materials purchased, and raw materials inventory levels; investigate differences.

Answer (D) is correct.
    REQUIRED: The procedure most likely to detect a purchasing fraud.
    DISCUSSION: The application of analytical procedures is based on the premise that, in the absence of known conditions to the contrary, relationships among information may reasonably be expected to exist and continue. Hence, the analytical procedures should identify an unexplained increase in materials used.
    Answer (A) is incorrect. Given that documents have been falsified, supporting documents exist for each cash disbursement. Answer (B) is incorrect. The vendors will confirm all transactions. Answer (C) is incorrect. Given that the improper orders are shipped to another location, observing receiving dock counts will not detect the fraud.

17. The chief of an organization's security received an anonymous call accusing a marketing manager of taking kickbacks from a media outlet. Thus, the marketing department is on the list of possible engagement clients for the coming year. The internal audit activity is assigned responsibility for investigating fraud by its charter. If obtaining access to outside media outlet records and personnel is not possible, the best action an internal auditor could take to investigate the allegation of marketing kickbacks is to

A. Search for unrecorded liabilities from media outlets.

B. Obtain a list of approved media outlets.

C. Develop a financial and behavioral profile of the suspect.

D. Vouch any material past charge-offs of receivables.

Answer (C) is correct.
    REQUIRED: The best action an internal auditor can take to investigate an allegation of kickbacks.
    DISCUSSION: A common indicator of fraud by an employee is an unexplained change in his or her financial status. A standard of living not commensurate with the employee's income may signify wrongdoing. The employee's behavior may also be suspicious (for example, constant association with, and entertainment by, a member of the media outlet's staff). The profile may help to corroborate illegal income and thereby provide a basis for tracing illegal payments to the employee.
    Answer (A) is incorrect. If the employee is taking kickbacks, unrecorded liabilities are not being created. Answer (B) is incorrect. A list of approved media outlets would not provide any information about kickbacks. Answer (D) is incorrect. The receipt of kickbacks would have no effect on accounts receivable.

18. The internal auditor reviewed documentation showing that a customer had recently returned three expensive products to the regional service center for warranty replacement. The documentation also showed that the warranty clerk had rejected the claim and sent it to the customer's local distributor. The claim was rejected because the serial numbers listed in the warranty claim were not found in the computer's sales history file. Subsequently, the distributor supplied three different serial numbers, all of which were validated by the computer system, and the clerk completed the warranty claim for replacements. What is the best course of action for the internal auditor under the circumstances?

A. Determine if the original serial numbers provided by the customer can be traced to other records, such as production and inventory records.

B. Notify the appropriate authorities within the organization that there are sufficient indicators that a fraud has been committed.

C. Verify with the appropriate supervisor that the warranty clerk had followed relevant procedures in the processing and disposition of this claim.

D. Summarize this item along with other valid transactions in the internal auditor's test of warranty transactions.

Answer (A) is correct.
REQUIRED: The action to be taken by the internal auditor in investigating suspicious warranty claims.
DISCUSSION: The best course of action for the internal auditor is to determine whether the related equipment had actually been reported in a sales transaction. This will allow the auditor to draw preliminary conclusions as to whether this is a case of error or of fraud.
Answer (B) is incorrect. The internal auditor should pursue additional information before alerting authorities. Answer (C) is incorrect. Verifying that the warranty clerk followed procedures does not provide more information about the validity of the warranty claim. Answer (D) is incorrect. The internal auditor should obtain more information about the validity of the transaction.

19. While reviewing a division's accounts, an internal auditor becomes concerned that the division's management may have shipped poor quality merchandise to boost sales and profitability and thereby increase the manager's bonus. For this reason, the internal auditor suspects that returned goods are being shipped to other customers as new products without full correction of their defects. Which of the following engagement procedures is the **least** effective in determining whether such shipments took place?

A. Examine credit memos issued after year end for goods shipped before year end.

B. Physically observe the shipping and receiving area for information of returned goods.

C. Interview customer service representatives regarding unusual amounts of customer complaints.

D. Require the division to take a complete physical inventory at year end, and observe the taking of the inventory.

Answer (D) is correct.
REQUIRED: The least effective procedure to determine whether merchandise returned has been reshipped without the correction of defects.
DISCUSSION: Taking a complete year-end inventory is an ineffective procedure because goods returned and reshipped without the correction of defects would not be on hand to be counted.
Answer (A) is incorrect. Credit memos provide the customer with proof that returned goods have been received by the organization and posted to the customer's account. Examining credit memos issued after year end for goods shipped before year end would show that customers are returning inferior goods. Answer (B) is incorrect. Physically observing the shipping and receiving area might reveal goods returned that are not yet accounted for. Answer (C) is incorrect. Unusual amounts of customer complaints may suggest a condition not explained by normal spoilage rates.

20. During a post-completion engagement related to a warehouse expansion, the internal auditor noted several invoices for redecorating services from a local merchant that were account-coded and signed for payment only by the cost engineer. The internal auditor should

   A. Compare the cost and description of the services with the account code used in the construction project and with related estimates in the construction-project budget.

   B. Consult with the cost engineer for assurance that these purchases were authorized for this construction project.

   C. Obtain a facsimile of the cost engineer's signature from the accounts payable group and compare it with the signature on the invoices.

   D. Recommend reclassifying the expenditure to the appropriate account code for redecorating services.

Answer (A) is correct.
   REQUIRED: The action taken when invoices are account-coded and approved by the cost engineer only.
   DISCUSSION: The internal auditor needs to determine the validity of the transaction because the engineer is performing incompatible tasks. Comparing the cost and description of the services with the account code and the budget will verify the transaction. However, normal controls over disbursements need to be established.
   Answer (B) is incorrect. The cost engineer's assurance would not confirm the authorization of these expenditures. Answer (C) is incorrect. The primary focus is the validity of the transaction within this construction project. Answer (D) is incorrect. There is no basis for reclassifying the transaction within this context.

21. Contributions to a nonprofit organization have been constant for the past 3 years. The audit committee has become concerned that the president may have embarked on a scheme in which some of the contributions from many sustaining members have been redirected to other organizations. The audit committee suspects that the scheme may involve taking major contributions and depositing them in alternative accounts or soliciting contributions to be made in the name of another organization. Which of the following procedures should be most effective in detecting the existence of such a fraud?

   A. Use generalized audit software to take a sample of pledged receipts not yet collected and confirm the amounts due with the donors.

   B. Take a sample that includes all large donors for the past 3 years and a statistical sample of others and request a confirmation of total contributions made to the organization or to affiliated organizations.

   C. Take a discovery sample of cash receipts and confirm the amounts of the receipts with the donors. Investigate any differences.

   D. Use analytical review procedures to compare contributions generated with those of other comparable institutions over the same period of time. If the amount is significantly less, take a detailed sample of cash receipts and trace to the bank statements.

Answer (B) is correct.
   REQUIRED: The procedure most effective for detecting misdirected contributions.
   DISCUSSION: The engagement objective is to determine whether contributions have been wrongly directed to alternate accounts or solicited for other organizations. Consequently, an appropriate procedure is to send confirmation requests to donors. However, testing transactions recorded by the accounting system will not result in sufficient information about solicitation of contributions for other organizations. The internal auditor must therefore make inquiries of the sustaining members about such solicitations.
   Answer (A) is incorrect. Sampling amounts listed as unpaid does not provide evidence about contributions previously paid or shifted to another organization. Answer (C) is incorrect. Sampling cash receipts that have been recorded by the organization provides no evidence about unrecorded receipts or contributions diverted elsewhere. Answer (D) is incorrect. Analytical procedures are of limited use. Also, the follow-up procedure only provides evidence that recorded receipts were also deposited.

22. The internal auditor suspects a disbursements fraud in which an unknown employee(s) is submitting and approving invoices for payment. Before discussing the potential fraud with management, the internal auditor decides to gather additional information. Which of the following procedures is most helpful in providing the additional information?

A. Use software to develop a list of vendors with post office box numbers or other unusual features. Select a sample of those items and trace to supporting documents such as receiving reports.

B. Select a sample of payments made during the year and investigate each one for approval.

C. Select a sample of receiving reports representative of the period under investigation and trace to approved payment. Note any items not properly processed.

D. Take a sample of invoices received during the past month, examine to determine whether properly authorized for payment, and trace to underlying documents.

Answer (A) is correct.
REQUIRED: The most helpful procedure related to a disbursements fraud.
DISCUSSION: A disbursements fraud may be accomplished through the use of fictitious vendors. Investigating vendors with suspicious characteristics appropriately focuses on payees as sources of additional information.
Answer (B) is incorrect. The individual perpetrating the fraud may have been in a position to obtain approvals. Answer (C) is incorrect. The problem is more likely to be with payments for which no valid support exists. Answer (D) is incorrect. Sampling invoices for the past month is not as effective as investigating suspicious vendors. It focuses only on a short period of time, and it does not emphasize the items most likely to be fraudulent.

23. During an engagement, the internal auditor found a scheme in which the warehouse director and the purchasing agent for a retail organization diverted a significant amount of goods to their own warehouse, then sold the goods to third parties. The fraud was not noted earlier because the warehouse director forwarded receiving reports (after updating the perpetual inventory records) to the accounts payable department for processing. Which of the following procedures most likely led to the discovery of the missing materials and the fraud?

A. Take a random sample of receiving reports and trace to the recording in the perpetual inventory record. Note differences and investigate by type of product.

B. Take a random sample of purchase orders and trace them to receiving documents and to the records in the accounts payable department.

C. Take an annual physical inventory, reconciling amounts with the perpetual inventory, noting the pattern of differences and investigating.

D. Take a random sample of sales invoices and trace to the perpetual records to see if inventory was on hand. Investigate any differences.

Answer (C) is correct.
REQUIRED: The audit procedure to detect the diversion of the goods.
DISCUSSION: Taking an annual physical inventory should lead to the identification of systematic shrinkages in the inventory. The pattern of the shrinkages should implicate the warehouse director. At that time, a fraud investigation should be undertaken.
Answer (A) is incorrect. Sampling receiving reports would not have detected the fraud. The warehouse director updates the perpetual inventory records before forwarding the false receiving reports to accounts payable. Answer (B) is incorrect. Taking a sample of purchase orders would not have detected the irregularities. All the goods were ordered, and the perpetrators colluded to falsify receiving reports even when the goods were diverted to another location. Answer (D) is incorrect. The warehouse director falsified the inventory records.

7.5 Fraud -- Awareness

24. After completing an investigation, internal auditing has concluded that an employee has stolen a significant amount of cash receipts. A draft of the proposed communication on this observation should be submitted for review to

- A. Legal counsel.
- B. The board.
- C. The chief executive officer of the organization.
- D. The organization's outside auditors.

Answer (A) is correct.

REQUIRED: The person(s) who should receive a draft of the proposed report on a fraud investigation.

DISCUSSION: The internal auditor must be concerned about the possibility of inclusion (and dissemination) of a statement for which the accused employee could sue the organization. Thus, a draft of the proposed final communications on fraud should be submitted to legal counsel for review. If the internal auditor wants to invoke client privilege, consideration should be given to addressing the report to legal counsel.

Answer (B) is incorrect. The board should receive a final draft of the report after it has been reviewed and approved by legal counsel. Answer (C) is incorrect. If appropriate, the CEO may receive a final draft of the report after it has been reviewed and approved by legal counsel. Answer (D) is incorrect. If it is customary to send the outside auditors copies of all internal auditing reports, they should receive a final draft that has been reviewed and approved by legal counsel.

25. The internal audit activity has concluded a fraud investigation that revealed a previously undiscovered materially adverse impact on the financial position and results of operations for 2 years on which financial statements have already been issued. The chief audit executive should immediately inform

- A. The external auditing firm responsible for the financial statements affected by the discovery.
- B. The appropriate governmental or regulatory agency.
- C. Senior management and the board.
- D. The internal accounting function ultimately responsible for making corrective journal entries.

Answer (C) is correct.

REQUIRED: The parties informed of the results of a fraud investigation.

DISCUSSION: The CAE is responsible for timely reporting of any incident of significant fraud or erosion of trust to senior management and the board. This includes a previously undiscovered materially adverse effect on the financial position and results of operations of an organization for 1 or more years on which financial statements have already been issued.

Answer (A) is incorrect. Management should communicate with the external auditors. Answer (B) is incorrect. Management should communicate with the governmental agencies. Answer (D) is incorrect. Management should communicate with the accounting function.

Practice even more exam-emulating questions in **Gleim CIA Test Prep!**

Have something to say?

Tell Gleim what's on your mind!

gleim.com/FeedbackCIA2

APPENDIX A
THE IIA GLOSSARY

This appendix contains the Glossary appended by The IIA to the *Standards*.

Add Value – The internal audit activity adds value to the organization (and its stakeholders) when it provides objective and relevant assurance, and contributes to the effectiveness and efficiency of governance, risk management, and control processes.

Adequate Control – Present if management has planned and organized (designed) in a manner that provides reasonable assurance that the organization's risks have been managed effectively and that the organization's goals and objectives will be achieved efficiently and economically.

Assurance Services – An objective examination of evidence for the purpose of providing an independent assessment on governance, risk management, and control processes for the organization. Examples may include financial, performance, compliance, system security, and due diligence engagements.

Board – The highest level of governing body charged with the responsibility to direct and/or oversee the activities and management of the organization. Typically, this includes an independent group of directors (e.g., a board of directors, a supervisory board, or a board of governors or trustees) If such a group does not exist, the "board" may refer to the head of the organization. "Board" may refer to an audit committee to which the governing body has delegated certain functions.

Charter – The internal audit charter is a formal document that defines the internal audit activity's purpose, authority, and responsibility. The internal audit charter establishes the internal audit activity's position within the organization; authorizes access to records, personnel, and physical properties relevant to the performance of engagements; and defines the scope of internal audit activities.

Chief Audit Executive – Chief audit executive describes a person in a senior position responsible for effectively managing the internal audit activity in accordance with the internal audit charter and the Definition of Internal Auditing, the Code of Ethics, and the *Standards*. The chief audit executive or others reporting to the chief audit executive will have appropriate professional certifications and qualifications. The specific job title of the chief audit executive may vary across organizations.

Code of Ethics – The Code of Ethics of The Institute of Internal Auditors (IIA) are principles relevant to the profession and practice of internal auditing, and Rules of Conduct that describe behavior expected of internal auditors. The Code of Ethics applies to both parties and entities that provide internal audit services. The purpose of the Code of Ethics is to promote an ethical culture in the global profession of internal auditing.

Compliance – Adherence to policies, plans, procedures, laws, regulations, contracts, or other requirements.

Conflict of Interest – Any relationship that is, or appears to be, not in the best interest of the organization. A conflict of interest would prejudice an individual's ability to perform his or her duties and responsibilities objectively.

Consulting Services – Advisory and related client service activities, the nature and scope of which are agreed with the client, are intended to add value and improve an organization's governance, risk management, and control processes without the internal auditor assuming management responsibility. Examples include counsel, advice, facilitation, and training.

Control – Any action taken by management, the board, and other parties to manage risk and increase the likelihood that established objectives and goals will be achieved. Management plans, organizes, and directs the performance of sufficient actions to provide reasonable assurance that objectives and goals will be achieved.

Control Environment – The attitude and actions of the board and management regarding the importance of control within the organization. The control environment provides the discipline and structure for the achievement of the primary objectives of the system of internal control. The control environment includes the following elements:

- Integrity and ethical values.
- Management's philosophy and operating style.
- Organizational structure.
- Assignment of authority and responsibility.
- Human resource policies and practices.
- Competence of personnel.

Control Processes – The policies, procedures (both manual and automated), and activities that are part of a control framework, designed and operated to ensure that risks are contained within the level that an organization is willing to accept.

Engagement – A specific internal audit assignment, task, or review activity, such as an internal audit, control self-assessment review, fraud examination, or consultancy. An engagement may include multiple tasks or activities designed to accomplish a specific set of related objectives.

Engagement Objectives – Broad statements developed by internal auditors that define intended engagement accomplishments.

Engagement Opinion – The rating, conclusion, and/or other description of results of an individual internal audit engagement, relating to those aspects within the objectives and scope of the engagement.

Engagement Work Program – A document that lists the procedures to be followed during an engagement, designed to achieve the engagement plan.

External Service Provider – A person or firm outside of the organization that has special knowledge, skill, and experience in a particular discipline.

Fraud – Any illegal act characterized by deceit, concealment, or violation of trust. These acts are not dependent upon the threat of violence or physical force. Frauds are perpetrated by parties and organizations to obtain money, property, or services; to avoid payment or loss of services; or to secure personal or business advantage.

Governance – The combination of processes and structures implemented by the board to inform, direct, manage, and monitor the activities of the organization toward the achievement of its objectives.

Impairment – Impairment to organizational independence and individual objectivity may include personal conflict of interest, scope limitations, restrictions on access to records, personnel, and properties, and resource limitations (funding).

Independence – The freedom from conditions that threaten the ability of the internal audit activity to carry out internal audit responsibilities in an unbiased manner.

Information Technology Controls – Controls that support business management and governance as well as provide general and technical controls over information technology infrastructures such as applications, information, infrastructure, and people.

Information Technology Governance – Consists of the leadership, organizational structures, and processes that ensure that the enterprise's information technology supports the organization's strategies and objectives.

Internal Audit Activity – A department, division, team of consultants, or other practitioner(s) that provides independent, objective assurance and consulting services designed to add value and improve an organization's operations. The internal audit activity helps an organization accomplish its objectives by bringing a systematic, disciplined approach to evaluate and improve the effectiveness of governance, risk management and control processes.

International Professional Practices Framework – The conceptual framework that organizes the authoritative guidance promulgated by The IIA. Authoritative Guidance is comprised of two categories – (1) mandatory and (2) strongly recommended.

Must – The *Standards* use the word "must" to specify an unconditional requirement.

Objectivity – An unbiased mental attitude that allows internal auditors to perform engagements in such a manner that they believe in their work product and that no quality compromises are made. Objectivity requires that internal auditors do not subordinate their judgment on audit matters to others.

Overall Opinion – The rating, conclusion, and/or other description of results provided by the chief audit executive addressing, at a broad level, governance, risk management, and/or control processes of the organization. An overall opinion is the professional judgment of the chief audit executive based on the results of a number of individual engagements and other activities for a specific time interval.

Risk – The possibility of an event occurring that will have an impact on the achievement of objectives. Risk is measured in terms of impact and likelihood.

Risk Appetite – The level of risk that an organization is willing to accept.

Risk Management – A process to identify, assess, manage, and control potential events or situations to provide reasonable assurance regarding the achievement of the organization's objectives.

Should – The *Standards* use the word "should" where conformance is expected unless, when applying professional judgment, circumstances justify deviation.

Significance – The relative importance of a matter within the context in which it is being considered, including quantitative and qualitative factors, such as magnitude, nature, effect, relevance, and impact. Professional judgment assists internal auditors when evaluating the significance of matters within the context of the relevant objectives.

Standard – A professional pronouncement promulgated by the Internal Audit Standards Board that delineates the requirements for performing a broad range of internal audit activities, and for evaluating internal audit performance.

Technology-based Audit Techniques – Any automated audit tool, such as generalized audit software, test data generators, computerized audit programs, specialized audit utilities, and computer-assisted audit techniques (CAATs).

APPENDIX B
THE IIA CIA EXAM SYLLABUS AND CROSS-REFERENCES

For your convenience, we have reproduced verbatim The IIA's CIA Exam Syllabus for this CIA exam part (global.theiia.org/certification/cia-certification/pages/cia-2013-exam-syllabus.aspx). Note that "proficiency level" means the candidate should have a thorough understanding and the ability to apply concepts in the topics listed. Those levels labeled "awareness level" mean the candidate must have a grasp of the terminology and fundamentals of the concepts listed. We also have provided cross-references to the study units and subunits in this book that correspond to The IIA's more detailed coverage. If one entry appears above a list, it applies to all items. Please visit The IIA's website for updates and more information about the exam. Rely on the Gleim materials to help you pass each part of the exam. We have researched and studied The IIA's CIA Exam Syllabus as well as questions from prior exams to provide you with an excellent review program.

NOTE: All items in this section of the syllabus will be tested at the Proficiency knowledge level unless otherwise indicated below.

PART 2 – INTERNAL AUDIT PRACTICE

I. **Managing the Internal Audit Function (40–50%)**

    A.   Strategic Role of Internal Audit

        1.   Initiate, manage, be a change catalyst, and cope with change (1.7)

        2.   Build and maintain networking with other organization executives and the audit committee (1.3)

        3.   Organize and lead a team in mapping, analysis, and business process improvement (1.6)

        4.   Assess and foster the ethical climate of the board and management (1.4)

            a.   Investigate and recommend resolution for ethics/compliance complaints, and determine disposition of ethics violations

            b.   Maintain and administer business conduct policy (e.g., conflict of interest), and report on compliance

        5.   Educate senior management and the board on best practices in governance, risk management, control, and compliance (1.1)

        6.   Communicate internal audit key performance indicators to senior management and the board on a regular basis (1.6)

        7.   Coordinate IA efforts with external auditor, regulatory oversight bodies and other internal assurance functions (1.5)

        8.   Assess the adequacy of the performance measurement system, achievement of corporate objective – **Awareness Level (A)** (1.6)

    B.   Operational Role of IA

        1.   Formulate policies and procedures for the planning, organizing, directing, and monitoring of internal audit operations (1.2)

        2.   Review the role of the internal audit function within the risk management framework (1.8)

3.   Direct administrative activities (e.g., budgeting, human resources) of the internal audit department (1.2)

4.   Interview candidates for internal audit positions (1.2)

5.   Report on the effectiveness of corporate risk management processes to senior management and the board (1.8)

6.   Report on the effectiveness of the internal control and risk management frameworks (1.8)

7.   Maintain effective Quality Assurance Improvement Program (1.9)

C.   Establish Risk-Based IA Plan

1.   Use market, product, and industry knowledge to identify new internal audit engagement opportunities (4.3)

2.   Use a risk framework to identify sources of potential engagements (e.g., audit universe, audit cycle requirements, management requests, regulatory mandates) (4.3)

3.   Establish a framework for assessing risk (4.3)

4.   Rank and validate risk priorities to prioritize engagements in the audit plan (4.3)

5.   Identify internal audit resource requirements for annual IA plan (4.4)

6.   Communicate areas of significant risk and obtain approval from the board for the annual engagement plan (6.3)

7.   Types of engagements

   a.   Conduct assurance engagements (2.1)

      a.1   Risk and control self-assessments (2.2)

         a)   Facilitated approach

            (1) Client-facilitated
            (2) Audit-facilitated

         b)   Questionnaire approach

         c)   Self-certification approach

      a.2   Audits of third parties and contract auditing (2.3)

      a.3   Quality audit engagements (2.4)

      a.4   Due diligence audit engagements (2.5)

      a.5   Security audit engagements (2.6)

      a.6   Privacy audit engagements (2.6)

      a.7   Performance audit engagements (key performance indicators) (2.7)

      a.8   Operational audit engagements (efficiency and effectiveness) (2.7)

      a.9   Financial audit engagements (3.2)

   b.   Compliance audit engagements (2.8, 3.1)

   c.   Consulting engagements (3.3-3.4)

      c.1   Internal control training
      c.2   Business process mapping
      c.3   Benchmarking
      c.4   System development reviews
      c.5   Design of performance measurement systems

II.   **Managing Individual Engagements (40–50%)**

   A.   Plan Engagements

   1.   Establish engagement objectives/criteria and finalize the scope of the engagement (4.1)

   2.   Plan engagement to assure identification of key risks and controls (4.2)

   3.   Complete a detailed risk assessment of each audit area (prioritize or evaluate risk/control factors) (4.2)

   4.   Determine engagement procedures and prepare engagement work program (5.1)

   5.   Determine the level of staff and resources needed for the engagement (4.5)

   6.   Construct audit staff schedule for effective use of time (4.5)

   B.   Supervise Engagement

   1.   Direct / supervise individual engagements (5.2)

   2.   Nurture instrumental relations, build bonds, and work with others toward shared goals (5.2)

   3.   Coordinate work assignments among audit team members when serving as the auditor-in-charge of a project (5.2)

   4.   Review work papers (5.3)

   5.   Conduct exit conference (5.3)

   6.   Complete performance appraisals of engagement staff (5.3)

   C.   Communicate Engagement Results

   1.   Initiate preliminary communication with engagement clients (6.1)
   2.   Communicate interim progress (6.1)
   3.   Develop recommendations when appropriate (6.2)
   4.   Prepare report or other communication (6.3)
   5.   Approve engagement report (6.5)
   6.   Determine distribution of the report (6.5)
   7.   Obtain management response to the report (6.6)
   8.   Report outcomes to appropriate parties (6.7)

   D.   Monitor Engagement Outcomes (6.8)

   1.   Identify appropriate method to monitor engagement outcomes

   2.   Monitor engagement outcomes and conduct appropriate follow-up by the internal audit activity

   3.   Conduct follow-up and report on management's response to internal audit recommendations

   4.   Report significant audit issues to senior management and the board periodically

III. **Fraud Risks and Controls (5–15%)**

    A.   Consider the potential for fraud risks and identify common types of fraud associated with the engagement area during the engagement planning process (7.1)

    B.   Determine if fraud risks require special consideration when conducting an engagement (7.1)

    C.   Determine if any suspected fraud merits investigation (7.2)

    D.   Complete a process review to improve controls to prevent fraud and recommend changes (7.3)

    E.   Employ audit tests to detect fraud (7.4)

    F.   Support a culture of fraud awareness, and encourage the reporting of improprieties (7.5)

    G.   Interrogation / investigative techniques – **Awareness Level (A)** (7.2)

    H.   Forensic auditing – **Awareness Level (A)** (7.4)

APPENDIX C
THE IIA STANDARDS AND PRACTICE ADVISORIES DISCUSSED IN PART 2

Gleim Subunit	Attribute Standard
1.9	1300 - Quality Assurance and Improvement Program
1.9	1310 - Requirements of the Quality Assurance and Improvement Program
1.9	1311 - Internal Assessments
1.9	1312 - External Assessments
1.9	1320 - Reporting on the Quality Assurance and Improvement Program
1.9	1321 - Use of "Conforms with the *International Standards for the Professional Practice of Internal Auditing*"
1.9	1322 - Disclosure of Nonconformance

Gleim Subunit	Performance Standard
4.3	2010 - Planning
6.2	2020 - Communication and Approval
4.4	2030 - Resource Management
1.2	2040 - Policies and Procedures
1.5	2050 - Coordination
6.2	2060 - Reporting to Senior Management and the Board
4.4	2070 - External Service Provider and Organizational Responsibility for Internal Auditing
1.1	2100 - Nature of Work
1.6	2110 - Governance
1.8	2120 - Risk Management
3.2	2130 - Control
4.1	2200 - Engagement Planning
4.2	2201 - Planning Considerations
4.1	2210 - Engagement Objectives
4.1	2220 - Engagement Scope
4.5	2230 - Engagement Resource Allocation
5.1	2240 - Engagement Work Program
5.2	2340 - Engagement Supervision
6.4	2400 - Communicating Results
6.4	2410 - Criteria for Communicating
6.4	2420 - Quality of Communications
6.4	2421 - Errors and Omissions
6.4	2430 - Use of "Conducted in Conformance with the *International Standards for the Professional Practice of Internal Auditing*"
6.4	2431 - Engagement Disclosure of Nonconformance
6.5	2440 - Disseminating Results
6.4	2450 - Overall Opinions
6.8	2500 - Monitoring Progress
6.8	2600 - Communicating the Acceptance of Risks

Gleim Subunit	**Practice Advisory**
6.4	1210-1: Proficiency
1.9	1300-1: Quality Assurance and Improvement Program
1.9	1310-1: Requirements of the Quality Assurance and Improvement Program
1.9	1311-1: Internal Assessments
1.9	1312-1: External Assessments
4.3	2010-1: Linking the Audit Plan to Risk and Exposures
4.3	2010-2: Using the Risk Management Process in Internal Audit Planning
6.2	2020-1: Communication and Approval
4.4	2030-1: Resource Management
1.2	2040-1: Policies and Procedures
1.5	2050-1: Coordination
6.2	2060-1: Reporting to Senior Management and the Board
1.6	2110-3: Governance: Assessments
1.8	2120-1: Assessing the Adequacy of Risk Management Processes
3.2	2130-1: Assessing the Adequacy of Control Processes
2.6	2130.A1-1: Information Reliability and Integrity
2.6	2130.A1-2: Evaluating an Organization's Privacy Framework
4.2, 5.1	2200-1: Engagement Planning
4.1	2210-1: Engagement Objectives
4.2	2210.A1-1: Risk Assessment in Engagement Planning
4.5	2230-1: Engagement Resource Allocation
5.1	2240-1: Engagement Work Program
2.6	2300-1: Use of Personal Information in Conducting Engagements
5.2, 5.3	2340-1: Engagement Supervision
6.5	2400-1: Legal Considerations in Communicating Results
6.3, 6.4	2410-1: Communication Criteria
6.4	2420-1: Quality of Communications
5.3, 6.5	2440-1: Disseminating Results
6.7	2440-2: Communicating Sensitive Information Within and Outside the Chain of Command
6.7	2440.A2-1: Communications Outside the Organization
6.8	2500-1: Monitoring Progress
6.8	2500.A1-1: Follow-up Process

APPENDIX D
THE IIA EXAMINATION BIBLIOGRAPHY

The Institute has prepared a listing of references for the CIA exam as of May 2013, reproduced below.* Thus, we have updated the bibliography for this Appendix. These publications have been chosen by the Professional Certifications Department as reasonably representative of the common body of knowledge for internal auditors. However, all of the information in these texts will not be tested. When possible, questions will be written based on the information contained in the suggested reference list. This bibliography for Part 2 is listed to give you an overview of the scope of the exam. The IIA also indicates that the examination scope includes

1. Articles from *Internal Auditor* (The IIA periodical)
2. IIA research reports
3. IIA pronouncements, e.g., The IIA's Code of Ethics and *Standards*
4. Past published CIA examinations

The IIA bibliography is reproduced for your information only. The texts you will need to prepare for the CIA exam will depend on many factors, including

1. Innate ability
2. Length of time out of school
3. Thoroughness of your undergraduate education
4. Familiarity with internal auditing due to relevant experience

SUGGESTED REFERENCES FOR PART 2 OF THE CIA EXAM

Part 2: Internal Audit Practice

Kotler, Philip. *Marketing Management*. 14th ed. Prentice Hall, 2011.

Kreitner, Robert. *Management*. 12th ed. Cengage Learning, 2012.

Porter, Michael E. *Competitive Strategy: Techniques for Analyzing Industries and Competitors*. The Free Press, 1998.

Reding, Kurt F., Paul J. Sobel, Urton L. Anderson, Michael J. Head, Sridhar Ramamoorti, Mark Salamasick, Cris Riddle. *Internal Auditing: Assurance & Advisory Services*. 3rd ed. The Institute of Internal Auditors Research Foundation, 2013. www.theiia.org/bookstore/product/internal-auditing-assurance-advisory-services-1668.cfm.

Sawyer, L.B. *Sawyer's Guide for Internal Auditors*. 6th ed. The Institute of Internal Auditors, Inc., 2012. www.theiia.org/bookstore/product/sawyers-internal-auditing-6th-edition-1597.cfm.

The American Institute of Certified Public Accountants. *Internal Control - Integrated Framework*. 2013. www.theiia.org/bookstore/product/coso-internal-control-integrated-framework-2013-framework-1684.cfm.

The Institute of Internal Auditors, Inc. International Professional Practices Framework (IPPF). 2013. global.theiia.org/standards-guidance/pages/standards-and-guidance-ippf.aspx.

The Institute of Internal Auditors, Inc. Practice Guides of International Professional Practices Framework (IPPF), including *Global Technology Audit Guide (GTAG)* and *Guides to the Assessment of IT Risk (GAIT)* series. 2013. global.theiia.org/standards-guidance/recommended-guidance/practice-guides/pages/practice-guides.aspx.

---

* At time of print, The IIA had not yet updated the bibliography to reflect current editions. We are confident that they are testing (and therefore candidates should be studying) the information in the most recent editions. Thus, we have updated the bibliography for this Appendix.

AVAILABILITY OF PUBLICATIONS

The listing on the previous page presents only some of the current technical literature available, and The IIA does not carry all of the reference books. Quantity discounts are provided by The IIA. Request a current catalog by phone or mail, or visit global.theiia.org/knowledge/pages/bookstore.aspx.

> The IIARF Bookstore
> 1650 Bluegrass Lakes Pkwy
> Alpharetta, GA 30004-7714
> iiapubs@pbd.com
> (877) 867-4957 (toll-free in U.S. and Canada) or (770) 280-4183

Contact the publisher directly if you cannot obtain the desired texts from The IIA or your local bookstore. Begin your study program with the Gleim CIA Review, which most candidates find sufficient. If you need additional reference material, borrow books mentioned in The IIA's bibliography from colleagues, professors, or a library.

APPENDIX E
ACCOUNTING CYCLES

On the following pages are five flowcharts and accompanying tables describing the steps in five basic accounting cycles and the controls in each step for an organization large enough to have an optimal segregation of duties.

NOTE: Except for manual checks and remittance advices, the flowcharts presented do not assume the use of either a paper-based or an electronic system. Each document symbol represents a business activity or control, whether manual or computerized.

NOTE: In the diagrams that follow, documents that originate outside the organization are separated by a thick border.

Sales-Receivables Cycle

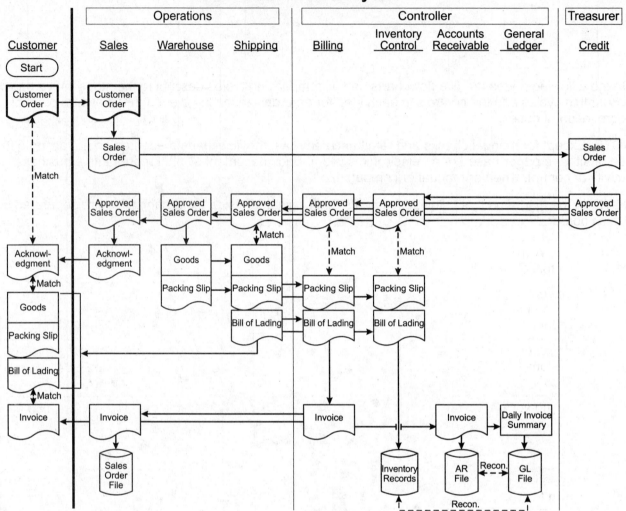

Figure E-1

Sales-Receivables Cycle

Function:	Authorization				Custody		Recording		
Department:	Customer	Sales	Credit	Billing	Shipping	Warehouse	Inventory Control	Accounts Receivable	General Ledger

Step	Business Activity	Embedded Control
1	Sales receives a **customer order** for merchandise, prepares a **sales order**, and forwards it to Credit.	Reconciling sequentially numbered sales orders helps ensure that customer orders are legitimate.
2	Credit performs a credit check on the customer. If the customer is creditworthy, Credit approves the **sales order**.	Ensures that goods are shipped only to actual customers and that the account is unlikely to become delinquent.
3	Credit sends the **approved sales order** to Sales, Warehouse, Shipping, Billing, and Inventory Control.	Notifies these departments that a legitimate sale has been made.
4	Upon receipt of an **approved sales order**, Sales sends an acknowledgment to the customer.	The customer's expectation of receiving goods reduces the chances of misrouting or misappropriation.
5	Upon receipt of an **approved sales order**, Warehouse pulls the merchandise, prepares a **packing slip**, and forwards both to Shipping.	Ensures that merchandise is removed from Warehouse only as part of a legitimate sale.
6	Shipping verifies that the goods received from Warehouse match the **approved sales order**, prepares a **bill of lading**, and sends the shipment to the customer.	Ensures that the correct goods are shipped.
7	Shipping forwards the **packing slip** and **bill of lading** to Inventory Control and Billing.	Notifies these departments that the goods have actually been shipped.
8	Upon receipt of the **packing slip** and **bill of lading**, Inventory Control matches them with the **approved sales order** and updates the inventory system.	Ensures that inventory unit counts are updated once the goods have actually been shipped. Updating inventory and GL files separately provides an additional accounting control when they are periodically reconciled.
9	Upon receipt of the **packing slip** and **bill of lading**, Billing matches them with the **approved sales order**, prepares an **invoice**, and sends it to the customer. If the invoice is paper-based, a **remittance advice** is included for use in the cash receipts cycle.	Ensures that customers are billed for all goods, and only those goods, that were actually shipped. Reconciling sequentially numbered invoice transactions helps prevent misappropriation of goods.
10	Sales receives the **invoice** from Billing and updates the sales order file.	Prevents double shipment of completed orders and allows follow-up of partially filled orders.
11	Accounts Receivable receives the **invoice** from Billing and posts a **journal entry** to the AR file.	Ensures that customer accounts are kept current.
12	Accounts Receivable prepares a **summary of all invoices** for the day and forwards it to General Ledger for posting of the total to the GL file.	Updating AR and GL files separately provides an additional accounting control when they are periodically reconciled.

Cash Receipts Cycle

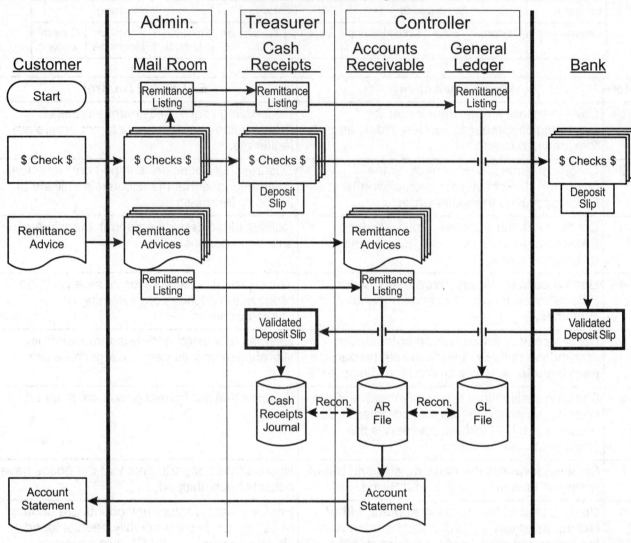

Figure E-2

Cash Receipts Cycle

Function:	Authorization		Custody		Recording	
Department:	Customer	Bank	Mail Room	Cash Receipts	Accounts Receivable	General Ledger

Step	Business Activity	Embedded Control
1	Mail Room opens customer mail. Two clerks are present at all times. Customer **checks** are immediately endorsed "For Deposit Only." **Remittance advices** are separated.	Reduces risk of misappropriation by a single employee.
2	Mail Room prepares a **remittance listing** of all **checks** received during the day and forwards it with the checks to Cash Receipts.	Remittance listing provides a control total for later reconciliation.
3	Cash Receipts prepares a **deposit slip** and deposits checks in Bank. Bank validates the **deposit slip**.	Bank provides independent evidence that the full amount was deposited.
4	Upon receipt of the **validated deposit slip**, Cash Receipts posts a **journal entry** to the cash receipts journal.	Ensures that the cash receipts journal is updated for the amount actually deposited.
5	Mail Room also sends the **remittance listing** to General Ledger for posting of the total to the GL file.	Updating AR and GL files separately provides an additional accounting control when they are periodically reconciled.
6	Mail Room also sends the **remittance listing** and **remittance advices** to Accounts Receivable for updating of customer accounts.	Ensures that customer accounts are kept current.
7	Accounts Receivable periodically sends **account statements** to customers showing all sales and payment activity.	Customers will complain about mistaken billings or missing payments.

Purchases-Payables Cycle

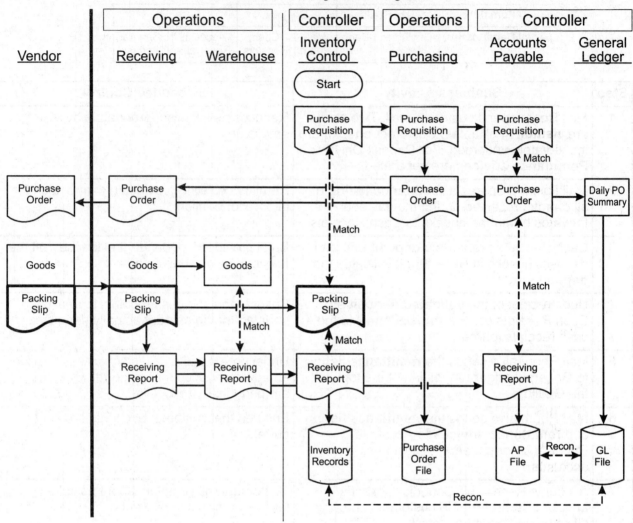

Figure E-3

Purchases-Payables Cycle

Function:	Authorization		Custody			Recording	
Department:	Inventory Control	Purchasing	Vendor	Receiving	Warehouse	Accounts Payable	General Ledger

Step	Business Activity	Embedded Control
1	Inventory Control prepares a **purchase requisition** when inventory approaches the reorder point and sends it to Purchasing and Accounts Payable.	Predetermined inventory levels trigger authorization to initiate purchase transaction.
2	Purchasing locates authorized vendor in vendor file, prepares a **purchase order**, and updates the purchase order file.	Ensures that goods are bought only from vendors who have been preapproved for reliability.
		Reconciling sequentially numbered purchase orders helps ensure that customer orders are legitimate.
3	Purchasing sends the **purchase order** to Vendor, Receiving, and Accounts Payable. Receiving's copy has blank quantities.	Vendor prepares merchandise for shipment.
		Receiving is put on notice to expect shipment.
		Accounts Payable is put on notice that liability to this vendor is about to increase.
4	Accounts Payable prepares a **summary of all purchase orders** issued that day and forwards it to General Ledger for posting of the total to the GL file.	Updating AP and GL files separately provides an additional accounting control when they are periodically reconciled.
5	Goods arrive at Receiving with a **packing slip**.	Because quantities are blank on Receiving's copy of the purchase order, employees cannot assume the order is correct as received and must count items.
6	Receiving prepares a **receiving report** and forwards it with the goods to Warehouse.	Detects discrepancies between the vendor packing slip and actual goods received.
7	Warehouse verifies that goods received match those listed on the **receiving report**.	Detects any loss or damage between Receiving and Warehouse.
8	Receiving sends the **receiving report** and **packing slip** to Inventory Control for matching with the **purchase requisition** and updating of inventory records.	Ensures that inventory records are current. Updating inventory and GL files separately provides an additional accounting control when they are periodically reconciled.
9	Receiving also sends the **receiving report** to Accounts Payable for matching with the **purchase order** and **purchase requisition** and updating of the AP file.	Ensures that vendor accounts are current.

Cash Disbursements Cycle

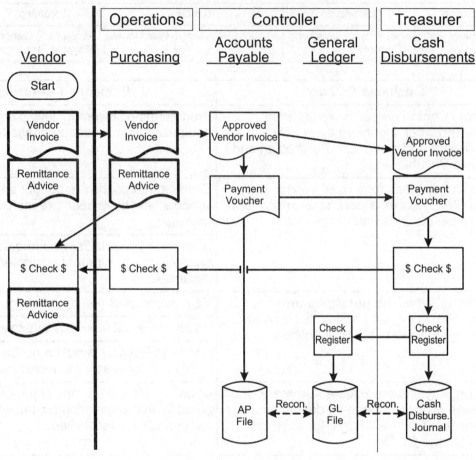

Figure E-4

Cash Disbursements Cycle

Function:	Authorization		Custody	Recording	
Department:	Vendor	Purchasing	Cash Disbursements	Accounts Payable	General Ledger

Step	Business Activity	Embedded Control
1	Purchasing receives a **vendor invoice** and **remittance advice**. The remittance advice is separated and filed. The invoice is matched with the purchase order file and approved for payment. The **purchase order** is marked as closed, and the approval is forwarded to Accounts Payable.	Ensures that vendors are timely paid for goods received and that Purchasing can follow up on partially filled orders.
2	Accounts Payable matches the **approved vendor invoice** with the AP file and issues a **payment voucher** to Cash Disbursements.	Ensures that the invoice is for goods actually received and that duplicate payment cannot be made.
3	Upon receipt of a **payment voucher** with an **approved vendor invoice**, Cash Disbursements issues a **check** and forwards it to Purchasing.	Ensures that payments are made only when goods have actually been received.
4	Purchasing sends the **remittance advice** with the **check** to Vendor.	Settles liability to Vendor.
5	Cash Disbursements prepares a **check register** of all checks issued during the day and posts a **journal entry** to the cash disbursements journal.	Ensures that the cash disbursements journal is updated for the total of checks requested.
6	The check register is also forwarded to General Ledger for posting of the total to the GL file.	Updating AP and GL files separately provides an additional accounting control when they are periodically reconciled.

Payroll Cycle

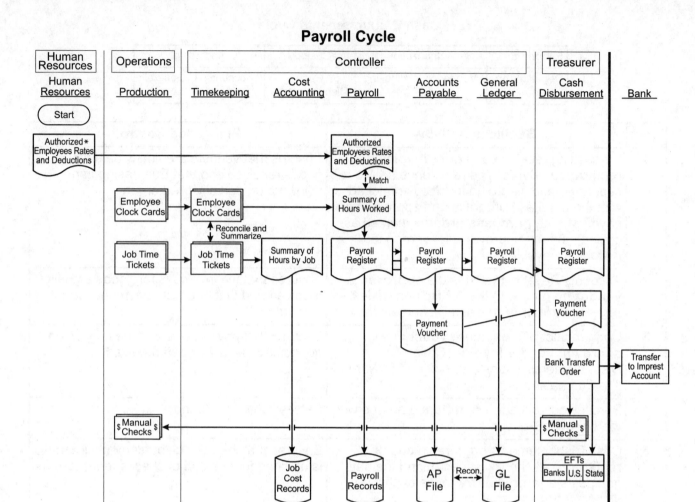

*Human resources receives only a list of authorized employee rates and deductions and does not have authority to change those rates.

Figure E-5

Payroll Cycle

Function:	Authorization		Custody		Recording				
Department:	Human Resources	Production	Cash Disbursements	Bank	Time-keeping	Cost Accounting	Payroll	Accounts Payable	General Ledger

Step	Business Activity	Embedded Control
1	Human Resources sends a **list of authorized employees**, pay rates, and deductions to Payroll.	Ensures that only actual persons are carried on the payroll and that rates of pay and withholding amounts are accurate.
2	Employees register the start and end times of their workdays on **clock cards**.	Mechanically or electronically captures employee work hours.
3	Employees record time worked on various tasks on **job time tickets**.	Allows accumulation of labor costs by job as well as tracking of direct and indirect labor.
4	At the end of the pay period, a production supervisor approves **clock cards** and **job time tickets** and forwards them to Timekeeping.	Ensures that employees worked only authorized hours.
5	Timekeeping reconciles the **clock cards** and **job time tickets**.	Ensures that employees are paid only for actual hours worked.
6	Timekeeping prepares a summary of **hours worked by job** and forwards it to Cost Accounting for updating of the job records.	Ensures that direct labor costs are appropriately assigned to jobs.
7	Timekeeping prepares a summary of **hours worked by employee** and forwards it to Payroll. Payroll matches it with the **authorized employee list**, prepares a **payroll register**, and updates the payroll records.	Ensures that employees are paid the proper amount.
8	Accounts Payable receives the **payroll register** from Payroll, prepares a **payment voucher**, and forwards it along with the payroll register to Cash Disbursements.	Ensures that a payable is accrued. Authorizes the movement of cash into the payroll imprest account.
9	Accounts Payable also forwards the **payroll register** to General Ledger for posting of the total to the GL file.	Updating AP and GL files separately provides an additional accounting control when they are periodically reconciled.
10	Cash Disbursements compares the **payment voucher** with the payroll register total and initiates appropriate **bank transfers**.	Ensures that the correct amount is transferred to the payroll imprest account and governmental authorities.
11	Cash Disbursements executes three **bank transfers**.	Use of an imprest payroll account allows idle funds to be invested and funds related to uncashed checks to be isolated.
		In the U.S., federal taxes withheld are transferred to the U.S. Treasury.
		In the U.S., state taxes withheld are transferred to the state government.
12	Employees paid by **manual check** are given checks by Treasury personnel, not by Payroll or their supervisors.	Ensures that Payroll or supervisory personnel cannot perpetrate fraud through the creation of fictitious employees.

APPENDIX F
GLOSSARY OF ACCOUNTING TERMS
U.S. TO BRITISH VS. BRITISH TO U.S.

U.S. TO BRITISH

U.S.	British
Accounts payable	Trade creditors
Accounts receivable	Trade debtors
Accrual	Provision (for liability or charge)
Accumulated depreciation	Aggregate depreciation
Additional paid-in capital	Share premium account
Allowance	Provision (for diminution in value)
Allowance for doubtful accounts	Provision for bad debt
Annual Stockholders' Meeting	Annual General Meeting
Authorized capital stock	Authorized share capital
Bellweather stock	Barometer stock
Bylaws	Articles of Association
Bond	Loan finance
Capital lease	Finance lease
Certificate of Incorporation	Memorandum of Association
Checking account	Current account
Common stock	Ordinary shares
Consumer price index	Retail price index
Corporation	Company
Cost of goods sold	Cost of sales
Credit Memorandum	Credit note
Equity	Reserves
Equity interest	Ownership interest
Financial statements	Accounts
Income statement	Profit and loss account
Income taxes	Taxation
Inventories	Stocks
Investment bank	Merchant bank
Labor union	Trade union
Land	Freehold
Lease with bargain purchase option	Hire purchase contract
Liabilities	Creditors
Listed company	Quoted company
Long-term investments	Fixed asset investments
Long-term lease	Long leasehold
Merchandise trade	Visible trade
Mutual funds	Unit trusts
Net income	Net profit
Note payable	Bill payable
Note receivable	Bill receivable
Paid-in surplus	Share premium
Par value	Nominal value
Pooling of interests method	Merger accounting
Preferred stock	Preference share
Prime rate	Base rate
Property, plant, and equipment	Tangible fixed assets
Provision for bad debts	Charge
Purchase method	Acquisition accounting
Purchase on account	Purchase on credit
Retained earnings	Profit and loss account
Real estate	Property
Revenue	Income
Reversal of accrual	Release of provision
Sales on account	Sales on credit
Sales/revenue	Turnover
Savings and loan association	Building society
Shareholders' equity	Shareholders' funds
Stock	Inventory
Stockholder	Shareholder
Stock dividend	Bonus share
Stockholders' equity	Share capital and reserves or Shareholders' funds
Taxable income	Taxable profit
Treasury bonds	Gilt-edged stock (gilts)

BRITISH TO U.S.

Accounts	Financial statements
Acquisition accounting	Purchase method
Aggregate depreciation	Accumulated depreciation
Annual General Meeting	Annual Stockholders' Meeting
Articles of Association	Bylaws
Authorized share capital	Authorized capital stock
Barometer stock	Bellweather stock
Base rate	Prime rate
Bill payable	Note payable
Bill receivable	Note receivable
Bonus share	Stock dividend
Building society	Savings and loan association
Charge	Provision for bad debts
Company	Corporation
Cost of sales	Cost of goods sold
Credit note	Credit Memorandum
Creditors	Liabilities
Current account	Checking account
Finance lease	Capital lease
Fixed asset investments	Long-term investments
Freehold	Land
Gilt-edged stock (gilts)	Treasury bonds
Hire purchase contract	Lease with bargain purchase option
Income	Revenue
Inventory	Stock
Loan finance	Bond
Long leasehold	Long-term lease
Memorandum of Association	Certificate of Incorporation
Merchant bank	Investment bank
Merger accounting	Pooling of interests method
Net profit	Net income
Nominal value	Par value
Ordinary shares	Common stock
Ownership interest	Equity interest
Preference share	Preferred stock
Profit and loss account	Income statement
Profit and loss account	Retained earnings
Property	Real estate
Provision for bad debt	Allowance for doubtful accounts
Provision (for diminution in value)	Allowance
Provision (for liability or charge)	Accrual
Purchase on credit	Purchase on account
Quoted company	Listed company
Release of provision	Reversal of accrual
Reserves	Equity
Retail price index	Consumer price index
Sales on credit	Sales on account
Share capital and reserves or Shareholders' funds	Stockholders' equity
Shareholder	Stockholder
Shareholders' funds	Shareholders' equity
Share premium	Paid-in surplus
Share premium account	Additional paid-in capital
Stocks	Inventories
Tangible fixed assets	Property, plant, and equipment
Taxable profit	Taxable income
Taxation	Income taxes
Trade creditors	Accounts payable
Trade debtors	Accounts receivable
Trade union	Labor union
Turnover	Sales/revenue
Unit trusts	Mutual funds
Visible trade	Merchandise trade

INDEX